The
American
History Highway

Also Available:

The History Highway: A 21st Century Guide to Internet Resources

The European History Highway: A Guide to Internet Resources

The US History Highway: A Guide to Internet Resources

The World History Highway: A Guide to Internet Resources

The
American
History Highway

A GUIDE TO INTERNET RESOURCES ON U.S., CANADIAN, AND LATIN AMERICAN HISTORY

DENNIS A. TRINKLE AND SCOTT A. MERRIMAN

EDITORS

M.E.Sharpe
Armonk, New York
London, England

Library of Congress Cataloging-in-Publication Data

The American history highway : a guide to Internet resources on U.S., Canadian, and Latin
American history / edited by Dennis A. Trinkle and Scott A. Merriman.
p. cm.
Includes bibliographical references and index.
ISBN: 978-0-7656-1629-6 (pbk.: alk. paper)
1. America—History—Research. 2. History—Computer network resources—Directories.
3. History—Research—Methodology. 4. Internet. I. Trinkle, Dennis A., 1968– II. Merriman,
Scott A., 1968–

E16.5.A46 2007
973.0285′4678—dc22   2006033212

Printed in the United States of America

The paper used in this publication meets the minimum requirements of
American National Standard for Information Sciences
Permanence of Paper for Printed Library Materials,
ANSI Z 39.48-1984.

BM (p)   10   9   8   7   6   5   4   3   2   1

In honor of the next generation,
Caroline Bradshaw Merriman and John Thomas Trinkle,
and the one before, especially Gayle Trinkle

Contents

Acknowledgments

The idea for *The History Highway* was conceived nearly a decade ago. That the work is now entering its fifth incarnation is a testament to its value to students, instructors, and lovers of history. It is also a tribute to the many individuals who have contributed directly and indirectly to the project over the past ten years. We cannot possibly thank everyone who has played a role in writing, so we hope you know that your efforts and support are recognized and appreciated. We would especially like to thank the contributors to this and past editions of *The History Highway*. We extend our sincere thanks and hearty apologies to Stephen Kneeshaw, whose chapter, "History and Social Studies Organizations," was not correctly attributed to him in the last edition of the work.

Dennis A. Trinkle would like to thank the faculty, staff, and students of DePauw University for their many tangible and intangible contributions to the development of the *History Highway* series. DePauw is a lively learning community, and I want to thank President Robert Bottoms and Executive Vice President Neal Abraham for their support and encouragement of my many activities. I also want to especially thank several former colleagues at DePauw who made my teaching, research, and work better and more successful: Annette Coon, Aaron Dzuibinsky, Bob Hershberger, Julianne Miranda, Ken Owen, Rick Provine, Nate Romance, and Carol Smith.

I would also like to thank the members of my other professional family—the American Association for History and Computing. In particular, my sincere appreciation is extended to David Staley, Charles Mackay, Jeffrey Barlow, Kelly Robison, Jessica Lacher-Feldman, Steve Hoffman, and Deborah Anderson. It is a genuine pleasure to work with so many creative and passionate teachers and scholars. Finally, but certainly not least, special thanks to my wife, Kristi, my greatest blessing John Thomas, my brother Keith, my mother Gayle, and all the members of my extended family. Your constant energy and care are a great inspiration.

Scott A. Merriman would like to thank his family, friends, and teachers, both past and present, for their support and guidance. Special thanks to my wife, Jessie, for her assistance, both in this writing effort and in many others, and to my daughter Caroline for all the smiles and ducks (red, white, blue and yellow) that she has brought into my life. I would also like to recognize the History Department of the University of Kentucky, faculty, staff, graduate students, and fellow part- and full-time instructors alike, for their support and encouragement. Especially deserving of gratitude for serving as mentors are, among others, Robert Ireland and Robert Olson. My years at UK have been enriched by my friendships with, among many others, Jessica Flinchum, Amber Fogle, Elizabeth Hill, Stephanie May, Erin Shelor, Jeremiah Taylor, and Jennifer Walton.

In my larger travels, I have been ably assisted by many people, far too many to mention, and I would be remiss if I did not thank at least some of them here. I am truly grateful for my continuing friendships and professional relationships with Jeffrey Barlow, Rowly Brucken, Bud Burkhardt, Randal Horobik, Jen McGee, Kelly Robison, David Staley, and Paul Wexler. I am thankful to my family for their perpetual support. Finally, for all those who have supported me, but who are not specifically mentioned, thanks!

Introduction

More than 60 percent of American households now report that they regularly access the Internet. This figure represents a stunning historical transformation. The number of Web pages is increasing so rapidly that no reliable estimate exists, though best guesses suggest more than 8 billion Web pages. The growth rate and proliferation are staggering and historically unprecedented. Radio, television, and the telephone became part of American daily life at a comparatively glacial pace. Such dizzying expansion and alteration make the Internet a tremendously exciting phenomenon, but also unsettling and unwieldy.

When we wrote the first edition of *The History Highway* in 1996, we lamented that trying to explore and sample the Internet was like trying to sip water from a fire hose. When *The History Highway 2000* appeared, and when *The History Highway 3.0* followed, the metaphor might have been changed to sipping water from a rushing river or Niagara Falls. Today, that first fire hose might be replaced by a roaring ocean. The pace of expansion and change is accelerating.

To novices and even seasoned users, the information superhighway can be information overload at its worst, often more intimidating and frustrating than exciting. For anyone interested in history, however, the Internet simply cannot be ignored. The resources are richer and more valuable than ever. There are hundreds of thousands of sites dedicated to the American Revolution alone. Students can find the complete texts of millions of books, work with previously inaccessible primary documents, and explore thousands of first-rate sites dedicated to historical topics. Publishers can advertise their wares, and professors can find enormous databases devoted to teaching suggestions, online versions of historical journals, and active scholarly discussions on a wide variety of research topics. The Internet is quite simply the most revolutionary storehouse of human knowledge in history.

For most of us, however, whether we are students, professors, librarians, editors, or just lovers of history, there are not enough hours in our already busy days to go chasing information down an infinite number of alleyways, no matter how useful or interesting that information might be. The aim of this book is to offer detailed information about the thousands of quality resources that are out there and how to find them.

Part I is a short primer for those with limited experience using the Internet. It discusses what exists and what you can do with it. It explains how to gain access to the Internet and outlines what types of software are necessary. There is also an important section on the manners and rules that govern the Internet—"netiquette," as seasoned users call it. A valuable new section on evaluating Internet resources has been added to the chapter as well.

Part II is the heart of the book. It lists thousands of sites that will appeal to anyone interested in history and that our specialist section authors have determined to be reliable and useful for the serious study of history. This section will allow you to avoid the helter-skelter databases, such as Yahoo!, Excite, Google, and DogPile, that take you to information regardless of quality and utility. You will not find sites created by first-graders in Indianapolis or by biased, ahistorical groups like the Holocaust Deniers of America. Bon Voyage!

Part I

Getting Started

Chapter 1

The Basics

Dennis A. Trinkle

History of the Internet

Since this book is directed at those interested in history, it seems sensible to begin with a brief history of the Internet itself. The story of the Internet's origins is as varied, complex, and fascinating as the information the Net contains. Ironically, the Net began as the polar opposite of the publicly accessible network it has become. It grew out of the Cold War hysteria surrounding the Soviet launch of Sputnik, the first artificial satellite, in 1957. Amid paranoia that the United States was losing the "science race," President Dwight D. Eisenhower created the Advanced Research Projects Agency (ARPA) within the Department of Defense to establish an American lead in science and technology applicable to the military. After helping the United States develop and launch its own satellite by 1959, the ARPA scientists turned much of their attention to computer networking and communications. Their goal was to find a successful way of linking universities, defense contractors, and military command centers to foster research and interaction, but also to sustain vital communications in case of nuclear attack. The network project was formally launched in 1969 by ARPA under a grant that connected four major computers at universities in the southwestern United States—UCLA, Stanford, the University of California at Santa Barbara, and the University of Utah. The network went online in December 1969. The age of computer networks was born.

In the early 1970s, it became clear to the initial developers of the ARPANET that the system was already stretching past its Cold War origins. Nonmilitary research institutions were developing competing networks of communication, more and more users were going online, and new languages were being introduced that made communication difficult or impossible between networks. To resolve this problem, the Defense Advanced Project Agency (which had replaced ARPA) launched the Internetting Project in 1973. The aim was to create a uniform communications language (a protocol, as the rules governing a computer language are termed) that would allow the hundreds of networks being formed to communicate and function as a single meganetwork. In an amazing display of scientific prowess comparable to the Apollo program, this crucial step in the development of the information superhighway was accomplished in a single year when Robert Kahn and Vinton G. Cerf introduced the Transmission Control Protocol/Internet Protocol (TCP/IP). This protocol made possible the connection of all the various networks and computers then in existence and set the stage for the enormous expansion of the Internet.

Over the next decade, the Department of Defense realized the significance and potential of the Internet, and nonmilitary organizations were gradually allowed to link with the ARPANET. Commercial providers like CompuServe then began making the Internet accessible for those not connected to a university or research institution. The potential for profiting from the Internet fueled dramatic improvements in speed and ease of use.

The most significant step toward simplicity of use came with the introduction of the World Wide Web (Internet), which allows interactive graphics and audio to be accessed. The World Wide Web was the brainchild of Tim Berners-Lee of the European Laboratory for Particle Physics, who created a computer language called hypertext that made possible the interactive exchange of text and graphic images and allowed almost instantaneous connection (linking) to any item on the Internet. Berners-Lee was actually developing this revolutionary language as the Internet was expanding in the 1970s and 1980s, but it was only with the introduction of an easy-to-use Web browser (as the software for interacting with the Web is called) that the Web became widely accessible to the average person. That first browser—Mosaic—was made available to the public by the National Center for Supercomputing Applications at the University of Illinois, Urbana-Champaign, in 1991. Three years later, Mosiac's creator, Marc Andreessen, introduced an even more sophisticated browser that allowed the interaction of sound, text, and images—Netscape Navigator. The next year Microsoft launched a browser of its own—Internet Explorer.

Today, there are many software options for exploring the Internet and access can be purchased through thousands of national and local service providers. A user need no longer be a military researcher or work at a university to "surf the Net." There are now more than 100 million users logging onto the Internet from the United States alone. Tens of thousands of networks now are connected by TCP/IP, and the Internet forms a vast communication system that can legitimately be called an information superhighway.

Uses of the Internet

This section of Part I will explain the most useful features of the Internet for those interested in history. It will discuss sending and receiving e-mail, reading and posting messages to Usenet newsgroups and discussion lists, logging on to remote computers with telnet, transferring files using the file transfer protocol, and browsing the World Wide Web. The next section will discuss in detail the software packages that perform these tasks and explain exactly how to get online.

Sending and Receiving E-mail

E-mail (electronic mail) is the most popular feature of the Internet. It offers almost instantaneous communication with people all over the world. Rather than taking days or weeks to reach their destination, e-mail messages arrive in minutes or seconds. A professor in Indianapolis, Indiana, can correspond with a student in Delhi, India, in the blink of an eye. A publisher, editor, and author can exchange drafts of a history book they are preparing with no delay. And e-mail does not involve the high costs of international postage, fax charges, or long-distance telephone premiums. E-mail is always part of the basic service arrangement provided with Internet access, and it is quite easy to use with the software packages discussed later.

E-mail Addresses

E-mail addresses are very similar to postal addresses. Like a postal address, an e-mail address provides specific information about where the message is to be sent along the Internet. For example, a friend's address might be something like:

Gkuecker@depauw.edu.

If you look at the end of the address, you will notice the .edu suffix. This means the e-mail message is going to an educational institution. In this case, it is DePauw University, as the second item indicates. Finally, the address reveals that the recipient is your friend Glen Kuecker (Gkuecker). This is just like providing the name, street address, city, state, and zip code on regular mail.

Although the names that individual institutions choose for their Internet addresses vary widely, all addresses in the United States are broken down into the computer equivalent of zip codes. We already noted the .edu in the above message indicates the recipient's account was at an educational institution. There used to be six key three-letter designations (the first six listed below) that provided a clue as to where your e-mail was going or coming from. However, that number has now grown exponentially. The following fourteen categories are just some of the many options available to today's Web surfer:

Category	Meaning
.com	commercial organizations
.edu	educational institutions
.gov	government organizations (nonmilitary)
.mil	military institutions
.net	network service providers
.org	miscellaneous providers
.aero	air-transport industry
.biz	businesses
.coop	cooperatives
.info	unrestricted
.museum	museums
.name	individuals
.pro	accountants, lawyers, and physicians
.country (.xx)	two-letter code designating the Web site's country of origin

A common naming system for American primary and secondary schools has also recently been introduced. This system uses the school name, the k12 designation, and the state where the school is located in the address. A typical address might read:

KeithTrinkle@howe.k12.in.us.

This indicates that a student, teacher, or administrator at Howe High School in Indiana sent the e-mail. The k12.xx.us will always be present in e-mail coming from a primary or secondary school, where the xx will be replaced by the abbreviation for the state.

These designations do not apply to e-mail addresses for accounts located outside the United States, but an equally simple system exists for identifying foreign messages. All mail going to or coming from foreign accounts ends with a two-letter country code. If you have a colleague in France, you might receive an e-mail message ending with .fr. You may receive an e-mail message from an editor in Canada ending in .ca. Or, if you met a historian with similar interests on that last trip through Tanzania, you might soon receive mail ending with .tz. Here is a partial list of these country extensions:

.af	Afghanistan
.al	Albania
.dz	Algeria
.as	American Samoa
.ad	Andorra
.ao	Angola
.ai	Anguilla
.aq	Antarctica
.ag	Antigua and Barbuda
.ar	Argentina
.am	Armenia
.aw	Aruba
.au	Australia
.at	Austria
.az	Azerbaijan
.bs	Bahamas
.bh	Bahrain
.bd	Bangladesh
.bb	Barbados
.by	Belarus
.be	Belgium
.be	Belize
.bj	Benin
.bm	Bermuda
.bj	Bhutan
.bo	Bolivia
.ba	Bosnia-Herzegovina
.bw	Botswana
.bv	Bouvet Island
.br	Brazil
.io	British Indian Ocean Territory
.bn	Brunei Darussalam
.bg	Bulgaria
.bf	Burkina Faso
.bi	Burundi
.kh	Cambodia

.cm	Cameroon
.ca	Canada
.cv	Cape Verde
.ky	Cayman Islands
.cf	Central African Republic
.td	Chad
.cl	Chile
.cn	China
.cx	Christmas Island
.cc	Cocos Islands
.co	Colombia
.km	Comoros
.cg	Congo
.ck	Cook Islands
.cr	Costa Rica
.ci	Côte d'Ivoire
.hr	Croatia
.cu	Cuba
.cy	Cyprus
.cz	Czech Republic
.dk	Denmark
.dj	Djibouti
.dm	Dominica
.do	Dominican Republic
.tp	East Timor
.ec	Ecuador
.eg	Egypt
.sv	El Salvador
.gq	Equatorial Guinea
.er	Eritrea
.ee	Estonia
.et	Ethiopia
.fk	Falkland Islands
.fo	Faroe Islands
.fj	Fiji
.fi	Finland
.fr	France
.gf	French Guiana
.pf	French Polynesia
.tf	French Southern Territories
.ga	Gabon
.gm	Gambia

.ge	Georgia
.de	Germany
.gh	Ghana
.gi	Gibraltar
.gb	Great Britain
.gr	Greece
.gl	Greenland
.gd	Grenada
.gp	Guadeloupe
.gu	Guam
.gt	Guatemala
.gn	Guinea
.gw	Guinea-Bissau
.gy	Guyana
.ht	Haiti
.hm	Heard and McDonald Islands
.hn	Honduras
.hk	Hong Kong
.hu	Hungary
.is	Iceland
.in	India
.id	Indonesia
.ir	Iran
.iq	Iraq
.ie	Ireland
.il	Israel
.it	Italy
.jm	Jamaica
.jp	Japan
.jo	Jordan
.kz	Kazakhstan
.ke	Kenya
.ki	Kiribati
.kp	North Korea
.kr	South Korea
.kw	Kuwait
.kg	Kyrgyzstan Republic
.la	Lao People's Democratic Republic
.lv	Latvia
.lb	Lebanon
.ls	Lesotho
.lr	Liberia

.ly	Libyan Arab Jamahiriya
.li	Liechtenstein
.lt	Lithuania
.lu	Luxembourg
.mo	Macau
.mk	Macedonia
.mg	Madagascar
.mw	Malawi
.my	Malaysia
.mv	Maldives
.ml	Mali
.mt	Malta
.mh	Marshall Islands
.mq	Martinique
.mr	Mauritania
.mu	Mauritius
.yt	Mayotte
.mx	Mexico
.fm	Micronesia
.md	Moldova
.mc	Monaco
.mn	Mongolia
.ms	Montserrat
.ma	Morocco
.mz	Mozambique
.mm	Myanmar
.na	Namibia
.nr	Nauru
.np	Nepal
.nl	Netherlands
.an	Netherlands Antilles
.nt	Neutral Zone
.nc	New Caledonia
.nz	New Zealand
.ni	Nicaragua
.ne	Niger
.ng	Nigeria
.nu	Niue
.nf	Norfolk Island
.mp	Northern Mariana Islands
.no	Norway
.om	Oman

.pk	Pakistan
.pw	Palau
.pa	Panama
.pg	Papua New Guinea
.py	Paraguay
.pe	Peru
.ph	Philippines
.pn	Pitcairn
.pl	Poland
.pt	Portugal
.pr	Puerto Rico
.qa	Qatar
.re	Réunion
.ro	Romania
.ru	Russian Federation
.rw	Rwanda
.sh	Saint Helena
.kn	Saint Kitts and Nevis
.lc	Saint Lucia
.pm	Saint Pierre and Miquelon
.vc	Saint Vincent and the Grenadines
.ws	Samoa
.sm	San Marino
.st	São Tomé and Príncipe
.sa	Saudi Arabia
.sn	Senegal
.sc	Seychelles
.sl	Sierra Leone
.sg	Singapore
.sk	Slovakia
.si	Slovenia
.sb	Solomon Islands
.so	Somalia
.za	South Africa
.es	Spain
.lk	Sri Lanka
.sd	Sudan
.sr	Suriname
.sj	Svalbard and Jan Mayen Islands
.sz	Swaziland
.se	Sweden
.ch	Switzerland

.sy	Syria
.tw	Taiwan
.tj	Tajikistan
.tz	Tanzania
.th	Thailand
.tg	Togo
.tk	Tokelau
.to	Tonga
.tt	Trinidad and Tobago
.tn	Tunisia
.tr	Turkey
.tm	Turkmenistan
.tc	Turks and Caicos Islands
.tv	Tuvalu
.ug	Uganda
.ua	Ukraine
.ae	United Arab Emirates
uk	United Kingdom
.us	United States
.um	United States Minor Outlying Islands
.uy	Uruguay
.uz	Uzbekistan
.vu	Vanuatu
.va	Vatican City State
.ve	Venezuela
.vn	Vietnam
.vg	Virgin Islands (British)
.vi	Virgin Islands (U.S.)
.wf	Wallis and Futuna Islands
.eh	Western Sahara
.ye	Yemen
.yu	Yugoslavia
.zr	Zaire
.zm	Zambia
.zw	Zimbabwe

E-mail Security

Because sending e-mail is so similar to sending a letter by postal service, many people forget that there are two major differences—federal laws discourage anyone from looking at (or intercepting) your mail, and sealed packaging provides a fairly reliable way to detect tampering, but, unfortunately, e-mail is not protected in the same ways. As your electronic message passes through the Internet, it can be read, intercepted, and altered by many individuals.

Some security measures have been developed to protect e-mail just as an envelope secures letters. The latest versions of many programs that process e-mail now include the ability to encrypt messages. Encryption converts your e-mail into a complex code that must be deciphered by an e-mail program or Web browser that is designed to convert the encoded message back into regular text. The latest versions of most e-mail programs include the ability to code and decode encrypted e-mail. If you purchase products and services over the Internet, you will also want to be certain that your account or credit card numbers are insured by some sort of encryption. Nevertheless, it is prudent to keep in mind that no security measure is completely reliable. Remember, too, never to give out your personal information via e-mail or to follow links from e-mails, which could redirect your browser to a false Web site designed to steal your personal information. Cut and paste e-mail addresses to your browser for safety, and only give out personal information using secure encrypted Web sites to sellers or individuals who have your personal trust. Look for the padlock icon at the bottom right-hand corner of some browser windows. If the icon is absent or the padlock open, the site is unencrypted. If the padlock icon is present and closed, the site is encrypted. Other browsers display encryption in different ways. Even on an encrypted site, you should still be sure you are working with a trusted seller before disclosing credit card or other personal data.

Reading and Posting Messages on Newsgroups

For anyone interested in history, newsgroups are another rewarding feature of the Internet. Newsgroups are the electronic equivalent of the old New England town meetings in which anyone could pose a question or make an observation and others could respond to it. Each newsgroup is regulated by a moderator who, like the editor of a newspaper, sets the quality and tone of the posts. There are groups that regularly discuss the Holocaust, the American Revolution, historical publishing, library concerns, and cartography, just to mention a few areas. Though newsgroups are declining somewhat in popularity, in favor of listservs and personal blogs, several remain popular among historians.

Several clues can help you determine the content and nature of groups. Like e-mail addresses, the addresses of newsgroups provide some insight into the nature of the group. Take the newsgroup:

alt.civilwar.

This address indicates that the group discusses the alternative topic—the Civil War. Each newsgroup has a similar address revealing its type and topic. The following categories will aid in determining which of the nearly ten thousand newsgroups are worth investigating:

Category	Meaning
alt.	alternative themes (most groups relating to history carry the alt. designation)
comp.	computer-related topics
misc.	miscellaneous themes
news.	posts about newsgroups
rec.	recreational topics
sci.	scientific discussions
soc.	social concerns
talk.	talk radio–style format

Reading and Posting Messages on Discussion Lists

Discussion lists are a hybrid mixture of e-mail and newsgroups. With discussion lists, the posts and replies that anyone can access in newsgroups are sent by e-mail only to those who have subscribed to the list. As with most newsgroups, there is generally an editor who screens the posts before they are sent to subscribers, maintaining quality and decency. There are discussion lists that target students, professors, editors, publishers, librarians, and general readers. Almost any historical topic imaginable has a list devoted to it. How open the discussion lists are to subscribers is determined by the moderators. Some limit membership to those with special interests, while others permit anyone who wishes to join. Part II discusses the lists focusing on history and explains their qualifications for subscription in more detail.

Part II will also provide more specific instructions on how to subscribe to each group. All discussion lists share a basic subscription format, however. To subscribe (or to unsubscribe), one simply sends an e-mail message to the computer that receives and distributes the messages. This computer is called the listserver (or listserv) because it serves the list. For example, to send a message to a list discussing the history of dogs (H-Dog), you would send the e-mail message:

> Subscribe H-Dog yourfirstname yourlastname

to the e-mail address:

> Listserv@ucbeh.san.uc.edu.

The listserv would quickly acknowledge your registration as a member, and e-mail posts from the other list members would begin arriving in your box.

Word of Warning About Discussion Lists

You should be careful to join only subscription lists that are truly of interest and be certain to read your e-mail several times a week. Most discussion lists are very active, sending out fifteen or more messages per day. If you get carried away at first, you may find yourself buried under an avalanche of several hundred e-mail posts awaiting your eager attention. So be careful to subscribe only to those lists that most interest you until you gain a feel for how much mail you are likely to receive.

Blogging

Blogs (Weblogs)—pages in which a single person or group of authors chronicles a particular topic—are of interest to oral historians and others seeking to capture history as it is experienced by the individual. There are two basic types of blogs, individual and interactive. Individual blogs are run by a single person or small group, and all messages posted come from that one person or small community. Interactive blogs allow posts from a much wider group and often spawn their own blogging communities. The environment created by bloggers and their readers is collectively known as the blogsphere.

Like readers of e-mail message chains, blog readers must generally start reading at the end of the blog and work backward, or else read in reverse chronological order, as the newest messages are added to the top of the page. Familiar readers thus will not have to wade through the entire blog to catch up on the most recent information. This convention can be disorienting for those used to standard front-to-back reading, but fans of back-to-front graphic novels can easily adapt to the practice. In interactive blogs, a single topic of great interest can generate a huge volume of posts, called a blog storm or blog swarm.

Blogs usually consist of a list of chronological entries, with the home page either containing all the entries or a hyperlinked entry list to facilitate faster reading. Blogs are equipped with technology that allows the blog owner to moderate conversations in his or her sphere. Bloggers have had an impact on politics already, and those studying their historical impact will doubtless have a challenging task.

Logging Onto a Remote Computer With Telnet

Although more and more libraries are migrating to more user-friendly, icon-based systems, most people who have used an electronic library catalog in the past ten years are familiar with the text-based systems used to search for a book in the library. These machines do not have their own microprocessors, but are linked to a central computer that shares information with all the terminals connected to it. Telnet is a program offered by all Internet service providers that permits your home or office computer to act just like those old terminals at the library. It enables you to temporarily connect to a remote computer and access its information as if it were on your own computer. Telnet has decreased in popularity in recent years as icon-based technology surpassed it in capability and accessibility. Moreover, library databases are now generally available to the public via the Internet without telnet software (though, to be sure, some libraries must still rely on text-based systems.)

Transferring Files With File Transfer Protocol (FTP)

File Transfer Protocol (or FTP) is similar to telnet, but it is still much more widely used. Like telnet, it is a program that connects you to a remote computer. FTP does not allow you to read the material on the remote machine; rather, it allows you to download it to your own computer, or to post your own files to the remote location. You can use FTP to get a copy of the U.S. Constitution or to download a program that teaches you the history of the Vietnam War. Thousands of sites with downloadable files, programs, and historical information are out there waiting to be tapped. Many of the best and most useful FTP sites will be discussed in Part II.

As with telnet, there are many packages that permit FTP access. For now, we will only mention that three main types of FTP access exist: anonymous FTP, identified FTP, and restricted FTP. Anonymous FTP allows anyone to connect to a computer and download information without giving identification. Identified FTP also allows anyone to copy materials, but it requires the provision of e-mail address and name, so the sponsors of the site can maintain statistical information about the use of their site. Restricted FTP is used by some commercial and private institutions that only allow FTP for a fee or for authorized users. Part II specifies which of these categories the sites fall into and explains how to gain access when a fee or password is required.

Browsing the World Wide Web

For most computer users, time on the Internet will mean using a Web browser. The Web is the most popular and fastest growing section of the Internet because it combines text, sound, and graphics to create multimedia sites. History buffs can find everything from an audio track of the "Battle Hymn of the Republic" to short film clips of JFK's assassination to a complete version of the French *Encyclopédie.*

The Web and Web browser packages owe much of their popularity and potential to their multimedia format, but they also profit from their ability to link information. Web page developers can create links to any other page on the Web, so by merely using your mouse to point at a highlighted image or section of text and then clicking the correct mouse button, you can almost instantly bring up that information. Thus, a link on a home page can connect you to any other site, just as a cross-reference in a textbook sends you to other related information. This makes the Internet an amazingly easy-to-use source of information or recreation.

The next section discusses the software that makes connecting to the Web possible, but as with e-mail, you will need to understand Web addresses in order to find information on the Internet. Do not feel intimidated by the techno-talk surrounding the Web. Web addresses, like everything Internet-related, have a technical name, "uniform resource locators," (URL). Every page on the Web has a unique URL. This makes it very easy to go directly to the information you need. They look something like strings of numbers or letters separated by dots (periods) and slashes. For example,

http://mcel.pacificu.edu/JAHC/JAHCiv2/index.html

is simply a link to the *Journal of the Association for History and Computing.* Some addresses are longer than this. Some are shorter. All contain three basic parts. Looking from right to left, the first designation you notice is index.html. This tells you that you are retrieving a file called index in the HTML format. HTML (Hypertext Markup Language) is the standard language of the Web for saving multimedia information. Other possibilities include .gif and .jpeg, which indicate graphic images files, .avi and .wav, which indicate audio files, and .mov, which signals a movie; XML is a markup protocol like HTML, but that also allows metatags, descriptive tags that encode content descriptions. Software can then do more sophisticated searches. Another common protocol is VRML, virtual-reality-modeling language, an Internet standard for rendering three-dimensional graphics.

The middle part of the address—mcel.pacificu.edu/JAHC/JAHCiv2—is just like an e-mail address, specifying what network and computer stores the information so that your software package can find it on the Internet. The .edu extension tells you the information is at an educational institution, and, as with e-mail, there will always be a three-letter code revealing the type of institution that sponsors the site.

The http:// lets you know that the browser is using the Hypertext Transfer Protocol to get the information. This is the standard language that governs the transfer and sharing of information on the Web. If you were using your browser to telnet or FTP, the http:// would be replaced by ftp:// or telnet:// and then the address, showing which function your computer is performing.

Of course, you can use the Internet and profit from the World Wide Web without spending hours studying the technical background, history, and terms. The next chapter tells you how to get on the Internet and what software you need.

Chapter 2

Signing On

Dennis A. Trinkle and Jessica Lacher-Feldman

Getting on the Internet

Dennis A. Trinkle

Once upon a time, getting connected to the Internet was the hardest part of going online. In the early days, if you did not work for the military or a research institution, you were out of luck. The introduction of commercial providers in the 1980s made access easier to obtain, but it might have cost you as much as a new car. Today, there are thousands of local and national Internet service providers, and the competition has made Internet access amazingly inexpensive. In most markets, you can now get almost unlimited access for $10 to $25 per month. For those fortunate enough to work for a library, college, university, or publisher, the price is often even better—free. Getting on the Internet has never been easier or less expensive.

Internet access is offered by three basic categories of service providers—corporate/institutional, national commercial, and local commercial providers. For those who do not have access to the Internet at work or school, there are several factors to consider in choosing a provider. Unless you use a cable modem or DSL, which do not require dial-up access, perhaps most important is finding a service that offers a local phone number or a toll-free number, so that you need not pay long-distance charges for your Internet access. The attractiveness of the Internet vanishes quickly in the presence of a $400 phone bill. Fortunately, there are now so many service providers it is usually easy to find a provider that offers a local phone number in your area, even in rural zones. Cable and satellite providers are also scurrying to offer other access options besides telephone connections.

The second consideration is the type of service you desire. Many national and local service providers in your city or state will offer almost unlimited access to the Internet, e-mail, FTP, and other basic services for very affordable rates. (Local service providers can be found by looking in your local phone book under "Internet Service Providers.")

Hardware

Convenient use of the Internet and its many tools is governed by speed. The faster your computer can send and process information, the more pleasurable and productive your time on the Net will be. Thus, there is a simple rule of thumb that guides the purchase of computer equipment for use on the Internet: Buy the best machine you can realistically afford. This does not mean to mortgage your house just to get better equipment. All new computers sold today are more than adequate for exploring the resources described in this book. Even most of those sold within the last four years have enough capacity to handle most Internet functions. More memory (RAM), a faster processor, and a speedier modem will all enable you to interact with the Net more quickly, however.

Software

While many educational institutions and the national service providers such as AOL and CompuServe offer their own software packages with directions and tutorials, those who choose local service providers can select the software they wish to use to access the Internet. Most local service providers will also give new users software needed to access the Internet along with detailed instructions. In principle, however, you can use any package you wish to connect to the Internet through a local provider. This section will present brief descriptions of some of the best packages and explain where to obtain them.

Web Browsers and E-mail Programs

The two powerhouse packages (Web browsers, as they are called) that most Internauts use are Netscape Communicator and Microsoft Internet Explorer. They combine all the tools for accessing the Web and sending e-mail. Both can display the combinations of graphics and text that make the Internet a lively and exciting resource. They are simple to use, come with tutorials and a help feature, and are good choices for all users from novices to experts.

Netscape Communicator and Microsoft Internet Explorer also can both be downloaded on the Internet free of charge. You can download Netscape at the following address (please note, addresses are case sensitive):

http://browser.netscape.com/ns8/.

Microsoft Internet Explorer can be downloaded at:

http://www.microsoft.com/windows/ie/default.mspx.

Netscape and Internet Explorer perform all the functions you need to explore the Internet, including e-mail. However, those who send and receive a lot of electronic correspondence, or who plan to send long files along with their messages, may prefer to use a package designed specifically to handle electronic mail. If you purchased some version of Microsoft Office, you may have received Microsoft Outlook as part of your package (this differs from Microsoft Outlook Express, a scaled-down version of the same program). This is a popular e-mail program that many companies and universities rely upon. Qualcomm's Eudora is also an excellent package for handling e-mail. It is available in free and paid versions, with the paid versions having better features and no ads. It also features an attractive graphic environment and menu, which makes it easy to use.

Eudora is available for download at:

http://www.eudora.com/.

Finally, Pegasus mail is available free from the Mercury Mail Transport system. It is compatible with all operating systems, including Linux. Its author, David Harris, intends to keep the system free to anyone who downloads it, so that information can be exchanged freely. Like Eudora, the system has user-friendly graphics and menus.

Pegasus is available at:

http://www.pmail.com/.

Netiquette and Copyright

There are some basic courtesies that keep the free and open communication of the Internet polite and enjoyable. Here are some netiquette hints that can keep you from accidentally offending someone.

General Netiquette

The most important thing to remember is that Internet communication is just like writing a letter. Electronic messages, however, can be seen by many individuals other than the intended recipient. They can be forwarded to countless people. They can even be printed and posted in public areas. Thus, the golden rule of Internet communication should never be forgotten:

> Never write anything you would not want a stranger to read.

It is also important to remember that e-mail is judged by the same standards as other written communication. Sometimes, the ease and speed of electronic communication lulls users into forgetting to check grammar and spelling. This can lead to your e-mail being forwarded to thousands of individuals, and you do not want people all over the Internet laughing because you innocently asked if it was Vasco de Gama who circumcised the world with a 40-foot clipper.

There are also several special grammatical conventions that govern the Internet. One important rule is not TO WRITE EVERYTHING OUT IN CAPITAL LETTERS or to underline everything, *italicize everything*, or **put everything in bold**. Seasoned e-mail readers consider this the equivalent of shouting at the top of your lungs, and it is considered the mark of a "newbie," or someone who has not yet learned how to behave on the Internet.

Because e-mail lacks a convenient way to convey emotion through text, you will also often encounter special symbols in e-mail correspondence. For example, a :) or :(is often put after a sentence to express happiness or sadness. A 0 may be added to express surprise. A :; may be inserted to indicate confusion, and history buffs who think they are Abe Lincoln may include a =|:-)= somewhere in their messages. Some users may also add full-fledged smiley face icons. These emoticons add a bit of charm to Internet communication, but it is important to remember that they are only appropriate in informal correspondence. They should not be overdone. Too many emotive symbols are considered another mark of a newbie.

Rules for Newsgroups and Discussion Lists and Blog Posts

Besides the netiquette governing general Internet communication, there are also some rules for those who wish to participate in newsgroups, discussion lists, and blogs.

1. Before you make a post to a group or list, it is wise to follow the group's posts for a while. This will help you to know what has already been asked and what type of questions/statements is considered appropriate. Asking repetitive or uninformed questions can get you off to a bad start.
2. Think before you write. Do not send off emotional or ill-considered responses to posts. (This is called "flaming" in Internet parlance.) Take time to consider criticisms, sarcasms, and insults carefully. Remember the Internet is not an anonymous frontier, and online remarks can be just as hurtful as any others. Moreover, it can be more difficult to convey with text an emotion that is easily transmitted by voice. A seemingly innocent remark can come off brash and rude because it was not phrased carefully.
3. Do not send private correspondence to groups or lists. If you just want to thank someone, send the message to the person directly. And be very careful when you reply to a message. The "reply all" feature of your e-mail program is both a boon and a potential bane. You do not want to accidentally tell several thousand readers about your date last night because you replied to the wrong address or to all of the original recipients.
4. Do not post advertisements to groups or lists. This is considered extremely rude and intrusive, and it is the surest way to become the victim of vicious flaming. Internauts are being careful to avoid the spread of junk mail to the Internet. Spam is already prevalent enough without any further contributions.

Copyright

The question of copyright is an important one for students, teachers, librarians, publishers, and all those on the Internet. Everyone wants to know what laws govern copying and sharing information on the Internet, and lawyers and lawmakers are working to develop clear rules that govern electronic mediums. For now, the issues of copyright as they pertain to the Internet are still somewhat hazy, but there are some certainties that can guide your steps.

Most important, all online correspondence, files, and documents are handled like other written documents. They are automatically held to be copyrighted in the individual author's name. When an Internet item is copyrighted by some other party, the copyright holder generally identifies himself or herself at the end of the document.

Students, teachers, and general users will be glad to know that Internet documents can be copied according to the fair use rules that govern printed sources. You can make personal copies of online documents and images, and you can incorporate them in instructional packages (if you are a student, teacher, or librarian) as long as the package is in no way intended to generate a profit, and only a small percentage of the overall work is copied. Other more precise rules governing copyright will undoubtedly be developed in the near future. For now, the safest course seems to be treating Internet sources just like other written documents. Students will be wise to cite their Internet sources *very* carefully and clearly in the texts of their papers or in footnotes. Copying and pasting work directly from the Internet into your term paper, without the use of *both* quotation marks *and* appropriate citation, is a form of plagiarism that is particularly simple to catch.

Evaluating Online Resources
Tools, Tips, and Terms
Jessica Lacher-Feldman

The Web Today

More and more we find ourselves dependent on the World Wide Web as a research tool. The way we seek and find information has changed remarkably: in just the past couple of years, a new term—a verb—has entered into the American linguistic landscape. We find ourselves saying things like "Just Google it. I bet you'll find what you're looking for." The use of Internet search engines as the first and only stop for information has completely changed the way that some students and teachers approach research and information seeking.

The challenge that this notion presents is that many people do not realize that these search engines are not magically verifying the veracity or adequacy of the information that they provide. Spiders and robots crawl the Web and look for terms that appear in the Web sites' content and in metatags. These robots do not discriminate—they grab everything and anything that they are programmed to find and happily give it all back to you in your search results.

As with any research endeavor, it is the responsibility of the end users to verify that the information that they use is good material—that it comes from reliable and unbiased sources and that it was written with no hidden agenda. This section will introduce you to the terms, tips, and tools you need to understand how to evaluate Internet resources, both in their content and their sources.

Information Literacy and Peer Review

As a general rule, much of the content of the World Wide Web has not been written with the same rigorous scholarship that you find in scholarly journals, newspaper articles, and books. The notion of peer review does not necessarily have an impact on the content of the vast majority of the materials on the World Wide Web, though there is certainly an abundance of free and easily accessible materials on the Web that reflects excellent scholarship. For example, numerous free online journals have undergone a rigorous peer review process, such as the *Journal for the Association for History and Computing* (*JAHC*), available online at http://mcel.pacificu.edu/JAHC/JAHCindex.HTM.

Traditionally, academic publishing involved a great deal of editorial control, and the distribution of scholarly work was greatly limited; subscription print journals found their way to libraries and to the offices of professors, and often not much further. Electronic publishing and the Internet have in many ways made it much easier to produce and distribute excellent scholarship to a broader and broader audience. Certainly a wealth of information exists on the Internet, and *The History Highway* helps to demystify much of the historical research information that exists online. The Internet can provide end users of all kinds with the information that they seek.

With all of this at your fingertips, one question needs to remain at the forefront of your mind and should be considered and reconsidered: *Are all Web resources created equal?*

The answer, unfortunately, is no. But that only requires you to be a better information consumer. The Web certainly offers a level of convenience never seen before. The speed with which you can retrieve information on a host of subjects is unprecedented. Students and other information consumers often come to the Internet believing it holds all the information they need for a research paper or other project. This is a dangerous assumption. Researchers and others who use only the Web invariably hinder their scholastic potential and, indeed, their own credibility.

Without question there is a great deal of wonderful, accurate, and valuable information on the Internet. Course syllabi from other colleges and universities shed light on a particular subject and provide still more resources, both print and online. Web sites of archival repositories and other cultural institutions identify and describe their collections online, providing users with authenticated digital surrogates as well as context for some of their holdings. The Internet offers an incredible bounty of information, but as with any type of research, the user must exercise good judgment in evaluating its value, authority, verity, and validity.

There is a term that is used often in describing this ability—information literacy. Information literacy is a skill set that allows individuals to "recognize where information is needed" and "to locate, evaluate, and use effectively the needed information."[1] These skills are critical in the era of the Internet. With the relative ease and access of the Internet, anyone with the ability to use Web development software and access to a bit of Web space can place any material at all online. This accessibility can create numerous challenges for researchers who fail to evaluate the information they retrieve.

The History Highway presents a broad range of history-related Web sites that have been evaluated and recommended by scholars in their respective fields. However, in such a volatile and rapidly evolving and changing environment, a Web site can disappear overnight, leaving frustrated and bewildered researchers behind. There have been efforts to archive the vast amount of information on the Web at given times, taking massive snapshots of the Internet on a regular basis. Sources such as the Internet Archive (http://Internet.archive.org/) are useful tools and excellent resources in researching the evolution of the Internet itself, but the constant shift—loss and gain of the availability of Web sites—remains frustrating for users. Sites are constantly being added and deleted from the Internet. Sites that were once free might begin charging a fee for use, limit access, or change their interface, editorial policy, or even overall mission.

The speed, breadth, and availability of online resources have changed the way that libraries do business, as well as the way a researcher might approach a project. For many researchers, serendipitous browsing of library stacks has been replaced by surfing the Web. There is room in the world for both approaches, and it is certain that one approach is not clearly better than the other.

Over the years, users have developed a degree of trust in regard to print sources. Editors review books and journals, and publishers are committed to printing and distributing these works. The process of publishing an article in an academic journal or a scholarly monograph through a commercial or university press is long and tedious. Copy editors carefully scrutinize these submissions, and a panel or group of peers reviews and edits them long before the material is presented in its final form to the public. Then, these print resources are sometimes reviewed by other journals, adding additional end value to the information they contain. These peer-reviewed sources are traditionally deemed reliable, accurate, and acceptable to use in research.

The Democratization of Information

One of the greatest things about the Web is that anyone with an Internet account, reasonable access to Web development tools, and a little bit of Web space can put something—anything—out there for the world to see. The Internet has democratized the distribution of information by offering this means to self-publish material. Much of the material on the Web has not been scrutinized by anyone. The vast majority of Web sites are not reviewed or refereed, certainly not to the extent that scholarly print materials are reviewed. Independent entities may review and award great Web sites, but they do not necessarily review content; their concern is rather appearance, functionality, and creativity. One such entity is the Webby Awards (http://Internet.webbyawards.com/).While these awards are prestigious, they are not the same as peer review.

The democratization of information—new materials being made available to the public every day—does not make it easier for the end user to do work. In fact, this makes it even more critical for all end users to learn to evaluate the online materials they consider using for research or information. The danger in finding faulty information on the Internet increases exponentially as more and more material is made available. By taking a Web source at face value without first trying to verify the information it contains as well as the source or sources for that information, users run the risk of perpetrating an untruth, not to mention personal and professional embarrassment.

Evaluating Web Sites: What to Look For

Many Web sites indicate on the index or home page that they are endorsed by a particular group or evaluating body. This endorsement does not necessarily hold the same weight as a peer-reviewed journal. However, depending on the endorsing body itself and its agenda, this simple piece of information offers initial evidence of the validity and informational value of the Web site.

With the ability to do research online at any time and from practically any place comes the responsibility to understand and evaluate online materials to make certain that these resources are accurate, unbiased, and of high quality. With practice, common sense, and a few skills, you become a good information consumer. You must develop critical thinking skills and an understanding of how to evaluate online sources—that is, you must gain a degree of information literacy. The ability to evaluate online resources when doing research is an extension of the ability to evaluate print resources and primary source materials. Indeed, developing skills to evaluate online resources has become a critical and absolutely necessary first step in the research process.

The Questions

Content: There are several questions that you need to ask as you view a site for the first time. When you first locate a Web site, take a look at the overall content. Are the title and the author of the site easily identified? Is the author credible? Are the author's credentials clearly listed and verifiable? Does the author document experience and expertise on the subject presented? Does the site represent a specific group or organization? Is this clearly indicated or buried within the site itself?

It is important to identify a corporate entity, political group, or religious body sponsoring the site. These bodies may have hidden agendas, despite the organization's attempt to present clear and unbiased information to its potential end users. Clues to the verity of this kind of site might be present in the URL.

If a Web address ends with .com, then this is corporate or commercial Web site. A site with the .edu suffix is from an educational institution, most likely a college or university. However, it should be noted that individuals affiliated with an institution can often place data on the institution's site. These sites generally display a tilde (~) somewhere in the URL and should be accessed with a bit more caution. The content may or may not be sanctioned by the host institution and may well contain biased or incorrect information. However, the page might just as easily be written by a noted professor in the field. Such a page might look like this:

http://Internet.ua.edu/~jdoe.html.

As a general rule, .gov, .org, and .edu sites contain the most reliable information on the Internet with regard to history and history-related sources.

Purpose: When looking at the content of a particular Web site, you must also seek out the purpose of the material presented. That is to say, does the material appear to be scholarly or popular? Who appears to be the intended audience for this Web site? Is it written for students, scholars, or peers? Does the language talk down to its audience? Does it oversimplify complicated information? Does it use language to complicate a simple or commonly understood topic?

Tone: It is critical to also look at the tone of the material presented. As with print material, the end user must be able to recognize the fundamental differences in language style, as well as the differences between a scholarly and nonscholarly work. A scholarly work is generally intended for a relatively narrow audience and is usually serious in content as well as overall appearance and presentation. (However, good scholars can also use humor in their works to good effect!) Popular works, in direct contrast, are written for a broader audience and therefore have broader appeal. While this may not always be the case, the Web site developed for a popular audience may have more graphics, bolder use of color, and broader, more general topics. For example, compare these two Web sites:

http://Internet.eonline.com/

and

http://mcel.pacificu.edu/JAHC/JAHCindex.HTM.

The first site is divided into numerous components, with several graphics, a scrolling bar of headlines, a slide show of alternating photographs and blinking text, and, most notably, advertising for various products. The second site is a sober white page with a simple graphic and blue and black text, and no advertising. The second site listed here is full of valuable information, but it is evident that neither its strength, nor its focus, is on grabbing the attention of a broad audience. It should be noted, however, that Web design is constantly getting more sophisticated, and even the most scholarly of Web sites now feature Flash, JavaScript, beautiful illustrations, and bold and stylish Web design. As with books, you cannot judge them by their covers—or home pages!

It is also important, as with print sources, to understand that Web sites may contain information that seems appropriate to your work, but does not have the level of scholarly value needed for your research. Some sites, while they do provide valuable information, are not geared toward the scholar or expert in a given field. Another type of site relies upon sensationalism, playing upon the curiosity and gullibility of its readers by using inflammatory language. For example, compare the following two sites:

http://scientificamerican.com

and

http://Internet.weeklyworldnews.com/.

While these two sites are obvious examples of the differences between types of online publications, comparing the style, content, and language serves as a useful exercise in understanding the broad range of online publications available with a simple search. A search for "prehistoric man" will generate results in both of these Web sites. However, the data on the *Scientific American* site is much, much more reliable. (And it does not hurt to note that *Scientific American* is also a peer-reviewed print journal with a Web arm.) While you may never consider using the *Weekly World News* in a research project, information that is just as inflammatory, inaccurate, or fictional exists throughout the Internet in much more subtle guises like the Holocaust Deniers of America.

Scope: You must also consider the scope of the material presented in the site being evaluated. Does the site appear to be narrowly or broadly focused on the subject at hand? How does it compare to other things you have read on this same topic? If the creator appears to have omitted important dates, events, or particular aspects of the issue or topic presented, this should immediately indicate a problem with the site. Has a list of related sources, a bibliography or webliography, been included on the site? If so, does the list appear to be biased in any way? Look at the other URLs listed. How does their inclusion reflect upon the site you are investigating?

Currency: The very basic question of currency is one that must be asked when evaluating a Web site. When was the material last updated? Is there a date for the last update? Does the site include the most recent editions of materials referenced? If the Web site has not been updated for a long time, or if citations refer to outdated editions of other sources, this should be a cause for concern. Though some historical discussions remain valid for years after their sites were last updated, many abandoned sites lack, at best, the most recent findings in a field. Is there more current and accurate information elsewhere? Has an old source been used in order to further an unpopular or outdated opinion? Are these opinions current? Does the language appear old-fashioned? Are the terms used considered politically incorrect or offensive? These biases may be especially evident when researching issues of race, gender, sexuality, or class online. You should consider whether the Internet is the best place to seek out the information you need. While a Web site mounted in 1996 may have the best information available online about a particular event, it is the responsibility of the researcher to verify this information and make certain that the site is the best possible source for the purpose it is being used.

Sources: When researching on the Internet, always seek out the sources used to create a site. All of this information should be clearly stated either on the home or index page or on a bibliography included in the site. Are there accurate and clear citations? Can these citations be readily verified? If the information is not easily accessible or readily available, there may be a problem. Check the links provided on the site. Are the linked sites appropriate, useful, and current?

Style: When it comes to Web sites, style is not just a question of simple aesthetics, but can often indicate if the creator of the site is skilled and serious about the information presented. An attractive Web site suggests to the researcher accuracy and authority, but this is certainly not always the case. In the information age, you must learn to be a good information consumer. This is done not only by reviewing all the components stated above, but also by taking note of things such as navigability, structure, and usability of any given Web site. Is there search capability on the site? If not, how does the lack of a search function interfere with the functionality of the site? How does the writing style correspond to the information in the site and the site's intended audience? All these factors should be noted carefully when considering any Web site for use in research of any kind. All information is not created equal.

Images: The Internet, among its many achievements, has created a venue for sharing information graphically as well as through the written word. Images on the Web can provide excellent historical evidence and are valuable tools for research. Images of handwritten letters, photographs, art, and other materials can be extremely interesting and valuable, enhancing the research experience immensely. But it is necessary to be aware that images can readily be altered in order to provide false evidence to support a controversial belief.

Such alterations of images are especially common in sites created by hate groups, most notably Holocaust deniers, who proliferate on the Internet and actively seek to spread their beliefs to others. Because the Web is accessible to anyone, both end users and creators, it has become an easy, effective way to make available materials that are misleading and perpetrate falsehoods. Some Web sites are blatant in that regard, but others manipulate users into believing that they are looking at vetted, accurate information. You must look for bias by investigating the creator of the site and the creator's agenda. The information may not be readily obvious to the end user. A legitimate nonprofit organization can have an .org Web address, but an .org site does not, by mere definition, house reliable or unbiased information.

When controversial information is presented to an audience in a slick, manipulative fashion, the novice researcher could easily be fooled into taking that information at face value as accurate. It is critical when using digitized surrogates of primary source material, including images of photographs, letters, or other correspondence, to take note of the Web address and trace its origin—verifying the source of that image. Compare these two URLs:

http://rmc.library.cornell.edu/FRENCHREV/Lafayette/exhibit/
ampolimages/iampol_lips.htm

and

http://rmc.library.cornell.edu/FRENCHREV/Lafayette
/images/screen/2_11.jpg

Both URLs are from the same collection but this is not immediately clear. The first offers an image of a handwritten recipe for Martha Washington's famous lip salve; the second is a portion of a letter presented on a page with no support documentation or transcription associated. In this case, the only indication that the material is probably reliable comes from the URL, which shows that the image is based in Cornell's library. While many older online exhibitions or digital collections may serve up images without accompanying information, the information in the URL is often enough to verify the validity and veracity of the image. The second URL here is clearly from a collection of images at Cornell University Library on the French Revolution and on Lafayette. By working from right to left and breaking down the URL, you can readily determine where the image is from and how it is being used, and if, in turn, it is an accurate and valid source.

Without the accompanying URL on the second site, all we have is a digitalized handwritten page with no information about the creator, the context, or anything else. By using a program such as Adobe PhotoShop, an unscrupulous creator of a Web site could alter a document or photograph with relative ease in order to support a personal agenda. While there is no great controversy in lip salve, it is critical to look for possible hidden agendas, as well as physical inconsistencies in the images themselves. Do they look altered? Is there evidence of pixelization or smudging concentrated in one area? Do other photographs on this site have similar problems or issues? Are there higher resolution images available to the end user as well?

Digitized Primary Sources: Digital surrogates, in the form of online exhibitions and collections, have increased dramatically over the past few years. Institutional repositories, digital archives, and virtual collections of all kinds are becoming de rigueur in libraries and archives across the United States and beyond. Theses exhibitions and digital collections provide excellent opportunities to gain access to materials that, without the advent of the Internet and its rich graphics capabilities, would be nearly impossible to see. It is important, however, to keep in mind that materials seen online are surrogates, digital images of an original document. Whether the surrogates are being accessed or made available as preservation copies in the same repository where you are doing your research, or are being accessed from halfway around the world, it is critical to review the URL to determine where these images are from and how they are being used.

Copyright and Fair Use: It is essential to consider issues of copyright and fair use when using any resource, including Web resources. Copyright laws are complicated and confusing to most people, but some general rules must be kept in mind. Even if copyright information is not presented on the Web site or is not made clear or evident, the material most probably still falls under copyright law. While access to the material may be free on the Internet, you must adhere to the same copyright laws as with print material.

Citing Online Resources: The most recent editions of *MLA Handbook for Writers of Research Papers,* the *Chicago Manual of Style,* and the *APA Stylebook* all provide information on citing Internet sources. As in any bibliography, it is important to adhere to a prescribed style. Citation information that might not be readily apparent may be part of a credits or an "about the Web site" page on the site you are referencing. You need to provide the most complete and accurate bibliographical information that you can find.

Bringing It All Together

When doing a search for online sources, it is critical to understand the types of sources you are looking for. A user doing historical research needs to seek out sites that are best suited for the project at hand, such as material presented by experts in the subject matter or cultural agencies that specialize in that particular area. While the Web site for a regional chamber of commerce might offer current demographics information on a given area, that resource will not help you if your research focuses on the same geographic area in the mid-nineteenth century. Before you even begin to search the Web, you should define your research and decide what particular types of Web sites will be most helpful. The sources, whatever they may be, should match your purpose and reflect your goals.

Searching the Web

Using a search engine to seek out information online is a task that many people have grown very comfortable with over the past few years. But there is a question that *must* be considered by anyone doing Web searches: How do you know if you are really doing an effective search? Identify a good search engine by first seeking out the advice of your academic institution's library. As mentioned previously, the ubiquitous google.com has taken over as the number one search engine used not only to search the Internet, but to power specialized searches of institutional sites such as colleges and universities. Google is not the only search engine available, and it is important to try different search engines, using the same search terms, in order to see how your results may vary. Here are some factors to consider:

- The search interface: Is it clear? Easy to use?
- How large is the database?
- Is the material indexed by machine or by people?

- How well do the search capabilities (Boolean searching, advanced searching) work?
- Are the results ranked?
- Is there advertising intermingled with the search results?

When in Doubt. . . . ASK!

Working with online resources can indeed be daunting. While the sites named here are plentiful and excellent, we know that more and more history sites are being added to the Web every day.

Brief courses in online search skills are offered frequently in educational institutions and libraries of all kinds. It is also important to never hesitate to ask a librarian for advice and instruction in online searching. A few minutes of instruction can be extremely valuable and ultimately save time as well. Effective searching is a skill that can be learned. Seek out your local information professionals, those who are trained to pass on their information-seeking skills.

If you have a strong interest in a particular topic, it is a good idea to check the Web frequently for information on that particular subject. Some Web sites offer alerts to new sites and updates to their own that may further your knowledge and interest. Bookmarking sites and printing out key materials for future reference will also save time and effort later on.

By keeping these few principles in mind, developing the skills needed to evaluate online resources is not difficult. *The History Highway* has done some of this work for the searcher by providing online sources that have been scrutinized by scholars in their respective fields. As the Web continues to grow and change, researchers from all levels and disciplines must be prepared to access and to interpret the very best the Web has to offer without risking the use of inaccurate, or inappropriate information. By asking the right questions and approaching online research with a critical eye, an open mind, and an arsenal of evaluative tools, the history researcher can reap the ever-growing bounty of the Internet.

Note

1. American Library Association (ALA). *A Progress Report on Information Literacy: An Update on the American Library Association Presidential Committee on Information Literacy: Final Report* (Chicago: American Library Association, 1998), available at http://www.ala.org/ala/acrl/acrlpubs/whitepapers/progressreport.htm.

Part II

Internet Sites
for Historians

The history sites on the Internet present an astounding amount of information. No one could ever hope to examine and read everything that is now online. Of course, no one could ever read every book in the Library of Congress, either. This is why the Library of Congress is meticulously organized and cataloged. When you need to find a book or a fact, you can go to an index or turn to a librarian for assistance. There is no single Internet librarian, but the subject-area specialists who have written the following sections offer the same guidance and assistance you would get from a knowledgeable librarian or seasoned teacher. Part II of *The History Highway* is designed to help you find specific information when you are looking for it and guide you to interesting and useful sites that are worth examining for pleasure or serious study.

As you read this guide, you will notice that the historical sites on the Internet have been created by a wide variety of people, ranging from history professors and students to publishers and history buffs. There is also a broad range of content on the Internet. Some sites are scholarly; others are informal. Some are composed entirely of links to other sites. The resources described in *The History Highway* have been screened for quality, utility, and reliability. In an age of information superabundance, however, it is important that everyone become a skilled critic of electronic information. To help you make personal determinations about each site, whenever possible the names and sponsoring institutions or organizations are clearly indicated. Nevertheless, we urge you not to assume that every argument or resource that you encounter on the following pages is credible or valid. Just as many excellent books contain some errors and misinterpretations and every library contains fallacious books, so some of the sites mentioned here contain a mixture.

Chapter 3

Futuring Methods, Practitioners, and Organizations

David J. Staley

In the popular imagination, professionals who think about the future are often confused with science fiction buffs. The relationship between the professional futurist and the science fiction buff is akin to the relationship between the professional historian and the history buff. Professional futurists today use a variety of disciplined techniques and work in very practical settings, such as business, government, think tanks, universities, and nonprofit corporations. Below is a list of several such organizations and futurist practitioners. The goal of this list is to provide a sense of the variety of methods futurists employ, describe their Web sites, and detail the types of problems and situations they seek to address.

Anticipating the Future

http://ag.arizona.edu/futures/

This is the Web site for an online course (but not a formal credit-granting course) at the University of Arizona maintained by Roger L. Caldwell. Links to Tutorials, Tours and Seminars; Paradigms, Driving Forces, and Trends; Scenarios, Foresight and Change; and Futures Related Sites and Resources.

The Arlington Institute

http://www.arlingtoninstitute.org

This is the consulting firm of futurist John Peterson. Click onto the links for scenarios, gaming, group process design, and modeling complex systems, each of which offers an excellent description of these futuring methods. Peterson is especially well known for his examination of "wild cards," which he defines as "low-probability, extremely high-impact events that are social and techno-logical developments or natural phenomena [that are] (a) global in scope and directly affect the human condition; (b) potentially disruptive (negatively and/or positively); (c) intrinsically beyond the control of any single institution, group or individual; and (d) rapidly moving."

Battelle

http://www.battelle.org/forecasts/default.stm

Battelle Memorial Institute is a research and development center that works with both government and business to develop new technologies and products. This site is a link to its "Technology Forecasts" page, which includes the institute's Top 10 list of predictions in areas such as the future of terrorism and security, consumer products, and technology generally. See next entry as well.

Battelle: Dr. Futuring

http://www.battelle.org/dr-futuring/

This is the site of Battelle futurist and thought leader Steven Millett. Includes descriptions of futuring methods such as trend analysis and IFS (Interactive Future Simulations), a tool that uses cross-impact analysis to develop multiple scenarios. Includes a link to the technology forecasts noted above.

Center for International Forestry Research

http://www.cifor.cgiar.org/acm/methods/fs.html

This is a CIFR Web page on "Future Scenarios." Includes a link where you can download a brief guide to the variety of scenario methods and the problems to which they can be applied, especially "adaptive management." The file may take a few minutes to download, but the resource is worth the wait.

The Centre for Future Studies

http://www.futurestudies.co.uk/

A UK-based think tank that consults with business and encourages discussion, debate, and creative thinking about the future. Click onto "Recent Publications," which includes topics such as scenarios, nanotechnology, and transport. Site includes access to several PowerPoint presentations as well.

Club of Amsterdam

http://www.clubofamsterdam.com/default.asp

The Club of Amsterdam is "an independent, international think tank that supports thought leaders and knowledge workers to form opinions, visions and agendas about preferred futures." Made up largely of corporate leaders. The site includes a journal and links to articles on a wide array of topics such as nanotechnology, media and entertainment, food and agriculture, and culture and religion. Provides an interesting European perspective on futuring methods and interpretations of the future.

Club of Rome

http://www.clubofrome.org/

The Club of Rome is perhaps best known for its 1972 report *The Limits to Growth,* which predicted dwindling oil supplies by the turn of the (last) century and the resulting effects on economic growth. The Club of Rome is an international think tank that explores "the World Problematique," which it defines as a concept "to describe the set of the crucial problems—political, social, economic, technological, environmental, psychological and cultural —facing humanity." On this site, look especially at the links, the downloadable publications (note that some of these are in languages other than English), and the reports, although these have to be ordered separately. Look carefully for the link "tt30," which is a small think tank for futurists around the age of thirty. Includes a link to its book *Exploring a Worthwhile Future for All.*

Deloitte Touche Tohmatsu

http://www.deloitte.com

A global consulting firm, specializing in thought leadership in technology, media and telecommunications; real estate; manufacturing; life sciences; and other areas. This site has links to Deloitte Research, including downloadable position papers on a variety of trends that affect global business. Click on "Insights and Ideas," then click "Deloitte Research." On this page, click on "Deloitte Research by Category" to find links to research on trends in energy and resources, manufacturing, financial services, and consumer business. A highly recommended site.

DonTapscott.com

http://www.nplc.com/

The Web site of futurist Don Tapscott, who works especially with business strategy. This site contains a few links to his recent publications, which offer a quick view of his thinking.

Foresight International

http://www.foresightinternational.com.au/

According to Richard Slaughter, Foundation Professor of Foresight at Swinburne University of Technology, a director of Foresight International, and one of Australia's leading futurists, a futurist is "someone who has learned how to study the future and how to use this knowledge to enable others to identify options and choices now. By studying the future you can move away from a passive or fatalistic acceptance of what may happen to an active and confident participation in creating the future you want." Includes his essay, "The Making of a Futurist."

Foresight (UK)

http://www.foresight.gov.uk/

Science-based futurist projects sponsored by the British government, such as intelligent infrastructure systems; brain science, addiction and drugs; and cybertrust and crime prevention. The links to each project include project reports, executive summaries, and other reports and publications. The site includes links to other future-related Web sites.

The Foundation on Economic Trends

http://www.foet.org/index.htm

The think tank of noted futurist Jeremy Rifkin, the Foundation on Economic Trends "[examines] emerging trends in science and technology and their likely impacts on the environment, the economy, culture and society." Rifkin is an "activist futurist"; note especially the "Campaigns" link, which include his legal challenges and activist work in the areas of human cloning, the hydrogen economy, civil society, and biotechnology patents. Each link describes the activities of Rifkin and his foundation and links to other useful sites.

Global Business Network

http://gbn.com/

Cofounded by Peter Schwartz and Stewart Brand, the Global Business Network is one of the leading futurist organizations. Schwartz especially has been a pioneer in the application of the scenario method to business strategy. An important site, with access to some articles; look especially at those dealing with scenarios. However, beware: many of the links here require a subscription (which is very expensive).

Institute for the Future

http://www.iftf.org

The site offers no free information, but does provide useful descriptions of the kinds of futuring work the institute performs for business and organizations.

KurzweilAI.net

http://www.kurzweilai.net/index.html?flash=2

This is the site of inventor and forward thinker Ray Kurzweil. The AI in the title refers to "accelerated intelligence," the site informs us. Visitors to the site are guided by Ramona, a photorealistic avatar. Links to articles based around themes such as "How to Build a Brain," "Will Machines Become Conscious?" "Dangerous Futures," "Virtual Realities," "The Singularity" (a reference to the accelerating pace of technological change), and "Living Forever," are of particular interest to Kurzweil. Challenging, outside-the-box thinking, too important to dismiss easily.

The Long Now Foundation

http://www.longnow.org/

The Long Now Foundation "hopes to provide counterpoint to today's 'faster/cheaper' mind set and promote 'slower/better' thinking" by encouraging a very long-term perspective (the "long now" is defined as 10,000 years). Board members include Brian Eno, Esther Dyson, Peter Schwartz, and Stewart Brand. The foundation has begun a number of "slow" projects, such as the 10,000-Year Clock, the Rosetta Project (an archive of all the world's languages), and the All Species Foundation, which is dedicated to cataloging all of the earth's species.

The Millennium Project: Global Futures Study and Research

http://www.acunu.org/

This is a project sponsored by the American Council for the United Nations University. The project is "a global participatory futures research think tank of futurists, scholars, business planners, and policy makers who work for international organizations, governments, corporations, NGOs, and universities." Includes links to "Future Scenarios for Africa," "Lessons of History," "Environmental Security," and "Applications of Futures Research to Policy." A very useful site, highly recommended.

The Next Twenty Years

http://www.tnty.com/

The Next Twenty Years is a conference series on trends and scenarios in bio-technology, nanotechnology, medicine, and security. The site maintains links to a number of "essays on the future" and both webcasts and transcripts of previous conferences.

On the Horizon

http://horizon.unc.edu

On the Horizon is located at the University of North Carolina-Chapel Hill, whose mission is "to inform educators about the challenges that they will face in a changing world and steps they can take to meet these challenges." This useful site has links to the various projects carried out by the organization, a link to *Innovate: Journal of On-Line Education,* and links to conferences. Look especially at the link for "ON-RAMP," which includes links to a wide array of data and materials.

Plausible Futures Newsletter

http://www.plausiblefutures.com/

Site maintained by the Norwegian futurist Ole Peter Galaasen. In addition to links to news stories on science and technology, includes section on different futuring methods, including scenario planning. The site is filled with data, which makes it both valuable and also a bit user-unfriendly, but worthwhile in any event.

The RAND Corporation

http://www.rand.org

Although not known as a futurist organization per se, the RAND Corporation nevertheless provides useful analysis and environment scanning on a number of important topics that are relevant for futurists. This site is filled with downloadable reports on a wide array of topics, including education, the environment, population and aging, science and technology, and terrorism and homeland security. Look especially at the "hot topics" link for research on important issues like bioterror-ism, Iran, Iraq, surveillance, and social issues in Islamic countries.

Scenario Planning Resources

http://www.well.com/~mb/scenario/

Site maintained by futurist Martin Börjesson. Includes links to articles and reports on scenario methods and their various applications and organizations that employ scenarios. A useful site.

Shaping Tomorrow

http://www.shapingtomorrow.com/

A UK organization that tracks trends in business, government, technology, and society. Many of the features on this site require a subscription, so it may not be useful for schools and teaching purposes; the site is aimed largely at business and government clients (and those who can afford to pay). There is a free e-mail newsletter service that provides summaries of articles. Still, an important site that shows a good range of futuring methods and topics.

Social Technologies

http://www.socialtechnologies.com/

A consulting firm that helps clients look five to ten years forward, then applies those insights to strategic thinking in the present. Much of the site describes the services performed by the firm, but note especially the link to "2025." This provides "immersion in the world of 2025." This link is grouped according to fifteen topics, each providing thoughtful scenarios on topics including the built environment, health, energy, the environment and sustainability, work and leisure, and transportation. Most of the material here requires payment, but there are some free downloads.

Toffler Associates

http://www.toffler.com/default.shtml

An executive advisory firm formed by the noted futurists Alvin and Heidi Toffler. "We help companies and governments create their future in the fast emerging 'Third Wave' economy," they note, referring to their 1991 book on the emergence of the information- and knowledge-based economy. Includes a link to a brief number of publications.

The World Future Society

http://wfs.org

The leading futurist organization in the United States, the World Future Society "strives to serve as a neutral clearinghouse for ideas about the future, [including] forecasts, recommendations, and alternative scenarios." Look especially as the regularly updated "Forecasts" link for predictions in the areas of demographics, government and politics, the economy, technology, and culture and lifestyles. Look also at the "The Future: An Owner's Manual" link, which provides a useful description of different futuring methods and applications.

Chapter 4

Future Issues

David J. Staley

Like historical inquiries, an inquiry about the future requires evidence. Since no "archives of the future" yet exist, the futurist must rely on information and data located in the present, such as statistics, trends, journalistic accounts, and government reports. Futurists call searching for and being receptive to a wide variety of such information "environment scanning." Using the information gathered through environment scanning, the futurist can then infer implications and effects, creating useful representations of the future.

Historians do not examine the whole of the past, but rather tend to light upon certain key issues as historiographically important (varieties of social history and gender history are important to historians right now, for example). Similarly, professional futurists also center upon a few key areas of interest or concern, rather than considering the whole of the future. In addition to serving as excellent ways to scan the environment, the sites listed below are grouped according to those key issues that are currently drawing the attention of futurists:

1. the hydrogen economy and alternative energy
2. the Internet and communications
3. demographic and environmental trends
4. terrorism and security
5. nanotechnology
6. biotechnology
7. intellectual property

The Hydrogen Economy and Alternative Energy

The Alternative Energy Institute

http://www.altenergy.org/

AEI is a nonprofit corporation, and this site provides links to various news reports, syllabi, and case studies from around the world. There is some uncertainty as to the authorship of the site (there is little way to determine who or what interests the AEI represents) but the site does offer a perspective very different from that of official government sites or research labs and universities. Use with caution.

HyWeb—The Hydrogen and Fuel Cell Information System in the Internet

http://www.hyweb.de/

This site is maintained by L-B-Systemtechnik, a German commercial firm that "supports industry, politics and non-governmental organisations in the identification of new products and services, in the development of strategies for the introduction of new products and concepts, with system studies, in finding new partners-networking, in the project management and co-ordination of projects, with strategic consultancy services." Supplies access to articles and other publications that provide a useful European perspective. Quality of the links on the site is uneven, however; therefore use with caution. The site is maintained in both English and German.

IEEE: Investigating the Hydrogen Economy

http://www.ari.vt.edu/hydrogen/

A virtual discussion held by the Institute of Electrical and Electronics Engineers after a conference held in April 2004 titled "The Hydrogen Economy: Its Impact on the Future of Electricity." The site includes links to a discussion (which requires a user login), links to other organizations working with hydrogen, background documents in pdf formats, and abstracts from the presenters at the conference.

U.S. Department of Energy Hydrogen, Fuel Cell and Infrastructure Technologies Program

http://www.eere.energy.gov/hydrogenandfuelcells/

Provides a useful introduction to the main issues concerning the hydrogen economy and the technology of fuel cells. Interesting sections on "The

Hydrogen Future" and teaching materials for elementary, secondary, and university teachers.

The Internet and Communications

Center for the Digital Future

http://www.digitalcenter.org

Supported by the University of Southern California Annenberg Center for the Digital Future, the site includes yearly reports from the project "Surveying the Digital Future: A Longitudinal International Study of the Individual and Social Effects of PC/Internet Technology." This is "a long-term longitudinal study on the impact over time of computers, the Internet and related technologies on families and society." Includes links to the first three annual reports as well as findings from the first World Internet Report and the use of the Internet by Latinos. An important source.

Centre for Quantum Computation

http://www.qubit.org/

Located at Cambridge University, the CQC "conducts theoretical and experimental research into all aspects of quantum information processing, and into the implications of the quantum theory of computation for physics itself." Quantum computing weds aspects of quantum mechanics to information processing. Click on "Research," which links to different working groups, and on "Library" for links to articles, books, and presentations on quantum computing. The "Community" link includes links to researchers (and their home pages). See also "Tutorials." Warning: the information here is quite specialized, but nevertheless provides a useful introduction to the dimensions of the research involved here.

CompSpeak2050: Institute for the Study of Talking Computers and Oral Cultures

http://www.compspeak2050.org

This is the Web site for William Crossman, philosopher and futurist, who maintains that computers and computing will soon evolve into what he calls VIVO (Voice In/Voice Out) "talking computers." One of his more controversial claims is that written language will eventually be phased out and that VIVO will facilitate the creation of a new kind of electronic oral culture by the year

2050. The site includes links to articles Crossman has published (although note that many of these are published in various European languages) and conferences at which he has presented. Culture Challenging Conceptualization that is important for all futurists to consider.

First Monday

http://www.firstmonday.dk/

An online, peer-reviewed journal dealing with the Internet. Excellent articles on a range of issues, including open source, the politics of information, and the digital divide, especially the Internet in the developing world. Highly recommended.

Future of Computing

http://www.infoweblinks.com/content/futureofcomputing.htm

Sponsored by a textbook publisher, this is a collection of links on issues dealing with quantum, molecular, and DNA computing. Very interesting and useful links for thinking about the future of computing.

The Journal of Digital Information

http://jodi.ecs.soton.ac.uk/

An electronic journal developed by the British Computer Society and Oxford University Press, centering on "the management, presentation and uses of information in digital environments." The journal is organized thematically, although published in traditional "issue" format. These themes are Digital Libraries, Hypermedia Systems, Hypertext Criticism, Information Discovery, Information Management, Social Consequences of Digital Information, and Usability of Digital Information. A useful resource.

Liquid Information

http://www.liquidinformation.org/

Liquid Information is a project developed by Frode Hegland and Doug Engelbart (who developed the mouse). The project aims to "make text more interactive —turning words into hyperwords." In their vision, all the words on a screen would be linked to other forms of information. Click on "Demo" to see, for instance, a live CNN.com page. Click onto any word and a screen pops up, allowing the user to look up the word in a dictionary, to do a Google search, or link to other paragraphs that contain the word. The site is experimental, but suggests a new way of thinking about text on the screen.

Pew Internet and American Life Project:
The Future of the Internet

http://www.pewinternet.org/pdfs/PIP_Future_of_Internet.pdf

A January 2005 report of a survey of technologists, scholars, and members of the public that considers a wide variety of issues, such as the impact of the Internet on news and publishing, security, education, families, and civic engagement. A useful and highly recommended source.

Wired.com

http://wired.com/

The online version of the technology magazine. Not a futurist publication per se, but very good at locating cutting-edge developments and thinking through some of the implications. Covers many types of technologies (including biotechnology and nanotechnology).

Demographic and Environmental Trends

Bureau of Labor Statistics

http://stats.bls.gov/

Includes statistics on employment and unemployment, demographics, occupations, productivity, inflation and consumer spending, business costs, and geography. Includes links to publications and research papers.

Child Trends Databank

http://www.childtrendsdatabank.org/

Reports, tables, and figures on trends in health, social and emotional development, income, education, demographics, and family/community as related to American children. Data are very accessible, as the audience here is journalists, researchers, students, policy makers, and child advocates. Very useful, highly recommended.

A Demographic Perspective on Our Nation's Future

http://www.rand.org/publications/DB/DB320/

A downloadable PDF file of a complete, forty-nine–page book from the RAND Corporation. Considers demographic trends such as declining birthrates, generation gaps, economic disparity, and increasing ethnic diversity. The study then addresses the policy implications of these demographic trends.

Energy Information Administration

http://www.eia.doe.gov/

The Energy Information Administration is a statistical agency of the U.S. Department of Energy. Statistical data on a wide variety of energy sources, including historical data. Look especially at the link to "Projections to 2025," which includes forecasts for such topics as market forces, coal, emissions, and electricity. Site includes links to downloadable publications, press releases, and weekly updates.

Global Trends 2015: A Dialogue About the Future With Nongovernment Experts

http://infowar.net/cia/publications/globaltrends2015/

A CIA Web site that is not a traditional intelligence publication. Considers seven key "drivers" of the future: demographics, natural resources and the environment, science and technology, globalization, national and international governance, future conflicts, and the role of the United States. Site also considers major uncertainties, including asymmetrical warfare, demographic challenges in Europe and Japan, and unpredictable conditions in the Middle East and China. Contains useful charts, graphs, and maps. An excellent resource for thinking about the future.

Google Zeitgeist

http://www.google.com/press/zeitgeist.html

A compilation of trends in Google searches. Interesting way to gauge attitudes in the culture at the moment, although perhaps less useful for spotting longer term trends.

Hispanic Trends

http://www.hispaniconline.com/trends/

Online version of the print magazine *Hispanic Trends*. Online version has compilations of newspaper reports dealing with arts and entertainment, sports, business, politics, and education.

National Statistics, UK

http://www.statistics.gov.uk

British statistics dealing with a range of social trends, from agriculture and commerce to crime, unemployment, and population/migration. Filled with data, although sometimes confusing to navigate. Recommended nevertheless.

Online Trends: A Compendium of Data on Global Change

http://cdiac.esd.ornl.gov/trends/trends.htm

Site maintained by the Carbon Dioxide Information Analysis Center, which is described as "the primary global-change data and information analysis center of the U.S. Department of Energy." Includes trend data on atmospheric trace gas concentrations, greenhouse gas emissions, climate, and ecosystems. This information also includes useful graphics and data sets.

Population Reference Bureau

http://www.prb.org/

The Population Reference Bureau provides "timely and objective information on U.S. and international population trends and their implications." The site incorporates links for educators which include lesson plans. Click onto "Datafinder" for a database of world population and health statistics. "PRB library" links to many useful free publications. The site, which can be searched by topic or by region, includes links to other PRB Web sites, such as the Center for Public Information on Population Research and the Interagency Gender Working Group. Highly recommended.

Trends in Europe and North America

http://www.unece.org/stats/trend/trend_h.htm#ch1

Site maintained by the United Nations Economic Commission for Europe. Note that registration is required to look at the comprehensive data on this site; however, there is a "restricted area" link that provides access, without any registration, to a wealth of useful compilations of statistics covering a wide variety of topics, from energy and environment to families and education. Look especially at the brief but very useful country profiles, which include many tables and charts.

Trends in Japan

http://web-jpn.org/trends/index.html

Very interesting site on trends in Japanese science and education, business and economics, sports, fashion, and popular culture and society. Provides short articles, which are compilations and summaries of Japanese news sources, on each trend.

U.S. Census Bureau

http://www.census.gov/

A necessary resource. Population, economic and business, and geographic data are accessible from this site.

U.S. Department of Justice, Bureau of Justice Statistics

http://www.ojp.usdoj.gov/bjs/welcome.html

Statistics on victims and crimes, prosecution, law enforcement, courts and sentencing, corrections, and drugs. Includes tables and charts.

WHO Statistical Information System (WHOSIS)

http://www.who.int/whosis/en/

Site maintained by the World Health Organization. Tabular data on a wide variety of health issues and epidemiological data from countries around the world. Click onto the "Publications" link for several downloadable WHO publications. The "Research tools" link includes geo-referenced databases. Somewhat awkward to navigate, but filled with useful statistical data nevertheless.

Worldwatch Institute

http://www.worldwatch.org/

Worldwatch Institute "offers a unique blend of interdisciplinary research, global focus, and accessible writing that has made it a leading source of information on the interactions among key environmental, social, and economic trends." Main topics include people, nature, economy, and energy. This site includes links to many of the institute's publications (these are not free, although they are moderately priced). Free information is included on the site by following the link under "Research Library." See also the "Press Room" link.

Terrorism and Security

Al Qaeda, Trends in Terrorism and Future Potentialities: An Assessment

http://www.rand.org/publications/P/P8078/

Link to a downloadable PDF document from Bruce Hoffman of the RAND Corporation. Considers the current and future state of the Al Qaeda network, as well as future trends in terrorism, especially thinking about the forms future terrorist acts might take.

Department of Homeland Security

http://www.dhs.gov/dhspublic/

Includes links to news and press releases. Note especially the links to "Research and Technology."

Facts on International Relations and Security Trends (FIRST)

http://first.sipri.org/

Searchable database on a wide array of trends in international security, such as nuclear weapons, military expenditures, peacekeeping activities, arms production and trade, and conventional weapons holdings. The site is aimed at politicians, journalists, researchers, and the general public.

Future Directions in Terrorism: Implications for Australia

http://www.aspi.org.au/uploaded/pubs/SI_understanding_terrorism.pdf

Not a metasite, but rather a PDF of an address by Aldo Borgu of the Australian Strategic Policy Institute (ASPI), delivered on September 8, 2004, to the Special Operations Command Senior Leadership Group. Lays out what Borgu perceives as "basic facts" about terrorism and its implications for Australia. Asks poignant questions about the future of terrorism. An important perspective from outside the United States.

Homeland Security Institute

http://www.homelandsecurity.org

The Homeland Security Institute's mission is "to assist the Department of Homeland Security (DHS), Science and Technology Directorate and the DHS Operating Elements, in addressing important homeland security issues, particularly those requiring scientific, technical, and analytical expertise." Includes links to the *Journal of Homeland Security,* which has articles, book reviews, interviews, and commentary, and to a newsletter with links to news and press releases.

U.S. State Department: Patterns of Global Terror

http://www.state.gov/s/ct/rls/pgtrpt/

An annual report to Congress from the State Department on the level and scope of terrorist activities across the globe.

Nanotechnology

Foresight Institute

http://www.foresight.org/

According to the site, the Foresight Institute is an "educational organization formed to help prepare society for anticipated advanced technologies," and its advisory board includes notable names from the worlds of business, academics, and medicine. The site includes links to news reports, to a threaded discussion page, and to *Foresight Update*, a publication of the Institute. Very useful site.

The Institute of Nanotechnology

http://www.nano.org.uk

Attached to the University of Stirling Innovation Park (United Kingdom). Site includes links to universities, government research centers, and others engaged in nanotechnological research. Includes links to images, although many of these are PowerPoint quality (they are not very high resolution and just average quality). Users must join in order to view the full Web site, but an associate membership is free. Many parts of the site can be accessed without a login.

Nanotech Now

http://nanotech-now.com/

According to its mission statement, Nanotech Now seeks to "provide a forum and format that helps clarify nanotechnology and nanoscale science, to laymen, general business persons, non-specialists, highly skilled technicians, professionals, and academics. Our most basic intentions are to stimulate public debate, and to provide a single-source information point." Note especially the "Possible Futures" and "Image Gallery" links.

National Nanotechnological Initiative

http://www.nano.gov

The NNI is an association of federal research and development projects. Includes links to media reports on nanotechnology, and an educational resource link for elementary, secondary, and university students and their teachers.

Technology Review.com

http://www.technologyreview.com/

The online version of the MIT publication. Centers on leading-edge technologies, especially those that are ripe for commercialization. Also useful for keeping up with trends in biotechnology and in computing.

The University of Wisconsin-Madison Materials Research Science and Engineering Center (MRSEC) Interdisciplinary Education Group (IEG)

http://www.mrsec.wisc.edu/edetc/index.html

Site that focuses on nanotechnology as a way to teach science and engineering concepts to college students. Includes links to a wide array of teaching materials, slide libraries, kits, and modules. Intended for science teachers rather than those interested in the future implications of the technology, but accessible nevertheless.

Biotechnology

Bio.com

http://www.bio.com/

This site, which is aimed largely at life scientists and biotech companies, features many industry reports, covering topics such as genomics, proteomics, bioinformatics, and drug discoveries. Bio.com seeks "the exchange of information within the life sciences, biotechnology and pharmaceutical industries." Although these are specialized topics, the articles are written in journalistic fashion and so are accessible.

BioPortal

http://www.bioportal.gc.ca/english/BioPortalHome.asp?x=1

This official site of the Canadian government contains information on "government policy and research activity; business support programs and market intelligence; a virtual library of educational resources; and regulations on biotechnology research and applications."

The Biotechnology and Development Monitor

http://www.biotech-monitor.nl/

An online journal sponsored by the Network University in the Netherlands. The journal presents "critical views on biotech, agriculture, sustainable development and food security issues for developing countries." Most of the articles are written for a broad audience of policy makers, scientists, students, and journalists, and so are user-friendly. Issues are free, but subscriber information is requested. The site also includes an extensive collection of links, grouped by topic, geographic region, and type of organization, and each of these is grouped into subcategories.

Biotechnology Australia

http://www.biotechnology.gov.au/

A Web site sponsored by the Australian government. The "links" link connects to a wide variety of Australian and international Web pages dealing with biotech associations and services and educational institutions.

Biotechnology Industry Organization

http://www.bio.org/

An information, advocacy, and business support group, the Biotechnology Industry Organization provides links to press releases, speeches and publications, government and business reports, and position papers covering topics such as health care, intellectual property, and bioethics. Note especially the link to "Science Updates."

Biotechnology Information Directory Section

http://www.cato.com/biotech/

A metasite sponsored by Cato Research, which is "a full-service contract research and development organization with international resources dedicated to helping pharmaceutical and biotechnology companies efficiently and expeditiously navigate the regulatory approval process in order to bring new drugs, biologics, and medical devices to the people who need them." Does not appear to be related to the Cato Institute. Links to many sites, covering such categories as publications, products, clinical trials, and software.

Biotechnology Law Resources

http://biotech.law.lsu.edu/blaw/

A metasite from Louisiana State University's law school, the site includes links to terrorism and bioterrorism resources, biomedical engineering and the law, and cases and briefs related to biotechnology. Not as extensive as the Working Group on Environmental Justice site listed below, but still useful.

Biozone International

http://www.biozone.co.uk/BIOTECHNOLOGY.html

Biozone International is a publishing house in New Zealand that produces educational materials for secondary school students. This site is a metasite with links organized according to topics such as general sites, biotechnology techniques, biotechnology processes, applications in biotechnology, and issues and ethics of biotechnology.

The Center for the Study of Technology and Society

http://www.tecsoc.org/biotech/biotech.htm

This Washington, DC, think tank "examines the interaction of technological change and society. The Center will strive to emphasize and clarify the point that advances in technology are neither inherently good nor inherently evil—but that every new technology has the potential to cause problems, and the capacity to solve problems." This page is its "Biotechnology" page (the Center maintains several other such pages), and it includes useful links to newspaper articles on biotechnology. A very useful site.

Council for Biotechnology Information

http://www.whybiotech.com/

The Council for Biotechnology Information "communicates science-based information about the benefits and safety of agricultural and food biotechnology. Its members are the leading biotechnology companies and trade associations." Site is chiefly composed of articles written by the CBI. Includes sections for consumers, farmers, teachers and students, and journalists.

The Electronic Journal of Biotechnology

http://www.ejbiotechnology.info/

Sponsored by UNESCO, this online journal contains articles dealing with a wide range of biotechnological issues, with particular focus on the impact of biotechnology in the developing world. The site includes links to news, organizations, publications, and other information sources.

European Federation of Biotechnology

http://www.efbweb.org/

The European Federation of Biotechnology is an association "of all national and cross-national Learned Societies, Universities, Institutes, Companies and Individuals interested in the promotion of Biotechnology throughout Europe and beyond." The association is interested in promoting biotechnology in a "socially and ethically acceptable manner" and so is interested in issues of sustainability. The site is a collection of links to Web pages featuring the Federation's sections, working groups, and task groups. These Web pages largely report on the activities of each of these groups and do not contain many reports or publications, but they are useful and inviting nevertheless. Look for "weblinks" to a wide variety of information services, various European associations, and other related sites.

The European Initiative for Biotechnology Education

http://www.eibe.info/

This site features nineteen units dealing with a broad array of topics on biotechnology, such as "Biotechnology and the Environment," "The Human Genome Project," and "Biotechnology: Past and Present." Designed as teaching materials for sixteen to nineteen-year-old (European) students, each unit contains experiments, debate topics, and role-playing activities. Easy-to-access PDF files.

Friends of the Earth Europe

http://www.foeeurope.org/GMOs/Index.htm

A grassroots environmental organization, the site is devoted to issues surrounding biotechnology and genetically modified organisms. Site includes links to a quarterly magazine, *Biotech Mailout*; other FoEE reports and publications; press releases; and European legislation. This antibiotechnology site provides a useful perspective that should be considered.

Union of Concerned Scientists

http://www.ucsusa.org/food_and_environment/biotechnology/page.
cfm?pageID=340

The Union of Concerned Scientists aims to "augment rigorous scientific analysis with innovative thinking and committed citizen advocacy to build a cleaner, healthier environment and a safer world." This site is entitled "What Is Biotechnology?" and includes reports and short position papers.

Working Group on Environmental Justice

http://ecojustice.net/biotechnology/

Located at Harvard, this is a metasite that includes links to news reports (and many audio clips) dealing with issues such as biosafety, genetic engineering, intellectual property rights, world trade, and international relations. Extensive list of links.

ZNet: Biotechnology

http://www.zmag.org/biotechwatch.htm

A site maintained by activists against biotechnology. Includes links to organizations as well as to articles—really more like blogs—on biotechnology issues. A challenge especially to global corporations and outside the mainstream, the site offers a useful and provocative perspective nevertheless.

Intellectual Property

The Consumer Project on Technology

http://www.cptech.org/

The Consumer Project on Technology was started by Ralph Nader. This site includes links to legal documents, government reports, articles, patents, and commentary by CPTech.

Copyfutures: The Future of Copyright

http://lsolum.typepad.com/copyfutures/2004/08/the_future_of_c.html

Copyfutures is the blog for Professor Lawrence Solum's Intellectual Property Seminar at the University of San Diego School of Law. Also includes links to news reports, other blogs, and Web sites of universities and other organizations devoted to copyright issues.

Creative Commons

http://creativecommons.org/

Stanford University law professor Lawrence Lessig's organization, Creative Commons advocates "flexible copyright" for creative works and is one of the driving forces for a relaxation of existing copyright laws. Site includes features on and links to various flexible copyright sites covering music, text, education, images, and audio.

Electronic Frontier Foundation

http://www.eff.org/

Founded by John Perry Barlow (of Grateful Dead fame) and John Gilmore, the Electronic Frontier Foundation is an advocacy group interested in "civil liberties issues related to technology." (Lawrence Lessig belongs to the board.) Site includes links to news reports, legal briefs, and congressional briefings.

IP @ The National Academies

http://search.nap.edu/shelves/ip/

The National Academies are the congressionally chartered National Academy of Sciences, the National Academy of Engineering, the Institute of Medicine, and the National Research Council. Topics here include antitrust, copyright, database protection, international harmonization, technology transfer, and trademarks, among others. Most of the links here are merely order forms for books, but the link to the newsletter is free and useful.

The Motion Picture Association of America

http://www.mpaa.org/

Links to PDF files stating the movie industry's take on issues of piracy, digital copyright, and creativity. A frequent target of scorn by those advocating for "free culture," but this is a needed site to balance the views of the other advocacy groups listed in this section.

Public Knowledge

http://www.publicknowledge.org/

Public Knowledge defines itself as an "advocacy group working to defend your rights in the emerging digital culture." Lawrence Lessig sits on the board of directors; Siva Vaidhyanathan (author of *Copyrights and Copywrongs: The Rise of Intellectual Property and How It Threatens Creativity*) is on the advisory board. Intended for policy makers, scholars, journalists, and artists, the site is filled with links to data, news reports, analysis of current intellectual property debates, and press releases. The "Issues" link is a good place to start in order to organize all the complex facets of this issue.

Chapter 5

General History

Mary E. Chalmers

Metasites (General and Specific History Categories)

Galaxy

http://www.galaxy.com/directory/34479/

Galaxy, claiming to be the Internet's first searchable directory, provides links to history sites in thirty-eight categories, including oral and other types of history; treaties, pacts, and agreements; museums; philosophy of history; and this day and week in history.

ECHO: Exploring and Collecting History Online: Science, Technology, and Industry

http://echo.gmu.edu/center.php

This Center for History and New Media at George Mason University Web site "catalogues, annotates, and reviews" more than 5,000 sites on the history of science, technology, and industry. Searchable by topic, historical period, and source type, the Web site also provides guidance to find and learn about projects collecting historical materials online.

Tennessee Technological University History Resources

http://www2.tntech.edu/history/

This site is a good starting place for students to find not only historical resources (documents, textbooks, audiovisuals, archives, and so on), but also sources about careers, study, travel, and scholarly groups. Some of the material on the site is directed toward TTU students, but scrolling down reveals resources of broader interest.

Visual Arts Sources and Images

http://library.concordia.ca/research/subjects/arthistory/visualart/
artvisualart.php

This research tool from the library of Montreal-based Concordia University provides access to significant art history guides, museums, and resources for finding visual images of art, architecture, and art history from around the world. Additional sites focus on Canadian resources.

WWW Virtual Library for History

http://vlib.iue.it/history/index.html

http://rmweb.Indiana.edu/history/vl/index.html

The Virtual Library (VL) for History, formerly at the University of Kansas, now has its central catalogue at European University Institute in Italy, with a mirror site at University of Indiana. The VL has grown so much that the catalog is now an "integrated and international network of indexes," accessible by clicking on "WWW VL History." The catalog is searchable through Google and by epoch, country or region, topic, and research methods and materials.

Topic-Specific Sites

Arctic Circle

http://arcticcircle.uconn.edu/index.html

Arctic Circle is an educational site on the peoples, cultures, natural resources, and history of the Arctic region. It explores questions of social equity and environmental justice as connected to the diverse cultures, histories, political economies, and interests of the Arctic Circle. This site also provides extensive links to other Internet materials on culture, science, education, and other related topics. Arctic anthropologist Norman Chance maintains the site.

Collated Web Index of Historians and Philosophers

http://www.scholiast.org/history/histphil.html

This Web site, created by Danish graduate student Peter Ravn Rasmussen, provides available links to ancient, medieval, and modern historians and philosophers. The links, not all of which remain valid, range from online archives to each historian's or philosopher's publications and home page to biographies and notes.

History of Money

http://www.ex.ac.uk/~RDavies/arian/llyfr.html

This site is a good place to start if you want to know about the history of money and related topics. Based on Glyn Davies's *A History of Money from Ancient Times to the Present Day,* the site contains both a chronology of money through time and essays on the Vikings, Celtic coins, third-world debt, the European Union, the U.S. dollar, and more. The site also has Web links to other sites about money, its value, and its history.

Maritime History

http://ils.unc.edu/maritime/home.shtml

This site brings together the vast resources (Web links and library databases) available for researching maritime history. The classification system for the online resources largely follows the fourth edition of R.G. Albion's *Naval & Maritime History: An Annotated Bibliography* and its *Supplement* by B.W. Labaree.

Popular Culture

http://www.uky.edu/Subject/popcul.html

The University of Kentucky Libraries maintains this subject catalog on popular culture. While it has not been updated in a couple of years, most of the URLs are still valid. Find access to top-notch libraries, colleges, and organizations devoted to popular culture as well as a diverse mix of resources on popular culture.

Professional Cartoonists Index

http://cagle.msnbc.com/

Daryl Cagle, the cartoonist for the online magazine *Slate,* maintains this site of newspaper editorial cartoons. The site includes cartoons by cartoonists from around the world, with access to cartoon archives for many of the cartoonists. Currently, the site also has separate sections of cartoons about Iraq and about the War on Terror. In addition, the site provides lesson plans for integrating political cartoons into the classroom.

A Walk Through Time

http://physics.nist.gov/GenInt/Time/time.html

This site, maintained by the National Institute of Standards and Technology, presents a short, illustrated narrative about time through the ages. It begins with a look at ancient calendars and early clocks and continues through mechanization, standardization, and developing technology.

World Rulers

http://rulers.org

A source to find out names of rulers of countries and territories, including subdivisions, often back to 1700. It also has chronological accounts of the changes in status of these entities, including disputed areas. Foreign ministers of the twentieth (and sometimes nineteenth) century are also listed. It also identifies the chronology of leaders of many world religions and international organizations.

Resources for Historians and Students of History

Guide to History Departments Around the World

http://chnm.gmu.edu/resources/departments

The Center for History and New Media at George Mason University manages this searchable database of more than 1,200 history department Web sites.

H-Net Home Page

http://www.h-net.org/

H-Net is an innovative, international organization of scholars and teachers dedicated to developing the potential of the Internet to facilitate "the free exchange of academic ideas and scholarly resources." The site contains links to more than 100 discussion lists, each with its own scholarly or pedagogical focus. Discussions from those lists and peer-reviewed scholarly book reviews are accessible and searchable.

Internet History Sourcebooks

http://www.fordham.edu/halsall

An excellent site for finding primary documents is the Internet Sourcebooks. This site provides copy-permitted primary sources and links to other Web sites of primary sources. Begun as the Medieval History Sourcebook, the site has now expanded to cover ancient, medieval, and modern eras. Additionally, sourcebooks cover a range of regional, topical, and thematic categories.

K–12 Teachers Website for History and Social Studies

http://school.discovery.com/schrockguide/history/histg.html

The administrator for technology for Nauset Public Schools (Cape Cod, Massachusetts) and a former library media specialist, Kathy Schrock has put together a diverse array of links to sites appropriate for K–12 teachers. Besides links to other sites identifying additional resources, she has links to engaging topical sites such as "Wacky Patent of the Month," Nobel winners and related sites, "Evening News Abstracts" since 1968, and newspaper advertisements from 1911 to 1955. She also has guides to U.S. and world and ancient history sites from this URL.

Maps for Historians

http://www.lib.utexas.edu/maps/map_sites/hist_sites.html

This University of Texas Library Web site allows access both to the Perry-Castañeda Library Map Collection (historical maps grouped by geographic region, plus historical astronomical charts) and to historical maps available on the Web.

Chapter 6

Canadian History

David Calverley

Metasites

Canada's Digital Collections

http://collections.ic.gc.ca/

Billed as the largest Canadian history resource on the Internet, this site has over 600 digital resources available to researchers and students. The majority of the sites, however, are more suited for secondary and first and second year undergraduate students than academic scholars. The sites maintained vary in range from national historical events to local and regional resources and stories.

Canadian Archival Resources on the Internet

http://www.archivescanada.ca/car/menu.html

This site provides links to numerous Canadian archives and archival resources on the Internet organized by province, region, academic institution, and theme. There are also links to colleges and universities that offer archivist training programs. Not all the links are useful as each archive maintains its own Web site. Some of the archives provide searchable databases of their holdings that are useful for historians considering an extensive research trip.

Canadian Museum of Civilization Corporation

http://www.civilisations.ca/

A stepping-stone into Canada's numerous federal museums, this is a crucial site for those interested in these institutions and the history that each is dedicated to. This site links into numerous elements of Canadian history, covering social, military, political, archaeological, and Aboriginal histories that are too numerous to provide a complete listing. Some outstanding specific links are offered later in this chapter.

Libraries and Archives Canada

http://www.collectionscanada.ca/

The National Library of Canada and the National Archives of Canada can be accessed through this site. By clicking on "Search Archival Materials," the user accesses a number of primary documents and resources, as well as search tools to locate call and reference numbers for the archives' extensive holdings. This is particularly useful for those resources on microfilm that can be lent to the researcher's local or university library. By clicking on "Browse by selected topics," users can access a number of online resources. The "Amicus" link allows users to search the National Library of Canada's holdings. Included with the National Library is a new feature: the Canadian Thesis Portal. Users can download theses written since 1998 as PDF files. Both the National Library and the National Archives sites maintain numerous links to educational resources pertaining to various aspects of Canadian history.

General Sites

The Applied History Research Group

http://www.ucalgary.ca/applied_history/tutor/

Based at the history department at the University of Calgary, the AHRG is composed of senior undergraduate and graduate students who research various topics in Canadian history and then produce fairly comprehensive Web sites highlighting their findings. This is primarily a secondary resource as few primary documents are made available on the site. Canadian subjects include The Peopling of Canada, Calgary and Southern Alberta, Canada's First Nations, Colonial North America, and Peopling North America.

Archives of Ontario

http://www.archives.gov.on.ca/

Users can search the AO's collection on this Web site. The databases available are very useful and fully searchable, covering a range of materials from general resource searches to more theme-specific databases. In addition, the site offers very thorough histories of various events and themes in Ontario history with links for unfamiliar terms, and primary documents, photographs, and maps. These histories are changed periodically.

Canadian Constitutional Documents

http://www.solon.org/Constitutions/Canada/English/index.html

The Solon Law Archives contains important Canadian political and constitutional documents. The earliest is Charles II's charter to the Hudson's Bay Company in 1670 and the most recent is the 2001 constitutional amendment that renamed Newfoundland the "Province of Newfoundland and Labrador." This is an excellent primary resource site for anyone interested in the main events of Canada's political and constitutional development.

Canadian Department of National Defence— History Directorate

http://www.forces.gc.ca/hr/dhh/engraph/home_e.asp

This is a very well developed and useful Web site. It contains numerous downloadable books and pamphlets written by departmental historians. An important primary document resource, which can also be downloaded, is the Canadian Military Headquarters Reports about Canada's various roles in World War II. Also provided on this site is a list of the department's library holdings. This is an excellent research site for those interested in Canada's military history.

The Canadian Encyclopedia

http://www.thecanadianencyclopedia.com/
index.cfm?PgNm=Homepage&Params=A1

Academics and leading researchers and writers in various fields of Canadian history write entries for the encyclopedia. A search engine makes it very accessible. The entries are suitable for beginning research into almost any topic in Canadian history, although the information here should be supplemented with more detailed sources.

Department of Indian Affairs and Northern Development—Historical Treaty Information Site

http://www.ainc-inac.gc.ca/pr/trts/hti/site/maindex_e.html

This site provides downloadable research reports on Canada's Indian treaties, written by leading scholars in the field. The site also provides numerous links to a large variety of other sites about First Nations' history in Canada. Included on this site is an excellent bibliography of further print resources. This is a useful site to access treaty documents and other primary sources concerned with Canada's First Nations.

Dictionary of Canadian Biography

http://www.biographi.ca/EN/

The DCB is one of the most important research sources on the Internet for Canadian history. Started in the 1970s, the DCB began as a print resource written by specialists. A fully searchable database of this twelve-volume work makes this an indispensable research tool. Volume twelve takes Canadian history into the 1920s. A useful bibliography of both primary and secondary resources is provided at the end of each entry. It is a resource to use after gaining some background knowledge on the event or person one is studying.

Early Canadiana On-Line

http://www.canadiana.org/eco/index.html

This site contains 1.6 million scanned pages of early Canadian primary documents and a fully searchable database. These generally are previously published, but out-of-print, documents. There are resource links with short essays, biographies, and documents suitable for senior high school and first- and second-year undergraduate students. There are also a number of links to lesson plans and educational resources for teachers. The free version gives users substantial access to documents, but there is also a subscription service for full access to this resource. The site is maintained by the Canadian Institute for Historical Microreproductions.

European Exploration From Earliest Times to 1497

http://www.heritage.nf.ca/exploration/early_ex.html

Maintained by the Newfoundland provincial government, this site contains general information about the early exploration and settlement of northeastern North America from the Vikings to John Cabot, as well as descriptions of early nautical techniques. There are few primary documents on this site, but a number of useful maps clearly outline the explorers' routes. Bibliographies and links to important archival sites and maritime history sites round out this Web page nicely.

A History of the Native People of Canada

http://www.civilisations.ca/archeo/hnpc/npint00e.html

This site is maintained by the Canadian Museum of Civilisation. It offers a précis summary of all the chapters in J.V. Wright's two-volume work, *A History of the Native People of Canada.* It is concerned mainly with precontact First Nations. Although a very useful source, it was written for those with substantial previous knowledge in this field.

The *Jesuit Relations* and the History of New France

http://www.collectionscanada.ca/jesuit-relations/index-e.html

This site contains links to Reuben Gold Thwaites's translation of the *Relations* on the Early Canadiana Web site. Maintained by the National Library and National Archives of Canada, it contains an excellent essay on the historical context of the *Jesuit Relations.* A similar site is offered at *The Jesuit Relations and Allied Documents, 1610–1671* (http://puffin.creighton.edu/jesuit/relations/). This is a more useful Web page since the *Relations* can be downloaded. There is also a search engine to find specific information in the *Relations.*

The Prime Ministers of Canada

http://www.primeministers.ca/

This site contains useful biographies of all of Canada's prime ministers. Of particular interest are the short interview snippets with leading historians and commentators. One weakness, however, is the lack of primary source material. The site is therefore cursory in its treatment of Canada's leaders and should be supplemented with appropriate entries from the *Dictionary of Canadian Biography.*

The War of 1812 Website

http://www.militaryheritage.com/1812.htm

Although a commercial Web site, this site provides excellent articles and primary documents pertaining to the War of 1812. A number of primary documents are also provided. Links on this page lead to a similar site about the Seven Years' War/French and Indian War (1756–1763). There is one glaring weakness on this site: there is no information about the importance of First Nations allies to the British in Upper Canada.

Chapter 7

Latin and South American History

Kathleen A. Tobin

Metasites

H-LatAm

http://www.h-net.org/~latam/

A discussion network created by Humanities Net (H-Net) at Michigan State University. It puts scholars in contact with other Latin American history scholars around the world and provides access to reviews, papers, archives, etc.

Integration in the Americas

http://www.unites.uqam.ca/gric/integration.htm

Maintained by the University of Quebec at Montreal, this site contains a vast number of links related primarily to commerce and trade in the Americas. A valuable resource for scholars of international economic relations.

Internet Resources for Latin America

http://lib.nmsu.edu/subject/bord/laguia/

This site, compiled and maintained by Milly E. Malloy at New Mexico State University, is an excellent collection of links to databases, library sources, Web directories, and online books. Very valuable in all areas of research on Latin America.

Latin America Data Base

http://www.ladb.unm.edu

A news and educational service on Latin America and an online publisher and information center. Access to articles in its online publications (*Sourcemex, NotiCen,* and *NotiSur*) requires a subscription, but the site also includes a wealth of information through links.

Latin America Home Page

http://www.casahistoria.net/latam.html

Created by a former instructor in Argentina to provide history students with guidance and access to valuable Web sites, this site is a good place to start when doing any kind of research in Latin American history.

Latin American Network Information Center

http://www.lanic.utexas.edu

This is the best place to start in conducting research on Latin America. Categorized by country, by topic, and by source of information, the collection of sites is comprehensive.

Latin American Studies Links

http://www.unl.edu/LatAmHis/LatAmLinks.html

Categorized by topics and sources, this site is a collection of links addressing a variety of subjects. Contains teaching resources, government sites, university sites, and sources for topics such as economics, labor, and human rights. Maintained by DeeAnna Manning in the Department of History at the University of Nebraska, Lincoln.

Political Database of the Americas

http://www.georgetown.edu/pdba/

Provides access to a substantial number of government documents and reference materials important to all Latin American countries. Reference materials include extensive bibliographies and links to organizations. Available in English, Spanish, French, and Portuguese.

Zona Latina: Latin American Media & Marketing

http://www.zonalatina.com/

An excellent source of news information. Through this site, researchers have access to newspapers and articles from across the political spectrum.

General History

The Conference on Latin American History

http://www.h-net.org/~clah/index.php

Home page of the Conference on Latin American Studies (CLAH), an organization that promotes the study and improved teaching of Latin American history. The site provides information about the organization and includes links useful to students and professionals in the field. It is affiliated with the American Historical Association (AHA).

The Council on Hemispheric Affairs

http://www.coha.org/

This is the home page of the Council on Hemispheric Affairs, an independent organization that monitors U.S.-Latin American relations. It offers information on politics, economics, and diplomatic issues, plus thorough investigative reports.

Historical Text Archive

http://historicaltextarchive.com

Compiled and edited by Donald J. Mabry, a retired professor and now independent scholar, this site contains articles, e-books, essays, documents, and photos on all aspects of history, many of them dealing with Latin America.

Library of Congress/*Handbook of Latin American Studies* Online

http://lcweb2.loc.gov/hlas/

An online version of the *Handbook,* with an extensive bibliography on Latin America. This format allows scholars to search thousands of works selected by humanities and social science scholars. It also offers abstracts and complete bibliographic information.

Oxford Latin American Economic History Database

http://oxlad.qeh.ox.ac.uk/

Hosted by the Latin American Centre at Oxford University, this site is aimed at social and economic historians of Latin America. It allows scholars to research a wealth of statistical data from Latin American regions (population, government expenditures, etc.) for the period from 1900 to 2000.

RetaNet, Resources for Teaching About the Americas

http://retanet.unm.edu/

This Web site, designed for secondary educators, acts as an interactive learning community of teacher peers. It offers lesson plans, curriculum materials, and news sources.

Society for Latin American Studies

http://www.slas.org.uk/

Home page of the Society for Latin American Studies, the principal association of Latin American studies scholars in the United Kingdom. It holds links to other associations in the UK and elsewhere, as well as information links. Maintained by Katie Willis of the Department of Geography at the University of London.

Sources and General Resources on Latin America

http://www.oberlin.edu/faculty/svolk/latinam.htm

Compiled by Steven Volk of the Department of History at Oberlin College, this site contains a wide variety of Web sources including bibliographies, databases, maps, and primary source documents, organized by topic and by country.

USAID: Latin America and the Caribbean

http://www.usaid.gov/locations/latin_america_caribbean/

This official Web site of the U.S. Agency for International Development provides current projects and links to country and region profiles created by USAID.

Pre-Columbian Latin America

Anthro.Net: The Andes
http://home1.gte.net/ericjw1/andes.html

Contains bibliographic references and links to Internet sources for Andean archaeology and ethnography.

Foundation for the Advancement of Mesoamerican Studies
http://www.famsi.org/

This Web site for the Foundation for the Advancement of Mesoamerican Studies contains maps, information on Maya writing, and links to many pre-Columbian Web sites.

Indigenous Peoples
http://lanic.utexas.edu/la/region/indigenous/

From the Latin American Network and Information Center, this page provides links to information on indigenous groups in Latin America and their histories. Categorized by region and by ethnic group.

MEXonline: Mexico Pre-Columbian History
http://www.mexonline.com/precolum.htm

Links to general sites promoting pre-Columbian history and archaeology. Some sites are devoted specifically to the Maya, the Aztecs, or other indigenous groups.

Colonial Latin America

Bibliography on History of Ideas in Colonial Latin America
http://www.h-net.org/~latam/bibs/bibideas.html

This is simply a bibliography, but it is a solid one offering an extensive list of sources. Housed on the H-LatAm section of Humanities Net.

Colonial Latin America
http://www.college.emory.edu/culpeper/BAKEWELL/

This site contains an extensive chronology of colonial Latin American history and links to interactive "ThinkSheets" exploring numerous topics. Also a good source for early maps and primary source documents. Excellent source for students.

Internet Modern History Sourcebook: Colonial Latin America

http://www.fordham.edu/halsall/mod/modsbook08.html

Part of the Internet History Sourcebooks Project, an independent project given Web space and support by Fordham University. It offers links to articles and documents relevant to colonial Latin American history.

Resources in Colonial Latin American History

http://lib.ollusa.edu/netguides/newspain.htm

Compiled by Steven Wise, reference/instruction librarian at Our Lady of the Lake University in San Antonio, Texas. Provides links to reference materials, primary sources, secondary sources, and Internet sources.

Central America and the Caribbean

AfroCuban History: A Time Line, 1492–1900

http://www.afrocubaweb.com/history.htm

This site contains a thorough time line, plus links to some related sites. It also contains very valuable sources examining race and identity in the history of Cuba.

Association of Caribbean States

http://www.acs-aec.org

This Web site of the Association of Caribbean States, established in 1994 to promote cooperation among its members, has links to news, trade information, and various projects. In English, French, and Spanish.

Caribbean Community and Common Market

http://www.caricom.org/

The Web site of CARICOM is a good source of information on its member countries.

Central America Panorama

http://www.elpanorama.net/

Source of news and information on various countries in Central America categorized by country. Available in English, Spanish, and German.

History of Cuba

http://www.historyofcuba.com/cuba.htm

This site is compiled by J.A. Sierra, an independent scholar. It is one of the few such sites that remains politically neutral. It contains brief synopses of historical episodes, a valuable timetable and bibliography, and links to primary source documents.

Latin American Network Information Center: Caribbean Nations

http://lanic.utexas.edu/region/caribbean.html

LANIC source, offering links and information on Caribbean countries. Categorized by country.

Latin American Network Information Center: Caribbean Regional Resources

http://lanic.utexas.edu/la/region/caribe/

LANIC source, offering links and information on the Caribbean region. Categorized by topic.

United Nations Economic Commission for Latin America and the Caribbean

http://www.eclac.cl/

This Web site of CEPAL, one of five regional commissions of the United Nations. This site provides links to publications, press releases, analysis and research reports, and statistical information. Available in English and Spanish.

Argentina

Argentine History: General

http://www.historiadelpais.com.ar/

Thorough history of Argentina, including military, political, and social history perspectives. Available only in Spanish.

Latin American Network Information Center: Argentina

http://www.lanic.utexas.edu/la/argentina/

LANIC source on Argentina. Provides links to organizations, newspapers, and educational institutions in Argentina or containing information about Argentina.

Bolivia

Boliviaweb

http://www.boliviaweb.com

Aimed toward a general audience, but contains some good links to information about Bolivian history and culture.

Brazil

The Brazilian Institute of Geography and Statistics

http://www.ibge.gov.br/

Provides statistical information and analysis of Brazilian development. Indicators include population, agriculture, industry, trade, and natural resources. Available in Portuguese and English.

Brazilian National Government

http://www.brasil.gov.br/

Official Web site of the Brazilian government. Information on policies, projects, socioeconomic indicators, public utilities, and social services. Only in Portuguese.

Chile

Chilean National Library of Congress

http://www.bcn.cl/

Electronic access to the Chilean National Library of Congress. This site is very valuable to scholars researching Chilean law. Provides links to historic legislative documents. Only in Spanish.

Latin American Network Information Center: Chile

http://www.lanic.utexas.edu/la/chile/

Valuable source of links on Chile. Information on business, economy, education, the environment, history, human rights, etc.

National Institute of Statistics

http://www.ine.cl/

Offers statistical information and analysis on development and related indicators of population, agriculture, mining, energy, labor, etc. Only in Spanish.

Colombia

Gobierno En Linea

http://www.gobiernoenlinea.gov.co/

Official Web site of the Republic of Colombia. Contains links to government documents and history. Provides numerous links to government departments and organizations related to education, social welfare, energy, agriculture, etc. Only in Spanish.

Republic of Colombia

http://www.colostate.edu/Orgs/LASO/Colombia/colombia.html#History

This Web site, created and maintained by the Latin-American Student Organization, contains general information about history and geography and links to organizations, universities, newspapers, and municipal resources.

Ecuador

Ecuador

http://newbabe.pobox.com/~leer/ecuador

Very good information source on Ecuador, with links to newspapers, educational institutions, government, and economic organizations.

Indigenous Peoples in Ecuador

http://abyayala.nativeweb.org/ecuador/

Good source of links to information about the indigenous people and to indigenous organizations. Some information is in Spanish, some in English.

Mexico

Latin American Network Information Center: Mexico

http://www.lanic.utexas.edu/la/mexico/

Valuable list of links from and about Mexico. Provides access to organizations, educational institutions, newspapers, and academic research resources.

Mexican Archives Project

http://www.lib.utexas.edu/benson/Mex_Archives/Collection_list.html

List of rare books and manuscripts held in the Benson Latin American collection at the University of Texas library. The collection also contains many works in Latin American studies and Mexican American and Latino studies. This site describes the holdings of rare books and manuscripts.

Mexico Online: History

http://www.mexonline.com/history.htm

History page of Mexico Online. Provides general information on Mexican history, plus links to primary source documents, constitutions, and biographies.

Peru

Parliamentary Portal of Peru and the World

http://www.congreso.gob.pe/

Official Web site of Congress. Contains general information about the country and a wealth of information about Peru's government. Links to organizations, legislation, and documents. Only in Spanish.

Venezuela

Embassy of the Bolivarian Republic of Venezuela in the United States of America

http://www.embavenez-us.org

Web site of the Venezuelan embassy in the United States, providing information on government, economy, business, culture, and tourism. Has numerous links to government organizations, documents, and services available to Venezuelan citizens.

Republica Bolivariana de Venezuela

http://www.venezuela.gov.ve/

Official Web site of the Republic of Venezuela. Much of the site is devoted to the powers and policy of the president, but a deeper look into the site finds significant information on history, culture, the economy, the indigenous people, etc. Only in Spanish.

Selected Library Catalogs With Major Latin American Holdings

Biblioteca Nacional: Brazil

http://www.bn.br/

Biblioteca Nacional: Chile

http://www.bibliotecanacional.cl/

Biblioteca Nacional: Panama

http://www.binal.ac.pa/

Biblioteca Nacional: Peru
http://www.bnp.gob.pe/portalbnp/

Biblioteca Nacional: Portugal

http://www.biblioteca-nacional.pt/

Biblioteca Nacional: Spain

http://www.bne.es/

Duke University Libraries
http://www.lib.duke.edu/

Stanford University Libraries: Latin American and Iberian Collections

http://www-sul.stanford.edu/depts/hasrg/latinam/index.html

Tulane University Latin American Library

http://lal.tulane.edu

University of California at Berkeley Library

http://www.lib.berkeley.edu/

University of Florida Library

http://www.uflib.ufl.edu/

University of Illinois Latin American and Caribbean Library

http://www.library.uiuc.edu/lat/

University of Miami Library

http://www.library.miami.edu/

University of North Carolina at Chapel Hill Libraries

http://www.lib.unc.edu/

University of Texas Library Online

http://www.lib.utexas.edu/

Vanderbilt University Library

http://www.library.vanderbilt.edu/

Chapter 8

United States History

General United States History

John A. King

General Sites

AcademicInfo: US History Gateway

http://www.academicinfo.net/histus.html

Although this site is a bit cumbersome to navigate and is plagued by advertising, it is vast in its annotated listing of Web sites related to American history—there are thousands of links! Its list of digital collections, for example, contains links to many primary source collections on the Web, while its Teaching US History section has links to sites specifically designed with classroom applications in mind. Sites are organized here both thematically and chronologically.

The Adoption History Project

http://www.uoregon.edu/~adoption/

This Web site provides a very complete treatment of the history of adoption in the United States, primarily in the twentieth century. This site is easy to use, and it has a nice repository of primary sources on the topic.

AMDOCS: Documents for the Study of American History

http://www.vlib.us/amdocs/

Part of the Virtual Library: United States History, AMDOCS provides a vast collection of primary sources in American history. The chronological organization makes it easy to locate both specific documents and documents representative a particular time period. Documents are mostly political in nature (presidential documents, Supreme Court decisions, treaties, political tracts, etc.), but some literary pieces and song lyrics are included as well.

The Authentic History Center

http://www.authentichistory.com/

The Authentic History Center presents artifacts from American popular culture, dating back to the antebellum period. Organized chronologically, the site includes audio files (songs, speeches, and radio broadcasts of major events, among other items), documents (a small collection of letters and diaries), and a substantial number of images of various types (posters, photographs, cartoons, and even some comic books!).

The Avalon Project

http://www.yale.edu/lawweb/avalon/avalon.htm

The Avalon Project, housed at Yale University, is a collection of legal, political, and diplomatic documents from the earliest years of the United States to the present. The collection includes not only official documents such as treaties and addresses, but also some private correspondence, presidential papers, and other materials. This is one of the best places to find the full text of a treaty or act.

Biography of America

http://www.learner.org/biographyofamerica/

From the Annenberg/CPB project, the Biography of America is a series of twenty-six lectures in video format, embedded with music and images, given by prominent historians. Each video episode is viewable online, and the Web site contains supplemental time lines, maps, Webographies, and interactive activities for each episode.

Digital History

http://www.digitalhistory.uh.edu/

Like the Gilder Lehrman site (below), Digital History provides a vast array of narratives of the major periods of U.S. history (see the "Guides" portion of the Web site), as well as features on special topics in American history, such as "science and technology" and "ethnic America." A wide variety of primary sources complements the descriptive sections of the Web site. Digital History also includes a separate section for teachers, with excellent handouts and fact sheets, lesson plans, background information, and other teaching aids.

Divining America: Religion and the National Culture

http://www.nhc.rtp.nc.us:8080/tserve/divam.htm

The National Humanities Center presents in this Web site a broad collection of articles, all richly illustrated, on the significance of religion in America from the seventeenth to the twentieth century. In addition, the site provides an extremely thoughtful teacher's guide for teaching each of the twenty-five articles in the collection. This is an excellent place to learn about any topic in American religious history, from religious pluralism to African-American religion to Islam in America.

Documenting the American South

http://docsouth.unc.edu/

Documenting the American South is an effort of the University of North Carolina to provide online access to the Southern perspective in American history by publishing online documents from its special collections. Documents include government documents, diaries, slave narratives songs, and many other texts on topics as wide-ranging as Carolina history to religion to World War I. The texts are diverse in their representation of race, gender, economic status, occupation, age, and other demographic criteria.

Eyewitness to History

http://www.eyewitnesstohistory.com/index.html

Although this site does not limit itself to U.S. history, much on the site is relevant. The site provides eyewitness accounts of historical events, "history through the eyes of those who lived it," as the Web site proclaims. It does contain some very interesting documents, which could be useful complements to textbook reading in a survey course. For example, students might enjoy reading William Bradford's description of his time on the *Mayflower,* the testimonies of those surrounding President James Garfield after he had been shot, Sheriff Pat Garrett's account of his shooting of Billy the Kid, or Branch Rickey's account of his meeting with Jackie Robinson in 1945, resulting in Robinson's signing with the Los Angles Dodgers, breaking the color barrier in major league baseball.

From Revolution to Reconstruction . . . and what happened afterwards

http://odur.let.rug.nl/~usa/

This is probably the best place on the Web to find a narrative of American history from pre-Columbian to present times. The narrative on this site is essentially a compilation of several publications of the United States Information Agency. In a limited number of hyperlinks in the texts, the site enhances the USIA accounts with a nice collection of biographies and bibliographies.

The Gilder Lehrman Institute of American History

http://www.gilderlehrman.org/

The Gilder Lehrman Institute presents online twenty "modules" covering the major periods in American history, from the colonial period to 9/11. Each module includes a narrative overview of the period; a unique selection of ten or so primary sources; visual aids, including maps, graphs, and images; lesson plans; guided readings of primary sources; and recommended Web sites, books, films, and other resources.

History Matters

http://historymatters.gmu.edu/

From George Mason University, the History Matters Web site is designed especially for teachers of American history, but contains resources that should be helpful to any student of American history as well. The site contains a rich collection of primary sources along with instructive guides for interpreting them. In addition, the site includes articles on various topics in the teaching of American history; a very impressive annotated list of Web sites in American history, organized chronologically and topically; sample syllabi; lesson plans incorporating the use of the World Wide Web; and samples of students' work.

Jensen's Web Guides

http://tigger.uic.edu/~rjensen/0.htm

Professor Richard Jensen of the University of Illinois has prepared guides to historical research on the Web in the following fields: American political history, politics research (general), military history, the Civil War and Reconstruction, Thomas Jefferson, railroad history, the Vietnam War, and world populations. The guides on political and military history are especially useful. The guides are quite comprehensive, including both electronic and print resources. Jensen updates his guides regularly, indicating sites that he especially recommends, and he is usually accurate.

Kingwood College Library

http://kclibrary.nhmccd.edu/research.htm

Designed specifically for researchers, the Kingwood College Library (in Kingwood, Texas) research page has a splendid collection of links to pages and Web
sites on American history, highlighted by decade-by-decade discussions of American cultural history. These pages are detailed expositions of American cultural
history, with illustrations and a plethora of hyperlinks embedded in the text to
related Web sites. A similar set of pages exists for American popular music.

Library of Congress Web Site

http://www.loc.gov/

The Library of Congress has much to offer students of American history, both
at the Library itself and online. The home page of the Library of Congress provides links to the subsites below, as well as a catalog search, "ask a librarian,"
a link to the "global gateway" for doing research on world affairs, and general
information and news about the library.

Library of Congress: American Memory

http://memory.loc.gov/ammem/index.html

The result of a fifteen-year project of the Library of Congress and other libraries
and archives to digitize the "American experience," the American Memory site
presents over 9 million documents, including maps, still and moving images,
and recorded sound. The materials are organized into a hundred collections, but
the archive is easily searchable by term, category, time period, and document
type. This is easily the richest collection of American history primary sources
to be found online.

Library of Congress: Especially for Researchers

http://www.loc.gov/rr/

The Especially for Researchers page provides all the instruction necessary for
doing research effectively in the collections of the Library of Congress, either
in person or online. Links to digital collections, databases, interlibrary loan,
and finding aids are all located here.

Library of Congress Exhibitions Gallery

http://www.loc.gov/exhibits

This is a collection of online exhibitions from the Library of Congress. Much
of the material here can also be accessed via the American Memory Web site.

Those included in this collection are excellent and wide-ranging, including an outstanding one on the role of religion in American life to the mid-nineteenth century, another on the contributions of Bob Hope, and many other topics.

Library of Congress: The Learning Page

http://memory.loc.gov/learn/

The Learning Page is specifically dedicated to teachers. In addition to information on professional issues, the page contains many lesson plans, activities, and instructions and recommendations on using the digital collections of the Library of Congress in the classroom.

Library of Congress: Thomas

http://thomas.loc.gov/

Another site sponsored by the Library of Congress, Thomas is the primary site for "legislative information on the Web." The site contains the full text of the *Congressional Record* from the 101st Congress (1989–1990) to the present, and many materials from Congresses as far back as the 93rd (1973–1974). Additionally, Thomas includes information on the workings of the legislative branch of government and various historical collections, including several primary source collections and congressional biographies and bibliographies dating back to the First Continental Congress (1774).

National Archives and Records Administration

http://www.archives.gov/

The NARA site contains a plethora of documents, as well as an electronic "Exhibit Hall" containing more than thirty online exhibits on important themes in American history, including "100 milestone documents in American history." The site is especially useful for teachers, as its "Digital Classroom" contains not only a great many lesson plans, but also a variety of teaching aids (including very effective document analysis worksheets) for using primary sources in the classroom.

National Park Service: Links to the Past

http://www.cr.nps.gov/

Links to the Past is the home page for the National Park Service's excellent collection of historical information. Ranging from special features to the Web sites for individual parks and Web courses on history, archaeology, and preservation, the site offers a wealth of information useful to history students, teachers, and scholars. Especially good for teachers are the lesson plans prepared by the Park Service, under the title "Teaching with Historic Places" (http://www.

cr.nps.gov/nr/twhp/). These are some of the most well-prepared and interesting lesson plans for American history on the Web, incorporating primary texts, secondary readings, images, maps, background information, and a variety of study questions and activities for students.

Nature Transformed: The Environment in American History

http://www.nhc.rtp.nc.us:8080/tserve/nattrans/nattrans.htm

Similar to the Diving America Web site Nature Transformed is a National Humanities Center project. A very thorough and richly illustrated survey of American environmental history, the site provides an excellent overview of the topic. Articles, such as "The Columbian Exchange," "The Puritan Origins of the American Wilderness Movement," and "Roads, Highways, and Ecosystems," are all complemented by detailed and original teachers' guides for using the resources of the Web site in the classroom.

Oyez: U.S. Supreme Court Multimedia

http://www.oyez.org/oyez/frontpage

The Oyez site provides concise summaries of all major cases heard by the Supreme Court and, for many recent cases, provides audio excerpts of the reading of the Court's decisions. The Oyez site also provides biographies of all the justices who have served on the Supreme Court. The Oyez content can be easily searched or browsed. Oyez also provides a link to FindLaw, the Web site where the full text of court decisions can be located, along with other information of interest to legal scholars.

PBS: *American Experience*

http://www.pbs.org/wgbh/amex/

One of the best television series on the history of America, PBS's *American Experience* has covered political, economic, cultural, and technological topics in American history. Many of the episodes have companion Web sites, found here, with special features, biographies, time lines, bibliographies, teachers' guides, and transcripts of the programs.

Professor Donna M. Campbell's "American Literature" Site

http://www.wsu.edu/~campbelld/

Although Professor Donna Campbell's Web site is focused primarily on topics in American literature, there is much here useful to students of history. Naturally, history and literature are interrelated, and everything on the Web site, such as the section on American authors, is discussed in its proper historical context. The time line is actually two time lines, one of developments in literature and a corresponding time line of developments in social history, and topics in "Literary Movements" include not only the movements one would expect, but jeremiads, slave narratives, travel narratives, and other genres that should appeal to the historian.

The Smithsonian

http://www.si.edu/

The national museum of the United States, the Smithsonian Institution has published online an extensive and wide-ranging array of materials and exhibits based on its vast collections. While the history and culture exhibits are the most relevant to historians, exhibits in other collections also may be useful. In addition to exhibit-specific lesson plans, the Smithsonian site also has a special section for teachers, including lesson plans.

Tax History Project

http://www.taxhistory.org/

The Tax History Project Web site is an excellent one for anyone wishing to learn more about tax history in the United States and, even more broadly, about American economic history. Rich in images and audio files, the site includes the "Tax History Museum," which chronicles the history of taxation in the United States (though it is weak on the later part of the twentieth century), as well as information on presidential tax returns; discussions of special topics, such as the debate over taxation in the *Federalist Papers;* a collection of images; and an extensive collection of articles on specific topics in tax history.

U.S. Census Bureau

http://www.census.gov/population/www/index.html

The U.S. Census Bureau Web site contains the most recent census data, as well as historical census data dating back to the first official census in 1790. Users should also consult the Historical Census Data Browser (http://fisher.lib.virginia. edu/collections/stats/histcensus/), which allows users to sort, manipulate, and map census data, to the county level, from 1790 to 1960. The data includes both demographic and economic statistics.

WWW Virtual Library—History: United States

http://vlib.iue.it/history/USA/

This site is a vast resource for researchers of American history. Its links are organized both chronologically and thematically. This would be an excellent starting place for a research project, as there seems to be nary a topic that is not represented by the links on this site.

State Histories

State governments, state archives, state museums, state historical preservations societies, and universities are responsible for many good Web sites and resources online for state, regional, and local history. Many provide excellent case studies and/or examples of state history with the broader context of general American history. These Web sites showcase both interactive historical presentations and some very rich resources from the collections of state archives that could be windfalls for researchers. Users should also examine Chapter 29, "State and Provincial Historical Societies," later in this volume. Here are some of the best examples of this kind of Web site:

Adirondack History Network

http://www.adirondackhistory.org/

Although its featured topics are somewhat limited in number, the exhibits on this Web site are original and informative, and they also encourage users to consult the online digital archives of the Adirondack Museum for further research. Mostly centered in the Gilded Age and Progressive Era, some topics included are "Women's Work" and "Mose Ginsberg: From Immigrant Peddler to Honored Citizen."

Exploring Florida

http://fcit.usf.edu/florida/

This site contains over 4,500 images and 3,000 maps, in addition to movies, audio files, documents, and other sources, documenting the history of Florida. The site offers an impressive collection of historical texts that could be integrated into a U.S. history course, including topics ranging from colonial life to railroad building, urbanization, and ethnicity and diversity.

Kansas History On-line

http://www.kansashistoryonline.org/ksh/Index.asp

Some portions of this site are still under construction, but the site provides a very detailed outline of Kansas history, highlighting many major themes and developments in American history (e.g., sectionalism, the frontier, reform movements). There are also several featured topics, such as buffalo and Bloody Kansas, which are treated in great detail.

The Library of Virginia

http://www.lva.lib.va.us/whoweare/exhibits/index.htm

The state Library of Virginia maintains a number of online exhibits on topics ranging from slave revolts to roots music and from women's history to art history. The exhibits are narratives that are richly illustrated and are complemented by extensive selections of digitized documents from the state archives.

Maryland State Archives Museum Online

http://www.mdarchives.state.md.us/msa/educ/exhibits/html/exhibit.html

One of the state archives with the best presence online, the Maryland State Archives Museum Online offers several excellent exhibits, such as Maryland in Focus, a robust collection of images documenting Maryland's history, as well as an extensive presentation of primary sources from the state's history, covering all periods from the colonial to the recent.

Washington State History Museum

http://www.wshs.org/

In its virtual "Great Hall of Washington History," the Washington State History Museum provides the experience of its brick-and-mortar Great Hall online. Visitors can explore a variety of themes in American history, such as early encounters, pioneer life, and art history, through this virtual tour. In addition, like many state and local museums, the Washington State History museum has published the full text of many articles in its journal, *COLUMBIA,* online. Readers can find articles here on such diverse topics as environmental history, labor history, and sport history.

The Way We Lived in North Carolina

http://www.waywelivednc.com/

Based on the publication of a book by the same name, this Web site details the social history of North Carolina through narrative text and the generous use of images and maps.

Publishing Companies' Web Sites

Bedford/St. Martins's History Resource Center

http://www.bedfordstmartins.com/history/

Students and teachers should be fond of this Web site. The site contains documents, images, maps, and a nice complement of secondary sources on a variety of topics. In addition, short "critical thinking" modules focus on particular issues in U.S. history. Instructors will find the maps archive useful, with over 600 maps, including printable blank maps. Students will find the student study guides that accompany the Bedford texts invaluable, as they include chapter summaries, terms lists, multiple choice quizzes, some very fine map exercises, and many other activities. Registration is required for students and instructors, but is free and does not require the use of a Bedford/St. Martin's textbook.

Wadsworth's American History Resource Center

http://www.wadsworth.com/history_d/special_features/ext/am_hist/
AmerHis-ch01.html

Teachers and students alike will find the American History Center an extremely useful resource. The site is easy to use and highly interactive. Some of the features are intertwined with Wadsworth's *American Journey* textbook. The site contains documents, images, maps, animated features on immigration and demographics, and an interactive time line with links to further information about the people and events on the time line.

Chapter 9

African-American History

Mary Anne Hansen

Metasites

Academic Info: African-American History: An Annotated Resource of Internet Resources on Black History

http://academicinfo.net/africanam.html

This extensive listing provides quality sites on African-American history for researchers, university students, and teachers. The site lists and briefly describes metaindexes, digital libraries and archives, online publications, museum presentations, library and archival catalogs, resources for teaching, and some topics such as Martin Luther King, jazz, and slavery. It is a useful source for locating primary materials. The directory is created and kept updated by Academic Info, a private organization compiling subject indexes for respected Web sites on a wide range of topics.

African American History and Culture

http://www.si.edu/resource/faq/nmah/afroam.htm

This is a list of the Smithsonian's resources on African-American history and culture.

African-American West

http://www.wsu.edu:8080/~amerstu/mw/af_ap.html#afam

This multicultural American West metasite links to numerous Web resources about blacks in the history of the American West. Local sites included.

American Identities: African-American

http://xroads.virginia.edu/~YP/african.html

Produced by the University of Virginia American Studies Program, this site links to a wide range of sites, some of them historical. Although these and other related sites are hosted at the University of Virginia, they are not directly connected.

A–Z of African Studies on the Internet

http://www.lib.msu.edu/limb/a-z/az.html

A–Z of African Studies on the Internet is another general clearinghouse of links to African and African-American sites. Two Michigan State University librarians, Peter Limb and Ibra Sene, maintain the site.

Black History Pages

http://blackhistorypages.com/

This directory site provides links to a wide variety of Web sites having to do with black history.

Black Soldiers in the Civil War

http://www.academicinfo.net/africanamcw.html

This site links to several other sites about African-American history during the Civil War, including Buffalo Soldiers.

Christine's Genealogy Web Site

http://ccharity.com/

Important for black history as well as genealogy, this privately maintained site contains a variety of governmental documents and lists. Although the contents are scattered and searching is somewhat difficult, materials include immigration records to Liberia, a Freedmen's Bureau list of "outrages," lists of lynchings, census records, and similar records useful in both research and teaching. Also links to black history by members of local communities.

Classic African-American Literature

http://curry.edschool.virginia.edu/go/multicultural/sites/aframdocs.html

Links to online sites of classic African-American documents, some more historical than literary. This site also contains a wide range of documents, familiar and unknown, many of them useful in teaching history. Part of the Multicultural Paths Project at the University of Virginia.

Historical Text Archive: African-American History

http://historicaltextarchive.com/

A metasite created by a professor at Mississippi State University who publishes high-quality articles, books, essays, documents, historical photos, and links, screened for content, for a broad range of historical subjects. It includes a wide variety of links, including some to black history in particular states and regions, exhibits about blacks, primary sources, genealogy sites, and teaching materials. Although Mississippi State University hosts the site, the university takes no responsibility for it.

Social Studies School Services: Black History

http://www.socialstudies.com

This commercial organization offers lesson plans, student exercises, RealVideo clips of materials it sells, catalogs of its other materials, reviews of other sites, and links. Extensive, but materials are not guaranteed for accuracy.

General Sites

Aboard the Underground Railroad

http://www.cr.nps.gov/nr/travel/underground/

Aboard the Underground Railroad: A National Register of Historic Places Travel Itinerary introduces travelers, researchers, historians, preservationists, and anyone interested in African-American history to the fascinating people and places associated with the Underground Railroad. The itinerary currently provides descriptions and photographs of sixty historic places that are listed in the National Park Service's National Register of Historic Places, America's official list of places important in our history and worthy of preservation. It also includes a map of the most common directions of escape taken on the Underground Railroad and maps of individual states that mark the location of the historic properties.

African-American Community

http://www.cmstory.org/african/default.htm

A large collection of online photographs and other information about African-Americans for Charlotte and Mecklenberg County, North Carolina, sponsored by the local public library.

African-American Heritage

http://www.cr.nps.gov/aahistory/

Provides an extensive listing of resources on the subject, including a list of physical locations, along with relevant Web sites that are important in African-American history.

African American Labor History Links

http://www.afscme.org/about/aframlink.htm

Created by the American Federation of State, County and Municipal Employees, the nation's largest and fastest-growing public service employees union.

African-American Mosaic: A Library of Congress Resource Guide for the Study of Black History and Culture

http://lcweb.loc.gov/exhibits/african/intro.html

The major site and starting place for African-American materials online from the Library of Congress and a rich sampling of its larger collections. Included are a comprehensive text and images from the nearly 500 years of the black experience in the Western Hemisphere. Lesser-known topics include Liberia, abolitionists, western migration, and documents from the Works Progress Administration, the Federal Writers Program, and the Daniel Murray Pamphlet collection. Items within the African-American Mosaic can be searched online. The American Odyssey is separate from the American Mosaic.

African-American Resources at the University of Virginia

http://etext.virginia.edu/services/courses/rbs/rbs16-95/

This site contains an initial online group of texts of documents and images relating to slavery assembled by a special seminar of the Rare Books Division of the Library of the University of Virginia.

African-American Resources: Electronic Text Center

http://etext.lib.virginia.edu/speccol.html

An extensive collection of original documents ranging from nineteenth-century African-American issues to dozens of letters from notable individuals, including Mildred Carr and Thomas Jefferson.

African Americans in the West

http://www.library.csi.cuny.edu/westweb/pages/black.html

This section of WestWeb provides information about African-Americans in the West. Like much of the rest of WestWeb, it is constantly changing and developing. Under "Texts" users will find examples of primary texts, such as the letters of African-American GIs in World War II and secondary texts, such as critical essays and historical studies (coming soon). Under "Resources" are biographies of Western African-Americans, bibliographies, and teaching materials. Under "Links to Other Sites," users will find a collection of links to sites dealing with various issues in African-American history, such as overland migration, the Black Panthers, and cowboy history. Finally, under "Images," users will find both general collections that include some images of Western African-American history and direct links to pictures available online.

African Genesis: Black History

http://afgen.com/history.html

This site offers contemporary and historic information concerning black America and the African diaspora. The music section is concentrated on jazz, gospel, blues, and a little bit of soul. In the history section are articles on abolitionists and African-American pioneers. The religion section is currently restricted to African traditional religions. In the African American Griot News section there are news articles and reports of interest to black America and the Diaspora.

AfriGeneas

http://www.afrigeneas.com/

AfriGeneas is a site devoted to African-American genealogy, to researching African ancestry in the Americas in particular and to genealogical research and resources in general. It is also an African ancestry research community featuring the AfriGeneas mail list, the AfriGeneas message boards, and daily and weekly genealogy chats.

Africans in America

http://www.pbs.org/wgbh/aia/home.html

An ambitious site with many of the strengths and weaknesses of original public television production. Extensive documents, text, maps, and images are included along with careful lesson plans for teachers. Although the impressive panel of scholars who assisted with the project is listed, little attention is given throughout to the identity and qualifications of writers and speakers, creating problems for students trying to put materials in historical context.

Afro-American Sources in Virginia: A Guide to Manuscripts

http://www.upress.virginia.edu/plunkett/mfp.html

This is an electronic edition of a print guide jointly produced by Michael Plunkett of the University Press of Virginia and the University of Virginia's Electronic Text Center.

American Slave Narratives: An Online Anthology

http://xroads.virginia.edu/~hyper/wpa/wpahome.html

Texts, photos, and recordings of some selected Works Progress Administration interviews are presented online. Developed for classroom use at the University of Virginia.

Archives of African-American Music and Culture

http://www.indiana.edu/~aaamc/index.html

This is a large database dedicated to all aspects of African-American music and culture, including many links to related sites. The site is a project of the Department of Afro-American Studies at Indiana University.

Behind the Veil: Documenting African-American Life in the Jim Crow South

http://cds.aas.duke.edu/btv/

This is a major project to collect and make accessible oral histories and photographs recording the experiences of African-Americans in the Jim Crow South. The Center for Documentary Studies at Duke University is responsible for the project, with involvement from other universities and communities.

Black History and Classical Music

http://chevalierdesaintgeorges.homestead.com/History.html

This Web site provides an introduction to black history and classical music. It includes a black history quiz and previews to companion pages.

Black Pioneers and Settlers of the Pacific Northwest

http://www.endoftheoregontrail.org/blakbios.html

Produced by the End of the Oregon Trail Interpretive Center, this site provides a time line of blacks in the state, biographies and photographs of early African-Americans there, discussion of the state's exclusion legislation and slavery, and a bibliography of sources.

Charlotte Hawkins Brown Memorial, North Carolina Historic Sites

http://www.ah.dcr.state.nc.us/sections/hs/chb/chb.htm

This excellent site, created by the North Carolina Division of Archives and History, gives information about Charlotte Hawkins Brown, a leading black educator, and the school that she founded. Online texts of documents by and about her give insight into her own thought. Very extensive bibliographies give references to manuscript collections, theses, and primary material. Articles and reports, books, and pamphlets are listed for those doing additional research.

Civil Rights in Mississippi Digital Archive

http://www.lib.usm.edu/~spcol/crda/

This important site makes available to a wider audience the oral histories collected in the fall of 1997 by the staff members at the University of Southern Mississippi's Center for Oral History and Cultural Heritage and at the Tougaloo College Archives. It contains online texts of interviews, searchable in various ways, and a bibliography. The Mississippi State Legislature, Mississippi Department of Archives and History, and the Mississippi Humanities Council funded the project.

Database of United States Colored Troops in the Civil War

http://www.itd.nps.gov/cwss/

The United States National Park Service and the Civil War Soldiers and Sailors created this database and made it available online. In addition to 235,000 names, information is presented in about 180 histories of USCT units and regiments and links to sites about the most significant Civil War battles in which African-Americans fought. Click on US Colored Troops under Origin in the database to limit your search to African-Americans.

A Deeper Shade of History

http://www.seditionists.org/black/bhist.html

A Deeper Shade of History is one of the premier resources on African-American history, film, and literature. Created and maintained by Charles Isbell of MIT, it is an excellent resource for biographies, with well-developed accounts of figures such as Thurgood Marshall and Paul Robeson.

Desegregation of the Armed Forces: Project Whistlestop Harry S. Truman Digital Archives

http://www.trumanlibrary.org/whistlestop/study_collections/desegregation/large/

The Truman Presidential Library has digitized Truman's Executive Order 9981, calling for desegregation of the armed forces, and other documents from the study leading up to that decision.

Duke University Library and John Hope Franklin Research Center for African and African-American Documentation

http://scriptorium.lib.duke.edu/franklin/collections.html

In association with Duke Library's Digital Scriptorium, the Franklin Center publishes digitized versions of finding aids, subject guides, and materials from selected collections. Exhibits include African-American Women; Retrieving African-American Women's History; and Third Person, First Person: Slave Voices from the Special Collections Library, Duke University.

Exploring *Amistad* at Mystic Seaport: Race and the Boundaries of Freedom in Antebellum Maritime America

http://amistad.mysticseaport.org/main/welcome.html

This site, produced by the Mystic Seaport Museum, is one of the best teaching sites focusing on a particular event and its participants. Included are a brief narrative, a time line, and links to other sites. The online historical documents related to the capture of the ship and its occupants provide little-known information, and the teacher's guide presents a variety of activities, including a reenactment of the capture.

Faces of Science: African-Americans in the Sciences

http://webfiles.uci.edu/mcbrown/display/faces.html

Faces of Science looks at the past, present, and future of African-Americans in the sciences. It presents biographies of famous African-Americans grouped by scientific discipline, examines the percentages of doctorates granted to African-Americans in each area of the sciences, offers a wealth of statistical and demographic data, and contains links to other related sites.

The Frederick Douglass Papers Project

http://www.iupui.edu/~douglass/

Information about the project at Indiana University—Purdue University at Indianapolis to edit and publish Douglass's papers not included in the Yale edition of Douglass's works. The site includes links to other sites and a bibliography of recommended sources.

Freedmen and Southern Society Project

http://www.history.umd.edu/Freedmen/

Scholars at the University of Maryland are in the process of editing a multivolume collection of papers from the National Archives by and about men and women who became free from slavery during and after the Civil War. The project is funded by the National Endowment for the Humanities.

Harlem 1900–1940: An African-American Community

http://www.si.umich.edu/CHICO/Harlem

This impressive site was created at the School of Information at the University of Michigan as part of its Cultural Heritage Initiatives for Community Outreach. Items came from the Schomberg Center and include digitized texts and photographs. Suggestions for teachers using the materials and links to other related sites are also presented.

History Makers

http://thehistorymakers.com/

The initial goal of the History Makers site is to complete 5,000 interviews of both well-known and unsung African-Americans within the next five years, creating an archive of unparalleled importance and exposing the archival collection to the widest audience possible. Not since the WPA project of the 1930s, when teams of writers and researchers were sent throughout the South to conduct 2,300 mostly hand-recorded interviews with former slaves, has there been such a methodic and wide-scale attempt to capture the testimonies of African-Americans.

Inventory of African-American Historical and Cultural Resources in Maryland

http://www.sailor.lib.md.us/MD_topics/his/af_am.html

A very extensive listing by county of structures, historical sites, and collections materials in Maryland relating to African-American history. The Maryland Commission on African-American History and Culture supports the project.

Martin Luther King Jr.

http://www.seattletimes.com/mlk/index.html

One of the best sites about King for classroom teachers and students. Produced by the *Seattle Times,* it includes editorials, interviews, news columns, and photographs from the newspaper. King is presented in historical context, with a series of classic pictures from the civil rights movement. The study guide provides probing questions relating to King's holiday and larger questions of racial equality.

Martin Luther King Jr. Papers Project of Stanford University

http://www.stanford.edu/group/King/

The scholars at Stanford University who are editing and publishing King's writings have begun to make a sampling of his papers available online, including some of his most well-known documents. In addition, the site contains a bibliography file containing about 2,700 references to published works dealing with King and the civil rights movement.

Museum of African Slavery

http://jhunix.hcf.jhu.edu/~plarson/smuseum/welcome.htm

The Museum of African Slavery in the Atlantic is designed to provide accurate, engaging, and provocative information to the public about the history of slavery. The site is aimed at primary and secondary students and their teachers. The primary author is Pier M. Larson, a professor of African history at Johns Hopkins University.

National Archives and Records Administration

http://www.archives.gov/

Primary documents about African-Americans from the National Archives and teaching activities for using them in the classroom. Topics include the *Amistad* case, black soldiers in the Civil War, and Jackie Robinson. Other African-American materials can be found by searching the National Archives Digital Library. See also John H. White: Portrait of Black Chicago content at this site.

National Civil Rights Museum

http://www.civilrightsmuseum.org/

This site discusses the National Civil Rights Museum in Memphis, Tennessee. It contains a virtual tour of the museum's exhibits and their aims. Color and black-and-white photos are included. In addition to the tour, there are links to related sites, membership information, and admission.

Negro League Baseball

http://www.negroleaguebaseball.com/

This site provides information on Negro League baseball, including team histories and player profiles.

North American Slave Narratives, Beginnings to 1920

http://metalab.unc.edu/docsouth/neh/neh.html

Books, pamphlets, and broadsides written by fugitive and former slaves before 1920 are being collected and put online by scholars at the University of North Carolina. This National Endowment for the Humanities project, when complete, will include all such works.

Prairie Bluff

http://www.prairiebluff.com/

B.J. Smothers's private Web genealogy project, this site provides links to cemetery records and other documents and resources, especially in the South.

Schomburg Center for Research in Black Culture

http://www.nypl.org/research/sc/sc.html

The Schomburg Center for Research in Black Culture at the New York Public Library is a national research library devoted to collecting, preserving, and providing access to resources documenting the experiences of peoples of African descent throughout the world.

Selected Library African-American Online Catalogs

http://www.library.ucla.edu/libraries/url/colls/africanamer/cats.htm

A listing of some online catalogs of African-American materials created and maintained by the UCLA Libraries. A good source for locating materials, even though not all such collections are included.

This Is Our War

http://www.afro.com/history/OurWar/intro.html

A series of articles written by black war correspondents during World War II for the *Baltimore Afro-American*. This is part of a larger site on black history produced by the newspaper.

Voices of the Civil Rights Era

http://www.voicesofcivilrights.org/

Voices of the Civil Rights Era is an audio archive, sponsored by Webcorp, containing different views of the future from Malcolm X, Martin Luther King Jr., John F. Kennedy, and others.

W.E.B. DuBois Virtual University

http://members.tripod.com/~DuBois/

This private site is a clearinghouse for information on DuBois. It offers links to online texts by and about DuBois, a bibliography of articles and dissertations in print about him, and a list of DuBois scholars.

Women and Social Movements in the United States, 1600–2000

http://womhist.binghamton.edu/projectmap.htm

This site from the University of New York-Binghamton contains about twenty document sets, dealing with African-American women's history. Compiled for college and high school classrooms, this site contains materials by and about black women seldom found elsewhere. The project is funded by the National Endowment for the Humanities.

Writing Black USA

http://www.learnnc.org/bestweb/writeblack

Writing Black USA contains full-text essays, books, and poems documenting the African-American experience in the United States from colonial times to the present.

Chapter 10

Native American History

J. Kelly Robison

Native American History—General Links

American Indian Studies

http://www.csulb.edu/colleges/cla/departments/ais/faculty/trj/

This site, created by Troy Johnson at California State University, Long Beach, contains a useful list of links to Native American sites, including recognized and nonrecognized tribal sites, history sites, and activist sites. Also includes a large number of images of Native Americans from the precontact period to the present.

Bureau of Indian Affairs, U.S. Department of the Interior

http://www.doi.gov/bureau-indian-affairs.html

The Bureau of Indian Affairs has information on the tribes, tribal governments, some history, the treaties, and documents on current affairs in Native America. The documents make this site important for researchers and teachers delving into the current situation among Native Americans. The index page is a clearinghouse of Web sites and other governmental sites dealing in some way with Native peoples.

First Nations Site

http://www.dickshovel.com

This very political site, maintained by Jordan S. Dill, contains many internal pages that are generally diatribes against the system rather than anything of real value to the historian. However, the list of offsite links makes this site a good resource.

Images of Native America: From Columbus to Carlisle

http://www.lehigh.edu/~ejg1/natmain.html

Professor Edward J. Gallagher's students at Lehigh University created a series of online essays on how Europeans and Euro-Americans imagined Native peoples. The essays are nicely written and contain links to related sites.

Native American Documents Project

http://www.csusm.edu/projects/nadp/nadp.htm

Located at California State University at San Marcos, this site contains primary material related to allotment and the Rogue River War, Indian Commissioner reports of the 1870s, and some digitized versions of legislation such as the Dawes Act.

Native American History and Culture

http://www.si.edu/resource/faq/nmai/start.htm

An excellent starting place for information on Native American history and culture. Includes online Smithsonian exhibits; resources for teachers, parents, and students; and a quite extensive list of readings for various topics. No links, but this site in itself is worth looking into.

NativeWeb

http://www.nativeweb.org/

An extensive collection of links and articles both for and about indigenous peoples in the Americas. These links and articles are not just of a historical nature, but also contain political, legal, and social materials. Includes search engines, message boards, lists of Native events, and articles about what is currently happening in Native America. An excellent site from which to begin research.

Recommended American Indian Web Sites

http://www.public.iastate.edu/~savega/amer_ind.htm

The list of links in this site by Susan A. Vega García can be found in many other locations, but the list of links to e-journals pertaining to Native issues is impressive.

This Day in North American Indian History

http://americanindian.net/

Phil Konstantine's Native American history and culture Web site seems, at first glance, an amateurish attempt by a history buff to have something on the Web. However, despite the somewhat cheesy "Moons" and other such things, Konstantine's links page includes an incredible 8,000 links. "Dates" is well worth clicking on.

Native American History—Topical

1492: An Ongoing Voyage

http://www.loc.gov/exhibits/1492/

This digital exhibit from the Library of Congress contains numerous short essays on life in the Americas and in Europe prior to the European voyages. The "voyage" then continues through a brief view of European conquest of the Americas from the Caribbean to the shores of North America. The thumbnail images within the essays are wonderful visual descriptors of the topics and can be viewed in larger format.

The Avalon Project: Relations Between the United States and Native Americans

http://www.yale.edu/lawweb/avalon/natamer.htm

A superb collection of primary documents relating to Native peoples compiled and digitized by the Yale Law School Avalon Project. The main focus of this site is treaties between the U.S. government and tribes. The site also includes statutes, presidential addresses, and a few court cases involving Native Americans. Although the list of documents on the main Native American page is relatively small, a search of the site will produce many other statutes in HTML format.

The Aztec Calendar

http://www.azteccalendar.com

Created by Rene Voorburg, this nicely done site examines the Aztec calendar. The opening screen depicts the current date in Aztec glyphs. Also contains a calculator that converts any date to its Aztec equivalent. The introduction is a brief, but thorough, essay on the calendar and its meaning.

Cahokia Mounds State Historic Site

http://www.cahokiamounds.com/cahokia.html

Run by the Illinois Historic Preservation Agency, Cahokia is the site of a pre-European city across the river from St. Louis, Missouri. The site lists upcoming events at the park and some information on the archaeology and history of Cahokia. This site seems to be a continual work in progress since it has very few new items posted within the past two years.

National Indian Law Library

http://www.narf.org/nill/

This site, maintained by the Native American Rights Fund, contains an extensive list of tribal documents, including constitutions and codes. Of equal interest are the links to Supreme Court cases concerning Native issues and extensive links on Native law issues, including primary documents and secondary resources.

Native American Authors

http://www.ipl.org/div/natam/

Part of the Internet Public Library, this section of the larger site can be browsed by author, title, or tribal affiliation. There is no search engine or subject browsing, however. Individual title "cards" contain basic bibliographic information plus some works by the authors.

Native American Nations

http://www.nativeculturelinks.com/nations.html

An alphabetical listing of Web sites either maintained by Native nations themselves or dedicated to a particular nation.

Sipapu: The Anasazi Emergence into the Cyber World

http://sipapu.ucsb.edu/

The site not only begs the reader to explore Anasazi architecture and archaeology, but also asks for contributions. The research section contains a database of Chaco outliers (great house communities) and a bibliography of related print works. It also links to several scholarly papers on the Anasazi. One interesting item is a wonderful little toy that allows 360-degree viewing of the Great Kiva of Chetro Ketl at Chaco Canyon National Monument. Created by John Kanter at the University of California at Santa Barbara.

Chapter 11

American West

J. Kelly Robison

The American West is generally thought of as the region of the United States west of the Mississippi River, though sometimes as the area west of the ninety-eighth line of meridian. Yet Western historians also study westward expansion, which brings in that area between the Appalachian Mountains and the Mississippi River. For many years, the "frontier" and the West have been synonymous, harking back to the debate over Frederick Jackson Turner's frontier thesis. In practice, thus, Western American history encompasses a wide scope of place and time. Chronologically, Western History embraces the entirety of human history of the West; from the beginnings to the present day. The study of the American West is a diverse field and the following World Wide Web sites reflect that diversity.

General Resources

America's West—Development and History

http://www.americanwest.com/

Though, at first glance, this site seems hokey and interested solely in the much-mythologized "Old West," it does contain a nicely organized series of pages of useful links to other sites.

New Perspectives on *The West*

http://www.pbs.org/weta/thewest/

The Web site for the PBS special on the American West produced by Ken Burns. An extensive site with links to a wide range of primary documents, articles on various Western topics, and biographies of Western figures.

WestWeb: Western History Resources

http://www.library.csi.cuny.edu/westweb/

A growing collection of topically organized links to Western history resources created and maintained by Catherine Lavender of the City University of New York. The site is broken down into thirty-one different chapters, each of which contains numerous links to sites that specialize in that topic. Some of the topic chapters also contain image thumbnails linked to National Archives photographs. The site is indexed. This site should be the first place anyone interested in Western history sites on the Web should go.

The American West—Topical

Buffalo Soldiers and Indian Wars

http://www.buffalosoldier.net

Although this site concentrates almost exclusively on the role of African-American soldiers in the campaigns against Native peoples, it provides a nice synopsis of that topic. Links embedded within the text (there are photographs as well) go to shorter essays on particular individuals or events or offsite to other pages that cover a topic in more detail.

California Heritage Collection

http://sunsite.Berkeley.EDU/calheritage/

From the Bancroft Library, this site is a collection of over 30,000 images of California's history and culture. The site, part of the Online Archive of California, also includes resources for K–12 instructors. Because of the sheer volume of images, some pages take a long time to load.

California Mission Studies Association

http://www.ca-missions.org/

Dedicated to the study and preservation of California's missions, this organization's Web site contains articles on the missions, a nice glossary of mission-related terms, and some wonderful photographs. The site also maintains both annotated and nonannotated links pages.

Frederick Jackson Turner, "The Significance of the Frontier in American History" (1893)

http://www.library.csi.cuny.edu/dept/history/lavender/frontier.html

Although brief, this page by Catherine Lavender contains not only a link to the hypertext of Turner's "Frontier Thesis," but also links to other sites on Turner and a short, but excellent, bibliography. For the teacher of Western history, Lavender has included a number of questions about the thesis that students could, and perhaps should, use in their examination of Turner.

Ghost Town Gallery

http://www.ghosttowngallery.com

This site is fun rather than of deep interest to the serious research historian. The reader can access photographs of the various ghost towns through either a listing by state or through a clickable map. Some information about the towns, such as dates of founding and significance, are given, though the reader could wish for more.

The Interactive Santa Fe Trail Homepage

http://www.kansasheritage.org/research/sft/

Created for Kansas Heritage, this site's most interesting feature is its extensive list of other sites related to the Santa Fe Trail. The sizable bibliography of Santa Fe Trail books and articles, print and online, primary and secondary, is also worth looking into. This site is a great starting point from which K–12 students can explore the history of the trail and the people who used it.

The Japanese-American Internment

http://www.geocities.com/Athens/8420/main.html

Contains a time line of the Japanese-American internment, basic information on the camps, and remembrances of internees. Numerous links to other Web sites and to primary documents are also available on this site by John Yu.

The Lewis and Clark Expedition

http://www.pbs.org/lewisandclark/

The Ken Burns PBS production companion site. Contains excerpts from the Corps of Discovery journals, a time line of the journey, maps of the expedition, and numerous other related materials. Also contains interviews with authorities on the expedition and classroom resources for teachers.

Mountain Men and the Fur Trade: Sources of the History of the Fur Trade in the Rocky Mountain West

http://www.xmission.com/%7Edrudy/amm.html

A resource for the study of the fur trade era. This site contains transcribed primary documents from the fur trade era, digitized business records, and a nice collection of digitized images of artifacts and art from the period. A nicely done site.

Multicultural American West

http://www.wsu.edu:8080/~amerstu/mw/

Essentially an online, annotated bibliography of sites relevant to the study of the American West. As the site's name implies, most of the resources and links are related to ethnicity in the West. The number of links and resources, including documents and first-person accounts, is impressive. Designed by Washington State University's American Studies program.

The Overland Trail

http://www.over-land.com/

A site dedicated to Ben Holladay's Overland Trail, created by Elizabeth Larson. Contains a large amount of information, including a clickable map to articles. The articles range from those strictly about the route and stopovers to Indian problems along the route. Links to other sites are categorized by topic and include brief descriptions.

The Silent Westerns: Early Movie Myths of the American West

http://xroads.virginia.edu/~HYPER/HNS/Westfilm/west.html

Mary Halnon's site devoted to the portrayal of the West in silent film. The brief, but excellent essays on the early film industry and mythologized elements in the Western movies are supplemented by footnotes and images of early films and silent movie stars.

Utah History Encyclopedia

http://www.media.utah.edu/UHE/

Just as the name implies, the UHE is encyclopedic in style and scope. Over 200 contributors wrote close to 600 articles, containing more than 200 photographs, on topics in Utah history. The site does not contain a search engine, though this hardly matters since the frames version of the site lists topics alphabetically and navigation is easy as long as readers know what they are looking for.

The Vigilantes of Montana: Secret Trials and Midnight Hangings

http://montana-vigilantes.org/

This site, maintained by Louis Schmittroth, contains a wealth of information on the Montana vigilantes. The site contains online books and articles by well-known Montana historians. The politics of the site are apparent, but the information contained within is well worth perusing.

Who Killed William Robinson?

http://web.uvic.ca/history-robinson/

A wonderful resource for teachers, this site by Ruth Sandwell and John Lutz takes the reader through a historical mystery to determine the identity of a murderer. Contains primary documents and asks pertinent questions dealing with race, politics, and settlement.

Women Artists of the American West, Past & Present

http://www.sla.purdue.edu/waaw/

Created by Susan Ressler of Purdue University and Jerrold Maddox of Penn State, this online exhibit of female artists provides essays on those artists or particular groups of artists. The Web site is originally from a distance-learning course, as the syllabus makes abundantly clear. But the syllabus also ties together the various elements of the site into a coherent framework.

Chapter 12

Mexican-American History

Ben Frederick

Association for the Advancement of Mexican Americans

http://www.aamainc.com/

The AAMA is focused on modern Mexican-American issues. This should be one of the first stops for research on current issues and policies.

The Azteca Web Page

http://www.azteca.net/aztec/index.shtml

Simple and useful, if very commercial, metasite. (The home page carries awards lists that amount to advertisements for the awarding agencies.) Topic links connect related themes on Mexican and Mexican-American culture. Some threads are outdated, referring to events long resolved, such as the discussion of California's Proposition 227, which dates back to a law enacted in 1998.

Beginning Library Research on Chicano/ Latino Studies

http://www-library.stanford.edu/depts/ssrg/adams/shortcu/chic.html

Stanford University Library site. Contains links to several online resources, as well as highlighting some important written works in Hispanic-American culture. Useful for beginning research in the area, but less helpful for those who have already studied the field for some time or completed a significant amount of research for a project.

Bilingual Education and English as a Second Language Resources

http://www.csun.edu/%7Ehcedu013/eslindex.html

This is the personal metasite of Dr. Marty Levine, a specialist in secondary education. It is specifically tailored to teachers of English as a second language (ESL), students in a bilingual classroom or people learning a foreign language abroad.

Border Crossings

http://www.uiowa.edu/~commstud/resources/bordercrossings/frontera.html

Metasite discussing the Mexico-Texas border, focusing not just on border crossings, but on their impact on cultures and peoples as well. Additional areas of the site discuss such cultural borders as queer identity and the use of cyborgs in science fiction.

Border Information Resources

http://lib.nmsu.edu/subject/bord/

A resource devoted to Latin American information, the Border Information Resources metasite has information relating to U.S.-Mexico border issues and several free databases of articles. This is a good starting point for research and a regularly updated resource to mine repeatedly.

California Ethnic and Multicultural Archives

http://www.library.ucsb.edu/speccoll/cema/cema.html

CEMA's mission is to make researching specific cultures and ethnicities easy. The site is specifically tailored for the University of California at Santa Barbara, but there are still quite a few resources useful to the larger population. The related links area is an excellent starting point, but the List of Guides will likely provide the most help in multicultural, not just Latin American, research.

Center for Mexican American Studies

http://www.utexas.edu/depts/cmas/

The Web site of the University of Texas at Austin's Center for Mexican American Studies has various resources, including sections on program information and summaries of publications. Also useful for research is the contact information for the program's professors.

Center for Multilingual, Multicultural Research

http://www.usc.edu/dept/education/CMMR/home.html

This University of Southern California site has a plethora of resources for public use. It has many useful links to other sites. Of specific interest to researchers are the USC Latino and Language Minority Teacher Projects (http://www-ref.usc.edu/~cmmr/LTP.html) and the Center for Research on Education, Diversity, and Excellence (http://www-rcf.usc.edu/~cmmr/crede.html).

Chicano and Chicana Space

http://mati.eas.asu.edu:8421/ChicanArte/html_pages/Protest-home.html

This site, focused on Chicano and Chicana art, is rich in resources. There are many images of Chicano and Chicana art, information about the works, and lesson plans for teaching the art.

Chicano/LatinoNet

http://clnet.ucr.edu/

CLNet, the Chicano Studies Research Center at UCLA, contains a huge categorized metasite for Latin American resources. Of particular interest are the "Electronic Publications" links, the "Chicana Resources" links, and the "Communities" links. The third contains a list of resources from selected cities with large Latino populations.

Chicano(a) Research Collection at Arizona State University

http://www.asu.edu/lib/archives/chicano.htm

Allows online searches for books, databases, and journals. Also lists the specific holdings included in the Chicano Collections and has links to a special Chicana area. Several links are to Arizona-specific resources, like the Sonora Arizona, 1907–1965 area of the site. Others detail general themes in Chicano(a) history.

Chicano Studies at the University of Wyoming

http://uwadmnweb.uwyo.edu/ChicanoStudies/

The course information section of this site gives detailed descriptions of the courses offered in the Chicano studies program. An excellent starting point for a research project or class syllabus.

Harvard Journal of Hispanic Policy

http://www.ksg.harvard.edu/hjhp/

The current issue of the *Harvard Journal of Hispanic Policy* is available online for no cost.

Hispanic Culture Review

http://www.gmu.edu/org/hcr/

Previous volumes of this journal, from 1992 to 2002, are available online.

Hispano America, USA

http://www.neta.com/~1stbooks/content.htm

An award-winning Web site focused on the Latin American contribution to the modern day United States. Much of the site is focused on military contributions. If users have trouble accessing the site, http://www.neta.com/%7E1stbooks/ allows them to download a Word file that will act as the home page for them to click and link from.

Inter-University Program for Latino Research

http://www.nd.edu/%7Eiuplr/

A comprehensive site from the University of Notre Dame containing research information, census data, and online community links. The IUPLR publications section contains a bibliography of the group's works, and the research aids section is a useful metasite for scholars at all levels.

Julian Samora Research Institute

http://www.jsri.msu.edu/

This Michigan State University site on Latin American studies contains hundreds of research reports, statistical briefs, and working papers. The site is fully searchable, making for a highly accessible resource.

LASPAU

http://www.laspau.harvard.edu/

The Latin American Scholarship Program of American Universities, housed at Harvard University, has an extremely useful search function that allows for full-text search of all digital information on the site, including its grants and scholarships section, its workshops section, and its online newsletter.

La Raza Studies at San Francisco State University

http://www.sfsu.edu/~raza/

The links portion of this site is still under construction and must be accessed by clicking the "links" button, then selecting the "links" option under the "under construction" message. However, the list accessed is a rich metasite of history resources.

Mauricio Gastón Institute for Latino Community Development and Public Policy

http://www.gaston.umb.edu/

The University of Massachusetts at Boston's Gastón Institute page has a useful metasite in its Other Resources section. It links to many Latin American and Mexican-American organizations throughout the country.

Mexican-American Library Program

http://www.lib.utexas.edu/benson/mals/mals.html

The Mexican-American and Latino studies Web site at the University of Texas at Austin houses the outstanding, voluminous Benson Latin American Collection, which should be the first stop in any Latin American research endeavor.

Mexican American Voices

http://www.digitalhistory.uh.edu/mexican_voices/mexican_voices.cfm

Digital History at the University of Houston combines many different resources into a coherent whole, with references, that tells a comprehensive story of Latin Americans in the United States. Contained within are links to many other resources.

Research Guide to the Records of MALDEF

http://www-sul.stanford.edu/depts/spc/guides/m673.html

For researching Mexican-Americans in the legal system, Stanford's Web site for the Mexican American Legal Defense and Education Fund should be the first stop.

Resource Center of the Americas

http://www.americas.org/

The Americas.org Web site is an extensive resource about current events in Central America. The most useful section, from a research perspective, is the

Southern Voices section, which contains links to many articles dealing with Central American issues.

Smithsonian Center for Latino Initiatives

http://latino.si.edu/

The most useful academic features here are the links to museums with Latin American exhibits. These frequently contain partial digitalizations of the exhibits, as does the main site.

Tomás Rivera Policy Institute

http://www.trpi.org/

Specializing in research focused on policies relating to Latin Americans, the research section of this site is an excellent resource. Most of the recent research publications are available as free downloads.

Chapter 13

Asian-American History

Ben Frederick

General Asian American Studies Resources

American Studies Crossroads Project

http://www.georgetown.edu/crossroads/#asia

This site compiles a number of resources and includes sections for an online community, curriculum information for professors planning a new class and students planning their academic careers, and an extensive research and reference section.

Asian American History Timeline

http://www.cetel.org/timeline.html

This time line includes links to selected historical documents, most of which are legal documents maintained by government agencies. Time line links are divided into a single two-century (1600–1799) and three fifty-year (1800–1849, 1850–1899, and 1900–1949) time periods, with a final link encompassing the period from 1950 to the present. Most entries in the time line are brief and serve largely as jumping-off points for researcher interest.

Asian American Studies Resources

http://sun3.1ib.uci.edu/%7Edtsang/aas2.htm

Compiled by Daniel Tsang, this site comprises a large number of resources for and about Asian-Americans, ranging from magazines and journals to libraries and movement groups. Users should watch for outdated links claiming to be new.

Asian Media Watch

http://www.asianmediawatch.net/

This site focuses primarily on promoting fair handling of Asians in the mainstream media. It has successfully protested many racially insensitive movies and television and radio programs. Though infrequently updated, it is a good litmus test of the popular reaction to movies, television shows, and advertisements featuring Asian themes. The site also has a link allowing visitors to receive e-mails when updates take place.

Asian Pages

http://www.asianpages.com/

This is the online edition of *Asian Pages*. The site has easy access to the current issue via the sidebar. The archive is online and is accessed through the search section. The publication discusses a wide range of Asian-American interests and includes sections focused on current events, education, the arts, and even short stories.

AsianWeek

http://news.asianweek.com/news/

The online version of the *AsianWeek* newspaper contains both current news and access to all past articles. Aimed at a popular rather than an academic audience, *AsianWeek* is nonetheless a good reference for scholars seeking information on specific topics.

Association of Asian American Studies

http://aaastudies.org/index.tpl

The AAAS Web site is a resource in progress, with a small links section. It contains links to a number of colleges with Asian-American history programs.

Census 2000 Briefs: The Asian Population: 2000

http://www.census.gov/prod/2002pubs/c2kbr01–16.pdf

This pdf file requires the use of the free Adobe Acrobat Reader. It is the official documentation and statistics for Asian-Americans from the 2000 U.S. Census. Included are maps and graphs of population distribution.

Digital History: Asian-America

http://www.digitalhistory.uh.edu/asian_voices/asian_voices.cfm

Digital History compiles many resources that would be found on a metasite into a single online textbook, with references, that tells a comprehensive story of Asians in America. Contained within are links to other resources and a time line. The home page links to primary sources, virtual exhibitions, and a thorough teacher resources area.

National Asian American Telecommunications Association

http://www.naatanet.org/

For a rental fee, visitors can view any of hundreds of Asian studies films.

Smithsonian Asian Pacific American Program

http://www.apa.si.edu/

This Smithsonian program has information on recent exhibitions and a resources section containing useful links to additional sources. The Research and Collections section highlights the Smithsonian's recent additions to its Asian studies program. Links can be difficult to use, so if the site appears unresponsive, users may have to repeat-click the link.

Chinese-Americans

Angel Island: California's "Immigration Station"

http://www.fortunecity.com/littleitaly/amalfi/100/angel.htm

The entirety of Mary Bamford's 1917 book on the process of immigration in the West is available here. Written by a white missionary, the book is an accurate presentation of the era's anti-Asian prejudices, best used to demonstrate historical white perceptions about Asians.

Angel Island Immigration Station Foundation

http://www.aiisf.org/

The official Angel Island Web site, dedicated to the preservation of this important landmark where many Chinese-Americans entered the United States between 1910 and 1940. Now owned by the California State Parks bureau, the location is preserved and maintained by a number of nonprofit agencies. The site includes an educator link offering access to the Pacific Link educational Web site, which houses a short Angel Island video.

Angel Island: Journeys Remembered by Chinese Houstonians

http://cgi.chron.com/content/chronicle/special/angelisland/

This Houston Chronicle Web site is an excellent primary source for interviews with people born in China who immigrated to America and were detained at Angel Island between 1910 and 1940. The site contains seven narratives from immigrants who finally moved to Houston, Texas, and includes images from the era before the administration building on Angel Island burned.

Asian Immigration to Hawaii

http://mcel.pacificu.edu/as/students/hawaii/index.html

This is a well-written article with additional resources linked throughout. It discusses Chinese, Japanese, and Asian islanders' migration to Hawaii to work on the sugar plantations. This site is part of Pacific University's Web ring that contains further resources, including discussions of interracial relationships and the social classes that emerged in Hawaii as immigrant laborers arrived.

Chinese Americans in Tucson, Arizona

http://parentseyes.arizona.edu/promise/

A Web site that examines the contributions of Chinese-Americans to Tucson, starting with the railroad workers in the late 1800s. Included here are some video clips and longer videos (all viewable online), a list of related publications, and short biographies of prominent Chinese-Americans from Tucson.

Chinese Culture Center Links

http://www.c-c-c.org/link/link.html

A fairly diverse metasite from San Francisco's Chinese Culture Center, with a wide variety of links to topics of interest for those studying Chinese-American culture and history. The site is divided into the following categories: Society and Culture, History and Genealogy, News and Magazines, Business and Software, Organizations, and Resource Areas. Since the site is updated only every few months, it would be wise to watch for broken links and outdated information.

Chinese Historical Society of America

http://www.chsa.org/

This Web site discusses the Chinese History Society's current exhibits and special collections. Also links to a Web log and a video of Chinese history in San Francisco from the earthquake of 1906 until 2006. The video requires the use of Macromedia Flash. Researchers will also be attracted to the links section.

Chinese Historical Society of Southern California

http://www.chssc.org/index.html

The historical resources available on the CHSSC Web site are impressive. There is a fairly extensive time line, a set of links, and sections on the Chinese population of San Luis Obispo and on the Chinese veterans of World War II.

Documents on the Chinese in California, San Francisco Museum

http://www.sfmuseum.org/hist1/index0.html

This San Francisco Virtual Museum site contains several written works and artworks relating to Chinese-Americans. The resources are mostly from the mid-1800s through the early 1900s, though there are a few works after that period. Of particular interest are the photographs from old Chinatown and the personal narratives of those who survived the 1906 earthquake and subsequent fire.

Gateway to Gold Mountain Exhibit

http://www.apa.si.edu/APA_Exhibits_gatewaytoGold.htm

The online site for the Smithsonian's exhibit Gateway to Gold Mountain. Contains a brief history of Angel Island.

Museum of Chinese American History in Los Angeles

http://www.camla.org/

In addition to museum-specific information, this Web site includes articles on a variety of topics, including silent film actress Anna May Wong, the Chinese-American experience in California's San Gabriel valley, and a history of the Los Angeles police department and the Los Angeles County sheriff's department.

Japanese-Americans

100th Battalion/442nd Regimental Combat Team

http://www.katonk.com/442nd/442/page1.html

This article focuses on one of the most highly decorated combat groups from the World War II era, the Japanese-American 100th Battalion/442nd Regimental Combat Team.

Ansel Adams's Photographs of Japanese-American Internment at Manzanar

http://memory.loc.gov/ammem/aamhtml/aamhome.html

This site, hosted by the Library of Congress, is home to Ansel Adams's dramatic photographs of the internment camp at Manzanar.

Chronology of Japanese American History

http://www.janet.org/janet_history/niiya_chron.html

A brief history of Japanese-Americans. The time line spans the mid-1800s to the late 1900s. Entries are generally a paragraph in length and offer data for keyword searches.

Documents, Reports, and Letters Related to Relocation on Bainbridge Island, WA

http://www.lib.washington.edu/exhibits/harmony/documents/

The University of Washington hosts text copies of original papers, letters, and documents relating to the wartime relocation and internment of Japanese-Americans in 1942.

Hirabayashi v. United States (1943)

http://caselaw.lp.findlaw.com/cgi-bin/getcase.pl?court=us&vol=320&invol=81

This is the full Supreme Court ruling in *Hirabayashi v. United States,* one of the cases upholding the internment of West Coast Japanese and Japanese-Americans during World War II.

Japanese American Exhibit and Access Project

http://www.lib.washington.edu/exhibits/harmony/default.htm

This page, hosted by the University of Washington, is focused on Japanese-American internment during World War II. It contains a virtual exhibit and a searchable archive.

Japanese American National Museum

http://www.janm.org/index.html

Contains exhibit information, both historical and contemporary, as well as a resources section with links to other useful sites.

Japanese American Network

http://www.janet.org/

JA Net is a group based in Little Tokyo in Los Angeles with the goal of using the Web to promote communication between Japanese-Americans. Many links are currently broken, but the forums still have frequent contributions.

Japanese Americans in San Francisco

http://www.sfmuseum.org/hist1/index0.1.html#japanese

This site contains a short list of links from the San Francisco Museum that cover the time period from the turn of the century through World War II.

Japanese Americans Internment Camps During World War II

http://www.lib.utah.edu/spc/photo/9066/9066.htm

Over 900 photographs of the Tule and Topaz internment camps are housed at this site, hosted by the University of Utah.

Korematsu v. United States (1944)

http://usinfo.state.gov/usa/infousa/facts/democrac/65.htm

The full ruling in *Korematsu v. United States*, which again upheld the discrimination and internment of Japanese-Americans during World War II.

A More Perfect Union: Japanese-Americans and the Constitution

http://americanhistory.si.edu/perfectunion/non-flash/index.html

The Smithsonian Museum's online exhibit focuses on the treatment of Japanese-Americans during the World War II era.

Photographs by Dorothea Lange

http://www.loc.gov/exhibits/wcf/wcf0013.html

The Library of Congress hosts the pictures of Japanese-American oppression taken by Dorothea Lange during the World War II era.

War Relocation Authority Camps in Arizona, 1942–46

http://parentseyes.arizona.edu/wracamps/camplife.html

This site contains a large photo collection documenting Japanese internment in Arizona along with articles, a good links page, and additional resources. This page is hosted by the University of Arizona.

Yasui v. United States (1943)

http://caselaw.lp.findlaw.com/scripts/getcase.pl?navby=search&court=
US&case=/data/us/320/115.html

A historic Supreme Court case during the Japanese-American internment in World War II that was decided at the same time as Hirabayashi and which held that a Japanese-American citizen did not lose his citizenship merely by being convicted of violating the curfew order, which a lower court had held.

Korean-Americans

Finding Home: Fifty Years of International Adoption: Korean Adoptees Remember

http://americanradioworks.publicradio.org/features/adoption/a1.html

The American Public Radioworks showcase contains a well-written article on Korean-American adoptees along with corresponding streaming audio.

Korean American Historical Society

http://www.kahs.org/

The Korean-American Historical Society has a large collection of links for Korean culture, history, communities, and networks. This should be one of the first stops for Korean-American research.

Korean American History Timeline

http://www.asianweek.com/2003_01_10/feature_timeline.html

This time line in *AsianWeek* gives an overview of Korean-American history since 1864.

Korean American Museum

http://www.kamuseum.org/

The museum site contains information on current and past exhibits. Of particular interest are the sections on Korean-American culture and community. The culture link discusses the relatively recent advent of Korean-American art, and the community link houses a good history discussion.

Korean Americans: A Century of Experience

http://www.apa.si.edu/Curriculum%20Guide-Final/index.htm

The Smithsonian Asian Pacific American Program produced this online work showcasing the last hundred years in Korean-American history. The site includes a very comprehensive links page for other resources and an excellent time line as well.

Korean Quarterly

http://www.koreanquarterly.org/

This magazine is the digital version of *Korean Quarterly*. All issues since 2001 are available online, and earlier issues are in the process of being digitized.

Philippine-American Links

Filipino American National Historical Society of Stockton

http://www.geocities.com/tokyo/pagoda/4534/filipino.html

This site, maintained by the Filipino American National Historical Society, contains a collection of links to Filipino-American sites and is a good starting point for research on the subject.

Filipino American Photographs of Ricardo Ocreto Alvarado

http://www.apa.si.edu/APA_Exhibitions.htm

The Smithsonian Asian Pacific American Program has limited details on online viewing of its current and past exhibits. The second exhibition discussed in the exhibitions link focuses on the photographs of Ricardo Ocreto Alvarado.

South Asian–Americans

Sikh Community: Over 100 Years in the Pacific Northwest

http://www.wingluke.org/pastexhibitions.html

The Wing Luke Museum Web site provides a summary of an exhibit devoted to Sikh culture.

South Asian–American Link

http://asnic.utexas.edu/asnic/countries/india/linta.html

This University of Texas metasite contains many resources mostly relating to current events and issues for South Asian–Americans.

South Asian Women's Network

http://www.sawnet.org/

SAWNET focuses on modern issues for South Asian women and is fully searchable.

Southeast Asian–Americans

Cambodian Genocide Program

http://www.yale.edu/cgp/

This Yale University page offers a database of information relating to the Cambodian genocide and a database of articles with full-text searching.

Hmong Studies Internet Resource Center

http://www.hmongstudies.org/

This award-winning research page has links to many different research threads available, including journals, reference sites, message boards, census data, and bibliographies. Of particular interest to researchers are the links to the *Hmong Studies Journal* and research bibliographies.

Hmong Studies Journal

http://www.hmongstudies.org/HmongStudiesJournal

Issues of the *Hmong Studies Journal* are available as free pdf downloads. This is an excellent resource.

Lao Studies Review

http://www.global.lao.net/laostudy/laostudy.htm

The resources on the *Lao Studies Review* Web site, while a bit dated, are free to download.

Laos WWW Virtual Library

http://www.global.lao.net/laoVL.html

This is the WWW Virtual Library for Lao studies. The Laos Research Resources are particularly useful, and the biographies include information for five prominent Lao individuals.

Southeast Asian Archive

http://www.lib.uci.edu/libraries/collections/sea/sasian.html

The University of California Irvine's library on Southeast Asian studies. It includes images of Hmong *paj ntaub* textiles, a virtual exhibit documenting the refugee experience, and useful links sections for several Southeast Asian groups.

Vietgate

http://www.vietgate.net/

Vietgate calls itself the portal to "all things Vietnamese on the Net." It has over 100,000 links to Vietnamese sites in business and history. It is fully searchable from the main page, making it easy to determine if it is a useful resource for individual research.

Vietnamese Studies Internet Resource Center

http://www.vstudies.org/

This site has a vast collection of data on Vietnamese studies, including photo essays and a link to a Vietnamese Studies Research Library.

WWW Hmong Homepage

http://www.hmongnet.org/

This metasite has hundreds of resources ranging from current events in Hmong culture to the distant past. This resource should be utilized for any Hmong research.

Chapter 14

Colonial American History (1492–1763)

Edward Ragan, Scott A. Merriman, and Dennis A. Trinkle

Metasites

From Revolution to Reconstruction

http://odur.let.rug.nl/~usa/usa.htm

This metasite, maintained by the Arts Faculty of the University of Groningen, Netherlands, is a massive resource for all aspects of American history. The site is divided into five general sections: Outlines, Essays, Documents, Biographies, and Presidents. This site is organized around several U.S. Information Agency publications: *An Outline of American History, An Outline of the American Economy, An Outline of American Government,* and *An Outline of American Literature.* While the text of these outlines has not been changed, they have been enriched with hypertext links to relevant documents, original essays, and other Internet sites. Currently this site contains over 3,000 relevant HTML documents.

Institutions (Museums, Libraries, Historical Societies, and Online Organizations)

Archives of Maryland Online

http://aomol.net/html/index.html

The site is sponsored by the Maryland State Archives. At present, it "provides access to over 471,000 historical documents that form the constitutional, legal, legislative, judicial, and administrative basis of Maryland's government." Researchers can gain access to full-text documents from Maryland's entire executive, legislative, and judicial history. This is a bold initiative to provide access to "records that are scattered among a number of repositories and that often exist only on rapidly disintegrating paper."

Colonial Williamsburg

http://www.history.org/

The official Web site for Colonial Williamsburg, one of the most extensive historical reconstructions in the United States. The well-illustrated site offers tourist information, educational resources, a colonial dateline, a historical glossary of names, places, and events in Colonial Williamsburg, photos of buildings and people, articles from *Colonial Williamsburg: The Journal of the Colonial Williamsburg Foundation,* and an extensive section on colonial lifestyles.

Common-place

http://www.common-place.org/

Common-place is sponsored by the American Antiquarian Society and the Gilder Lehrman Institute of American History in association with the Florida State University Department of History. It bills itself as a "common place for exploring and exchanging ideas about early American history and culture" in a way that is "a bit friendlier than a scholarly journal, [and] a bit more scholarly than a popular magazine." Published quarterly, this online journal includes essays, books reviews, roundtable discussions, and an open forum for commenting on articles that appear in *Common-place.*

H-OIEAHC Discussion Network

http://www.h-net.msu.edu/~ieahcweb/

This is the Web site of the H-OIEAHC discussion list, which is sponsored by the Omohundro Institute of Early American History and Culture (OIEAHC). Affiliated with H-Net, this group focuses on colonial and early American history. Its Web pages contain information about the discussion list and allow users to subscribe. They also include calls for papers, conference announcements, bibliographies, book reviews, articles, and links to related sites, including the Omohundro Institute.

Jamestown Rediscovery Project

http://www.apva.org/jr.html

The Jamestown Rediscovery Project, sponsored by the Association for the Preservation of Virginia Antiquities, is a ten-year comprehensive excavation of Jamestown that began in 1994. This site offers photographs and progress reports on the project to date, two online exhibits, and plans for the future.

The Library of Virginia Digital Library Program

http://www.lva.lib.va.us/dlp/index.htm

The Library of Virginia's Digital Library Program is an internationally recognized effort to preserve, digitize, and provide access to significant archival and library collections. Users can search births, deaths, marriages, wills, and Bible records, genealogy and biography databases, photograph collections, and maps, gazetteers, and geographical resources, among other things. Perhaps the most stunning accomplishment is the Land Office Patents and Grants Database, which is searchable by keyword and provides links to scanned copies of the original Virginia land patents. All in all, this is a remarkable tool for Virginia historians and genealogists.

Plimoth-on-Web: Plimoth Plantation's Web Site

http://www.plimoth.org

The official Web site for the living history museum of seventeenth-century Plymouth. Like the living history museum, the Web site brings 1627 Plimoth back to life.

Religion and the Founding of the American Republic

http://www.loc.gov/exhibits/religion/religion.html

This online exhibit, sponsored by the Library of Congress, is a nuanced presentation of America's rich religious traditions. Divided into sections that include downloadable JPEG images and scanned texts, the exhibit explores America's history as a seventeenth-century religious refuge. It also examines the Great Awakening of the eighteenth century and its influence on the religious attitudes of the American Revolution. Additional sections discuss the separation of church and state as well as the religious diversity of the early republic.

Society of Early Americanists Home Page

http://www.hnet.uci.edu/mclark/seapage.htm

The SEA aims to further the exchange of ideas and information among scholars of various disciplines who study the literature and culture of America up to approximately 1800. The society publishes a newsletter, operates an electronic bulletin board, and maintains the Web site. The site contains an excellent list of links on colonial and early American history.

Topical Histories

1492: An Ongoing Voyage

http://www.loc.gov/exhibits/1492/

1492: An Ongoing Voyage is an electronic exhibit of the Library of Congress. The site weaves images and text to explore what life was like in pre- and post-Columbian Europe, Africa, and the Americas. The site examines the effect that the discovery of America had on each continent, stressing the dark elements of colonization. There are excellent maps, documents, artwork, and supporting text.

1755: The French and Indian War Home Page

http://web.syr.edu/~laroux/

Created by Larry Laroux, a professional writer, this site serves as a prologue to Laroux's forthcoming book *White Coats,* which will examine the soldiers who fought in the French and Indian War of 1755. The site is presently under construction, but Laroux eventually aims to include histories of important battles, a list of French soldiers who fought in the war, and other statistical records. The site already contains a brief narrative account of the war, along with some interesting information and trivia.

Iroquois Oral Traditions

http://www.indians.org/welker/iroqoral.htm

This Web site is part of the American Indian Heritage Foundation's Indigenous Peoples' Literature page. The tradition of De-Ka-Nah-Wi-Da (the chief who brought peace and power in the traditional stories) and Hiawatha, who between them were traditionally credited with creating the Iroquois Confederation, is recounted here along with over twenty other Iroquoian stories about the people of the longhouse and their place in the world. Many of these stories were translated into English and recorded in the late nineteenth and early twentieth centuries.

Jonathan Edwards

http://www.jonathanedwards.com/

Mark Trigsted of Flower Mound, Texas, has created what he describes as the "World's Largest Edwards Web Site." And he may be right. Trigsted has transcribed nearly a hundred of Edwards's sermons on topics such as judgment, doctrine, shepherding, and charity. In addition to sermons, Trigsted has included extensive excerpts from Edwards's writings on theology, science, and religious revival in the eighteenth century.

Salem Witchcraft Trials: 1692 (Famous Trials in American History)

http://www.law.umkc.edu/faculty/projects/ftrials/salem/salem.htm

Doug Linder, a professor of law at the University of Missouri-Kansas City Law School, has compiled many of the relevant Salem witchcraft documents as part of his Famous Trials Web site. Linder has included a detailed chronology, several maps, selected images, information on the legal procedure in witchcraft cases, and brief biographies of all major participants in the trials. Also included is a wealth of relevant transcribed documents, such as Cotton Mather's *Memorable Providences,* the arrest warrants, examinations and evidence, various petitions, and several letters from New England governor William Phips. The evidence is presented objectively without the myriad of odd historical explanations.

Salem Witch Museum

http://www.salemwitchmuseum.com/

This site primarily presents travel information, including a map of witch trial sites with links to photographs. Also offered is an interactive FAQ section on witch trials and local history. Other resources are being added rapidly.

The Thanksgiving Tradition

http://www.plimoth.org/visit/what/exhibits/thanksgiving.asp

The research, education, and public relations departments at Plimoth Plantation: The Living History Museum of 17th-Century Plymouth present a cornucopia of information on the American Thanksgiving tradition. Included at this site are relevant primary documents, essays, a sample menu, and a list of alternate claimants for the "first Thanksgiving."

Virtual Jamestown: Jamestown and the Virginia Experiment

http://www.virtualjamestown.org/

Created by Crandal Shifflett, professor of history at Virginia Tech, the "Virtual Jamestown Archive is a digital research, teaching, and learning project that explores the legacies of the Jamestown settlement." Included are links to primary documents and images; digitized, 360-degree reconstructions of the fort; discussion of Indian, African, and English life around Jamestown; and time lines. This site has been included in the NEH EDSITEment Project. If you cannot go to Jamestown in person, this is the next best thing.

Wampum—Treaties, Sacred Records

http://www.kstrom.net/isk/art/beads/wampum.html

This site offers information on the construction and meaning of wampum to Native America. Included are images and descriptions along with links that provide more detail.

Documents and Images

18th Century Documents

http://www.yale.edu/lawweb/avalon/18th.htm

This first-rate collection of documents is part of the Avalon Project at Yale Law School. Included here are many of the significant American colonial legal documents of the eighteenth century. These documents detail the Anglo-American imperial relationship and the major political conflicts of the era of the American Revolution, as well as those of the early American national period. There are links to document sets such as *The Federalist Papers,* the state and federal constitutions, and early presidential papers.

American Colonist's Library: A Treasury of Primary Documents

http://www.freerepublic.com/forum/a3a6605427caf.htm

Compiled by Richard Gardiner, a history instructor at University Lake School (Hartland, Wisconsin), the American Colonist's Library is a comprehensive gateway to the early American primary source documents that are currently available online. Included in the list are links to historical sources that influenced American colonists, online collections of the work of major early American political leaders, the text of the Acts of Parliament concerning the American colonies, numerous

American Revolution military documents, and much more. The hundreds of documents are grouped chronologically from 500 BCE to 1800 CE. As the site boasts, "if it isn't here, it probably is not available online anywhere."

American Historical Images on File: The Native American Experience

http://www.csulb.edu/colleges/cla/departments/ais/faculty/trj/

This collection of historical images of Native American peoples was developed by Professor Troy Johnson of California State University, Long Beach. The images span the chronological range of Native America, from Paleo-Indians to the present. They are presented here with full permission of Facts On File, Inc., but take note of the copyright details before you use them for your own purposes.

A Briefe and True Report of the New Found Land of Virginia

http://docsouth.unc.edu/nc/hariot/hariot.html

This Web site includes the transcription of the 1590 folio edition of Thomas Hariot's *A Briefe and True Report of the New Found Land of Virginia*, which is "the first original book in English relating to what is now America, written by one of the first Englishmen to attempt new world colonization." The images from Hariot's volume, which were based on John White's watercolors and engraved by Theodore de Bry, are reproduced here in facsimile.

Colonial Charters, Grants and Related Documents

http://www.yale.edu/lawweb/avalon/states/statech.htm

The Avalon Project at Yale Law School has compiled a wide range of colonial-era charters. Many of the documents are general charters granted to individuals, such as *Priviledges and Prerogatives Granted by Their Catholic Majesties to Christopher Columbus* (1492) and Queen Elizabeth's 1584 charter to Sir Walter Raleigh. Organized by colony, the site includes founding documents as well as updated charters and related material.

Columbus and the Age of Discovery

http://muweb.millersville.edu/~columbus/

A searchable database of over 1,100 text articles pertaining to Columbus and themes of discovery and encounter. The site, which allows unrestricted access, was built by the History Department of Millersville University of Pennsylvania in conjunction with the U.S. Christopher Columbus Quincentenary Jubilee Commission of 1992.

Early America

http://earlyamerica.com/earlyamerica/index.html

The main focus of Early America is primary source material from eighteenth-century America. The site is the public access branch of the commercial American Digital Library, which sells reproductions of hundreds of early American documents from the Keigwin and Mathews Collection of eighteenth- and nineteenth-century historical documents, as well as images, maps, and other items.

Gottlieb Mittelberger, *On the Misfortune of Indentured Servants* (1754)

http://www.let.rug.nl/~usa/D/1601-1650/mittelberger/servan.htm

In 1750 the German immigrant Gottlieb Mittelberger arrived in Philadelphia, where he taught school. When he returned to Germany in 1754, he wrote this account describing the miserable life that servants endured in the colonies.

The Jesuit Relations and Allied Documents: 1610 to 1791

http://puffin.creighton.edu/jesuit/relations/

This impressive undertaking is the work of Rev. Raymond A. Bucko, a Jesuit priest and professor of anthropology at Creighton University in Omaha, and Thom Mentrak, a historical interpreter at the Ste. Marie Among the Iroquois Museum in Syracuse, New York. This site contains the scanned and transcribed version of the seventy-one-volume edition edited by Reuben Gold Thwaites in the late nineteenth century. *The Jesuit Relations* began as private reports between the Jesuit missionaries in New France and their superiors in Paris. The Jesuits made extensive reports on the native peoples they encountered, making this source a must for serious research into Huron and Haudenosaunee (Five Nations) culture in the seventeenth century.

John White Drawings/Theodore de Bry Engravings

http://www.virtualjamestown.org/images/white_debry_html/introduction.html

By a special licensing agreement with the British Museum, Virtual Jamestown (see above) has digitized a collection of John White's fabulous watercolors that depict coastal Algonquian life around the Roanoke colony in 1585. These watercolors were the basis of Theodore de Bry's engravings.

The Leslie Brock Center for the Study of Colonial Currency

http://etext.lib.virginia.edu/users/brock

This Web site seeks to take some of the confusion out of understanding and working with colonial currencies. Included here are eighteenth-century pamphlets and other contemporary writings that relate to currency, as well as more recent articles on the various colonies and currencies and links to additional resources covering currency rates and monetary history.

Mayflower History

http://www.mayflowerhistory.com/

Caleb Johnson, a *Mayflower* descendant, has authored this detailed site about the people who settled at Plymouth colony. Includes a *Mayflower* passenger list with biographies for each passenger and a history of the voyage and early settlement. There is also a genealogy of the early Plymouth settlers along with passenger lists from other voyages to Plymouth colony. The site also contains full-text primary sources from the first three decades of Plymouth settlement as well as links to *Mayflower* societies, museums, and other resources.

Notes on the State of Virginia

http://etext.lib.virginia.edu/toc/modeng/public/JefVirg.html

Constructed as a series of answers to questions posed by foreign observers, Thomas Jefferson's *Notes,* first published in 1787, provides a unique description of the natural and human landscapes of Virginia in the late eighteenth century. This e-text version is sponsored by the University of Virginia Library Electronic Text Center.

Perry-Castañeda Library Map Collection (University of Texas)

http://www.lib.utexas.edu/maps/histus.html

The University of Texas Library presents its impressive collection of historical maps in JPEG format for convenient downloads. These historical maps of the United States are categorized under the following headings: Early Inhabitants, Exploration and Settlement, Territorial Growth, Military History, and Later Historical Maps. Also included are links to additional historical map resources.

The Plymouth Colony Archive Project at the University of Virginia

http://www.people.virginia.edu/~jfd3a/

The Plymouth Colony Archive presents a collection of searchable texts, including seminar analysis of various topics, biographical profiles of selected colonists, probate inventories, wills, "Glossary and Notes on Plymouth Colony," and "Vernacular House Forms in Seventeenth-Century Plymouth Colony: An Analysis of Evidence from the Plymouth Colony Room-by-Room Probate Inventories 1633–1685," by Patricia E. Scott Deetz and James Deetz. The site itself is maintained by the Deetzs, pioneers in material culture studies.

Rare Map Collection—Colonial America

http://www.libs.uga.edu/darchive/hargrett/maps/colamer.html

The Hargrett Rare Book and Manuscript Library at the University of Georgia has digitized an impressive collection of rare maps. The Colonial America section includes maps that date from 1625 through 1774. In addition, there are links to maps from earlier and later periods.

Theodore de Bry Copper Plate Engravings

http://www.csulb.edu/~aisstudy/woodcuts/

This collection of historical images of Native peoples is the digitized versions of copperplate engravings made by the Flemish engraver and publisher Theodore de Bry. The engravings are based on the watercolor paintings of the sixteenth-century English explorer John White. The site was developed by Professor Troy Johnson of California State University, Long Beach.

Chapter 15

Revolutionary America

Robert Lee

Metasites

American Revolution

http://www.americanrevolution.org/

This comprehensive metasite contains over 1,900 links to nearly every topic on the American Revolution available through the Internet. The links are broken down into three sections—for historians, genealogists, and reenactors—and spread out over 300 pages. Visitors may also peruse a vast and growing library of exclusive content. The Scholar's Showcase, featuring historical essays and e-books, especially warrants a visit.

Eighteenth-Century Resources

http://www.andromeda.rutgers.edu/~jlynch/18th/

A self-described "labor of love" by Jack Lynch, an English professor at Rutgers University, this metasite houses an expansive collection of links covering the "very long" eighteenth century. Topics run the gamut of arts and sciences, with an emphasis on British history and literature. In assembling the site, Lynch targeted the needs of students and researchers, providing links to e-texts, professional resources, and Web pages of other eighteenth-century scholars.

WWW Virtual Library: Revolutionary Era, 1765–1783

http://vlib.iue.it/history/USA/ERAS/revolutionary.html

Dr. Lynn H. Nelson launched the Virtual Library at the University of Kansas in 1993 and the site has since been transferred to the domain of the European University Institute in Florence, Italy. It has a voluminous, bulleted index with a spartan design that allows visitors to follow chronological, geographical, or topical orientations across a bevy of sites. Relevant content also appears in a separate index covering the constitutional era, 1786–1800.

General Sites

The Adams Family Papers: An Electronic Archive

http://www.masshist.org/digitaladams/aea/index.html

The Massachusetts Historical Society's collection of John Adams's papers cuts across the revolutionary era and offers valuable insight into Massachusetts politics, the fledgling American government, international affairs, and the personal lives of the Adams family. The archive is divided into three sections: John Adams's diary, his autobiography, and his correspondence with his wife, Abigail Adams. In addition to illuminating eighteenth-century courtship and married life, John and Abigail's letters provide a female perspective on the events of the period.

The American Revolution and Its Era: Maps and Charts of North America and the West Indies, 1750–1789

http://memory.loc.gov/ammem/gmdhtml/armhtml/armhome.html

This large and growing Web site will eventually display digital images of over 2,000 period maps and charts held by the Library of Congress. Simply put, there is no better online resource on the geography of North America as it was visualized during the revolutionary era.

The American Revolution Educational New Media Project

http://independence.nyhistory.org/

Funded by the U.S. Department of Education, this Web site initiates the New-York Historical Society's plan to bring its vast revolutionary era records to the Internet. The project's first installment, an online exhibition titled Independence and Its Enemies in New York, showcases dozens of digital documents, games for students, and lesson plans for educators.

The American Revolution: Lighting Freedom's Flame

http://www.nps.gov/revwar/

The National Park Service created Lighting Freedom's Flame to promote awareness of federally owned revolutionary parks. The invitingly designed site integrates links to relevant national parks with stories from the period, biographies of major figures, and various educational resources for students and teachers. It also offers virtual tours of these parks, announces upcoming public history events, and features a section on the "unfinished Revolution." The emphasis falls as much on the Revolution's legacy as the war itself, providing an interesting introduction to the subject of public memory.

American Revolution

http://www.americanrevolution.com/

This site features a wealth of material on the Revolution, organized in over fifty topical links. All the information is put forth in a straightforward, encyclopedic style, interlaced with hyperlinks to simplify navigation. Topics range widely, including traditional discussions of military and political issues, social histories of the roles played by women, African-Americans, and immigrants, and even some quirky accounts like the "History of Yankee Doodle Dandy."

The American Revolution

http://theamericanrevolution.org

Along with two time lines and short biographies of political figures, this site contains solid accounts of key battles in the American Revolution. Each brief description includes a battle synopsis and an analysis of the event's place in the scope of the war, as well as humanizing details like the temperature, weather, and casualty statistics. In an attempt to build the relationship between online and traditional secondary sources, most pages direct readers to recent monographs pertinent to the topic at hand.

Archiving Early America

http://earlyamerica.com

Web surfers undeterred by a few flashy ads will be rewarded with this site's archive of eighteenth-century primary sources, including images of period maps, newspapers, and pamphlets, all displayed in their original format. The content varies from the well-known Articles of Confederation to a rare issue of *The Maryland Gazette* recounting George Washington's trip to the Ohio Valley in 1754. There are also sections on notable women, famous obituaries and portraits, and an online journal, *The Early American Review*.

Avalon Project at the Yale Law School: 18th Century Documents

http://www.yale.edu/lawweb/avalon/18th.htm

This frequently updated site should be one of the first stops for students and researchers looking for primary sources on revolutionary America. It archives full-text transcriptions of state constitutions, colonial acts and edicts, government treaties, political pamphlets, and various other records of eighteenth-century history, law, and diplomacy. The documents appear in alphabetical order, but the site's user-friendly format also permits navigation by subject or time frame. A search function on a full copy of *The Federalist Papers* is one of the project's many useful features designed to expedite research.

Bibliographies of the War of American Independence

http://www.army.mil/cmh-pg/reference/revbib/revwar.htm

These extensive bibliographies, amassed by the U.S. Army Center of Military History, are a helpful source to consult before venturing out to the library. However, the bibliographies were originally compiled for the 1983 publication *The Continental Army* and the site was last updated in 2000, so be sure to heed the introduction's advice to cross-reference.

Documents From the Continental Congress and Constitutional Convention, 1774–1789

http://memory.loc.gov/ammem/collections/continental

One of American Memory's many revolutionary era collections, this site features hundreds of keyword-searchable broadsides and other records on the Continental Congress and Constitutional Convention. The broadsides cover the well-known drafting and ratification of the Constitution, but also pertain to Congress's more workaday tasks of holding committee meetings and issuing resolutions. The additional documents include petitions, political pamphlets, diplomatic and financial reports, and papers from state and local governments. To see how some of these documents have been interpreted, check out the online exhibits, Declaring Independence: Drafting the Documents and Religion and the Founding of the American Republic, available through the site's related resources page.

The History Place: American Revolution

http://www.historyplace.com/unitedstates/revolution/index.html

The History Place's six-part time line spans from early colonial history up to 1790 and is especially detailed during the war years from 1775 to 1783. Its simple format makes it easy to get a general sense of the chronology of the Revolution or quickly find specific dates. For anyone taking a course or writing a paper on this era, this site merits a bookmark.

The Thomas Jefferson Papers

http://memory.loc.gov/ammem/collections/jefferson_papers/index.html

As a slave owner whose articulation of natural rights in the Declaration of Independence framed the Revolution, Jefferson is a case study in the complexities of early American life. The Library of Congress holds 27,000 Jefferson documents and has greatly simplified serious research by posting digital images of many of them on its American Memory page. The papers come in a variety of forms, including correspondence, addresses, legal documents, and scientific writings. Students and teachers looking for a more public history-oriented introduction to Jefferson will find one at the media-rich Monticello home page at http://www.monticello.org/.

Journals of the Continental Congress

http://lcweb2.loc.gov/ammem/amlaw/lwjc.html

Between 1904 and 1937, the Library of Congress published the thirty-four-volume *Journals of the Continental Congress, 1774–1789,* based on the original journals kept by Secretary Charles Thompson and on other congressional records. The American Memory project has digitized the work and equipped it with a search function, bringing easy access to this immense chronicle of the legislative process that transformed America from a confederation of rebellious colonies into a unified nation under the current Constitution.

Omohundro Institute of Early American History & Culture

http://www.wm.edu/oieahc/

This Web page is an online hub for scholars studying early America. Visitors will find recent tables of contents for *The William & Mary Quarterly,* conference and colloquia announcements, the institute's newsletter, and a variety of links. The page also provides access to the institute's H-Net discussion forum, an excellent resource designed for (but not limited to) academics.

The Online Institute for Advanced Loyalist Studies

http://www.royalprovincial.com/

This Web page provides an interesting introduction to the Tory worldview during the American Revolution. A good—albeit far from comprehensive—sampling of documents related to the Loyalist experience appears in the sections titled History and Military. The site is aimed chiefly at those interested in military research, genealogy, and living history, but could also be used effectively for class discussions on point of view in historical narratives.

Thomas Paine National Historical Association Web Archive

http://www.thomaspaine.org/newarch.html

Thomas Paine did as much as anyone to foment the Revolution when he published *Common Sense* in 1776. Along with biographies of Paine and a chronology of his writings, this site hosts a full-text archive of Paine's corpus—essential reading for anyone interested in the ideology of the Revolution.

RevWar75

http://www.revwar75.com/

Primarily for researchers interested in the microhistory of the Continental Army and, to a lesser extent, the British Crown Forces, this site dons an impressive index of surviving orderly books. Since its inception, the site has grown to include a library with scholarly articles and primary sources pertaining to the life of the common soldier, as well as indexes of land and sea battles and Revolutionary War articles from the journal *Military Collector & Historian*. Those studying specific military units or campaigns will find this page particularly helpful.

Spy Letters of the American Revolution

http://www.si.umich.edu/spies/

Covert intelligence on enemy location, troop strength, and strategy gathered by spies and traitors was an integral component of the execution of the Revolutionary War. This online exhibit, assembled from the Sir Henry Clinton Collection at the University of Michigan, offers a rare window into the intelligence operations of the American and British armies. The site provides multifaceted access to primary sources on subjects ranging from the infamous Benedict Arnold to lesser-known female spies.

The Sullivan-Clinton Campaign: History, The Iroquois & George Washington

http://sullivanclinton.com/

This multimedia site focuses on the Sullivan-Clinton Campaign against the Iroquois in 1779, with a particular emphasis on Indian dispossession in New York. Along with contemporary texts and brief articles, the site features photo galleries, original animation, and interactive maps that together provide an excellent overview of the Six Nations role in the Revolution.

USHistory

http://www.ushistory.org/

The Independence Hall Association in Philadelphia developed this "Congress of Web sites" focused on Pennsylvania in the revolutionary era. On these colorful and informative pages, Web surfers can take a virtual tour of Philadelphia's Historic Mile, delve into the myth and history of the American flag at Betsy Ross's house, be introduced to the life of Benjamin Franklin, and learn the history of the Liberty Bell. Additional sections on Valley Forge, Brandywine Battlefield, and the Philadelphia Campaign of 1777 analyze Pennsylvania as a military front.

George Washington: A National Treasure

http://www.georgewashington.si.edu/index.html

This online companion to the National Portrait Gallery's touring exhibition of Gilbert Stuart's George Washington portraiture is a study in national memory. The centerpiece is an interactive version of the iconic Landsdowne portrait that highlights the painting's symbolism. The site's "Patriot Papers," which follow the exhibition across the country, tell Washington-inspired stories and the "Town Hall" hosts discussion forums. Along with puzzles for kids, there are educational aids for teachers and families. The links page functions as an authoritative metasite on Washington. From here, the general public can visit the virtual Mount Vernon and researchers can access extraordinary digital archives at the Library of Congress and the University of Virginia.

Chapter 16

Early United States History (1783–1860)

Edward Ragan

Metasites

From Revolution to Reconstruction

http://odur.let.rug.nl/~usa/usa.htm

This metasite, maintained by the Arts Faculty of the University of Groningen, Netherlands, is a massive resource for all aspects of American history. The site is divided into five general sections: Outlines, Essays, Documents, Biographies, and Presidents. This site is organized around several U.S. Information Agency publications: *An Outline of American History, An Outline of the American Economy, An Outline of American Government,* and *An Outline of American Literature.* While the text of these outlines has not been changed, they have been enriched with hypertext links to relevant documents, original essays, and other Internet sites. Currently this site contains over 3,000 relevant HTML documents.

The Making of America

http://www.umdl.umich.edu/moa/

The Making of America is a digital library of primary sources in American social history from the antebellum period through Reconstruction. Contained in this collection are approximately 8,500 books and 50,000 journal articles on subjects as far ranging as education, psychology, American history, sociology, religion, and science and technology. The project, sponsored by the University of Michigan and Cornell University, "represents a major collaborative endeavor in preservation and electronic access to historical texts." These texts are searchable by keyword with links to digitized copies of the nineteenth-century imprints. This is an outstanding site for those who need access to nineteenth-century documents.

Nineteenth-Century Documents Project

http://www.furman.edu/~benson/docs/

Lloyd Benson has prepared an extensive collection of primary documents. The period is categorized topically, and all topics seem to emphasize increased sectional differences and the coming of the Civil War. The documents are grouped under the following headings: Early National Politics, Slavery and Sectionalism, the Nebraska Bill, the Sumner Caning, the Dred Scott Decision, John Brown's Raid on Harpers Ferry, an 1850s Statistical Almanac, the 1860 Election, Secession and War, and the Post–Civil War Era.

Institutions (Museums, Libraries, Historical Societies, and Online Organizations)

American Treasures of the Library of Congress

http://lcweb.loc.gov/exhibits/treasures/

This is a substantial virtual exhibit from the Library of Congress collections that contains a variety of items, including letters by Thomas Jefferson and John Quincy Adams's notes from the *Amistad* case. Substantial detail and historical context are provided for each component of the collection. Jefferson, whose personal library became the core of the Library of Congress, arranged his books into three types of knowledge, corresponding to three faculties of the mind: memory (history), reason (philosophy), and imagination (fine arts).

Amistad: Race and the Boundaries of Freedom in Antebellum Maritime America

http://amistad.mysticseaport.org/main/welcome.html

This site is part of the Mystic Seaport Museum. It contains information on the *Amistad* slave ship, the revolt of its cargo, and the Supreme Court trial of its slave mutineers. The focus of this site is living history. A time line of events is provided as are classroom lessons for teachers.

The Early America Review

http://www.earlyamerica.com/review/

This electronic "Journal of Fact and Opinion on the People, Issues and Events of 18th-Century America" is edited by Don Vitale. The journal contains wide-ranging articles about the social, political, and military developments of this period. An excellent example of the ways in which modern scholarship seeks to combine traditional formats with technology.

Historic Mount Vernon—The Home of Our First President, George Washington

http://www.mountvernon.org

Visitors to the official Mount Vernon Web site will find information designed to meet a variety of needs. In addition to a virtual tour of the house and grounds, this site contains a biography of Washington written at the fifth-grade level, teaching aids such as quizzes, and an electronic image collection.

The Gerrit Smith Virtual Museum

http://www.NYHistory.com/gerritsmith/index.htm

The New York History Net has detailed information about the abolitionist leader Gerrit Smith. Includes a biographical essay, bibliography, and portrait gallery of Smith and his family. This site was developed in cooperation with the Syracuse University Library Department of Special Collections and Hamilton College (Clinton, New York), both of which hold substantial portions of Gerrit Smith's papers.

Topical Histories

African Canadian Heritage Tour

http://www.ciaccess.com/~jdnewby/heritage/african.htm

The African Canadian Heritage Tour celebrates the history of those who made the arduous journey to freedom in Canada via the Underground Railroad. This site is the central Internet presence for a collection of five historical sites that provide information about the Underground Railroad and the African-Canadian settlement of southwestern Ontario: the Buxton Historical Site and Museum, the North American Black Historical Museum, the Sandwich Baptist Church, the Uncle Tom's Cabin–Josiah Henson Interpretive Site, and the Woodstock Institute Sertoma Help Centre.

Abolition: The African-American Mosaic

http://www.loc.gov/exhibits/african/afam005.html

The Library of Congress provides information on the history of the antislavery movement in America that led to the formation, in 1833, of the American Anti-Slavery Society. Includes references to Library of Congress holdings such as abolitionist publications, minutes of antislavery meetings, handbills, advertisements, songs, and appeals to women. Demonstrates the tradition of the abolition movement in America before 1833.

The American Whig Party (1834–1856)

http://odur.let.rug.nl/~usa/E/uswhig/whigsxx.htm

Essay by Hal Morris that describes the rise of the American Whig Party as an opposition to President Andrew Jackson's kinglike tendencies. Included is a history of the Whig Party and links to biographies of Whig presidents and political leaders in America.

John Brown

http://www.pbs.org/weta/thewest/people/a_c/brown.htm

This PBS-sponsored site contains a biography of the radical abolitionist John Brown.

James Fenimore Cooper (1789–1851)

http://odur.let.rug.nl/~usa/LIT/cooper.htm

Kathryn VanSpanckeren's literary biography evaluates James Fenimore Cooper's role in the development of the American novel. Traces the familial and cultural influences that led Cooper to create Natty Bumppo, his chief protagonist.

Chronology of the Secession Crisis

http://members.aol.com/jfepperson/secesh.html

James F. Epperson charts the chronology of events that culminated with the firing upon Fort Sumter, South Carolina. The site includes links to relevant documents.

Democracy in America: De Tocqueville

http://xroads.virginia.edu/~HYPER/DETOC/home.html

The American studies program at the University of Virginia maintains this site, which explores American democracy in the 1830s. De Tocqueville traveled across the United States in the 1830s, and his itinerary, letters, and journal entries are here combined with cultural artifacts from the period to provide a glimpse of American democracy and culture in the early nineteenth century. Among other topics, this site examines issues of gender, race, and religion for the period.

The Founding Fathers

http://www.archives.gov/national-archives-experience/charters/
constitution_founding_fathers.html

The National Archives and Records Administration has compiled biographies of the delegates to the Constitutional Convention of 1787. This is an excellent place to start when studying the U.S. Constitution and the Founding Fathers.

Benjamin Franklin: A Documentary History

http://www.english.udel.edu/lemay/franklin/

J.A. Leo Lemay, the Henry Francis du Pont Winterthur Professor of Colonial American Literature at the University of Delaware, gives visitors a peek into the research that he is doing for a Franklin biography. He offers a detailed chronology of Franklin's life that is divided into three stages: early life, professional interests, and political career. Each event in Franklin's life is verified with citations that are connected to a bibliography of primary documents.

Benjamin Franklin: Glimpses of the Man

http://www.fi.edu/franklin/rotten.html

The Franklin Institute maintains this site, which celebrates the life and work of Benjamin Franklin. It emphasizes his work as statesman, printer, scientist, philosopher, musician, economist, and inventor.

Horace Greeley (1811–1872)

http://equinox.unr.edu/homepage/fenimore/greeley.html

David H. Fenimore of the University of Nevada, Reno, offers a detailed biography of Greeley complete with photographs, quotations, a Greeley bibliography, and links to related information.

Sarah Grimké, Angelina Grimké (Biographies)

http://www.gale.com/free_resources/whm/bio/grimk_sisters.htm

Gale Publishing has created these biographies of Sarah Grimké and Angelina Grimké that focus on their work for abolition and women's suffrage.

Thomas Jefferson: A Film by Ken Burns

http://www.pbs.org/jefferson/

This PBS-sponsored site is the online version of Ken Burns's documentary about Thomas Jefferson. It features selections of Jefferson's writings used in the film, the transcripts of interviews conducted for the film, tips for educators on teaching about Jefferson, and classroom activities for students.

The Thomas Jefferson Memorial Foundation

http://www.monticello.org

The Thomas Jefferson Memorial Foundation has prepared a virtual tour of life at Monticello to demonstrate how Jefferson spent an average day. Included here is a discussion about Jefferson's interests, inventions, family, slaves, and grounds. Lengthy essays seek to explain Jefferson's world to the twentieth-century student. Links connect the reader to additional information about Monticello, its owner, inhabitants, and visitors. "The Jefferson-Hemings DNA Testing: An On-Line Resource" is a valuable link for understanding the current controversy about Jefferson's legacy.

Lewis & Clark

http://www.pbs.org/lewisandclark/

This is the PBS-sponsored online companion to Ken Burns's documentary series on the Lewis and Clark expedition. The site includes biographies for all members of the Corps of Discovery along with equipment lists, time lines, maps, and excerpts from the journals kept. Also included are short histories of the Native American tribes that were encountered on the journey. Burns discusses the making of the series, and PBS provides teaching resources. Overall, this is an excellent site.

Manifest Destiny

http://odur.let.rug.nl/~usa/E/manifest/manifxx.htm

This essay by Michael Lubragge traces the history of this concept in America.

The Mexican-American War (1846–1848)

http://www.pbs.org/kera/usmexicanwar/

This PBS-sponsored site is the online companion to the television documentary. The site provides a detailed analysis of the war from both sides with the perspective that "there are many valid points of view about a historical event." The war is placed in its larger context as a war for North America. Also included here are a bibliography, a teacher's guide, a time line of events, historical analysis by experts, and information on the making of the documentary. This site is available in Spanish and English.

The Mexican-American War, 1846–1848

http://www.dmwv.org/mexwar/mexwar.htm

Sponsored by the Descendants of Mexican War Veterans, this site offers a history of the war with sections on the countdown to war, the various conflicts fought across Mexico and California, and the peace that followed. Also provided are maps, documents, images, and links to related resources.

Mountain Men and the Fur Trade: Sources of the History of the Fur Trade in the Rocky Mountain West

http://www.xmission.com/~drudy/amm.html

This site is devoted to the mountain men of the Rocky Mountains through 1850. It includes digitized personal and public records and a bibliography for further reading.

New Perspectives on *The West*

http://www.pbs.org/weta/thewest/

This is the PBS-sponsored online companion to the eight-episode documentary on the American West produced by Ken Burns and Stephen Ives. Burns and Ives introduce the production and provide a time line with relevant biographies of key figures. Also included are sample primary source documents that were used to create the series and links to related sites.

Orphan Trains of Kansas

http://www.kancoll.org/articles/orphans/

Connie Dipasquale and Susan Stafford present their research about children brought to Kansas from New York on Orphan Trains. This site includes firsthand accounts, a time line, newspaper descriptions, and partial name lists of children on the Orphan Train.

Peabody Museum: The Ethnography of Lewis and Clark

http://www.peabody.harvard.edu/Lewis_and_Clark/

The Peabody Museum of Archaeology and Ethnology at Harvard University has developed this site to examine the cultural implications of the Lewis and Clark expedition. Included here are artifacts (with detailed descriptions) from Native Americans, route maps, and a resources page with links.

Politics and Sectionalism in the 1850s

http://odur.let.rug.nl/~usa/E/1850s/polixx.htm

Stephen Demkin has written this essay that examines the major political issues of the 1850s, such as the Compromise of 1850, the Kansas-Nebraska Act, and the Dred Scott decision. Also included are links to related sites.

Presidents of the United States

http://www.whitehouse.gov/history/presidents/index.html

The official White House Web site provides excellent biographies of the presidents along with links to relevant documents and biographies of the first ladies.

Presidents of the United States

http://www.ipl.org/div/potus/

The Internet Public Library has produced a useful collection of presidential Web sites. Sections contain presidential election results, cabinet members, notable events, and links to Internet biographies. The information here is laid out in a very accessible format.

A Roadmap to the U.S. Constitution

http://library.thinkquest.org/11572/?tqskip=1

Jonathan Chin and Alan Stern of ThinkQuest have developed this site on the U.S. Constitution. The authors have tried to re-create the milieu out of which the Constitution emerged. In addition to providing an annotated copy of the Constitution, essays explore the origins of this document. The authors also examine constitutional crises and the relevant Supreme Court decisions. This site provides a discussion board for those with specific questions.

Secession Era Editorials Project

http://history.furman.edu/~benson/docs/index.htm

Lloyd Benson of the Furman University Department of History has reproduced newspaper editorials from four critical events that highlighted America's growing sectional divide. Included are the Kansas-Nebraska Bill (1854), the caning of Massachusetts senator Charles Sumner by South Carolina representative Preston Brooks (1856), the *Dred Scott* decision (1857), and the raid on Harpers Ferry by radical abolitionist John Brown (1859). The project includes "at least one complete run of editorials from each major political party in each state of the Union." Users can search the editorials by text. Benson has also developed "mapping and statistical tools for placing the editorials into their analytical context."

"The Star Spangled Banner"

http://odur.let.rug.nl/~usa/E/banner/bannerxx.htm

Amato F. Mongelluzzo offers an essay that relates the events and dispels several myths surrounding the creation of this poem that became the national anthem.

Henry David Thoreau Home Page

http://www.walden.org/Institute/index.htm

This site, sponsored by the Walden Woods Project, the Thoreau Society, and the Thoreau Institute, is the essential Thoreau site. Emphasized here are Thoreau's biography, images, electronic texts, and scholarly analysis of Thoreau's work.

To the Western Ocean: Planning the Lewis and Clark Expedition

http://www.lib.virginia.edu/small/exhibits/lewis_clark/planning.html

The site is part of a map exhibition at the Tracy W. McGregor Room, Alderman Library, University of Virginia. To the Western Ocean is the fourth chapter of a larger exploration of nation building and mapmaking. This site is valuable because it places the Lewis and Clark expedition into a larger historical context.

Uncle Sam: An American Autobiography

http://xroads.virginia.edu/~CAP/SAM/home.htm

The American studies program at the University of Virginia has created this site to discuss the origin of this American icon. The forgotten origin of Uncle Sam during the War of 1812 is placed alongside his evolution as a symbol and national icon, including his official adoption and standardization by the U.S. State Department in the 1950s.

The Valley of the Shadow

http://valley.vcdh.virginia.edu/

Edward L. Ayers, the Hugh P. Kelley Professor of History at the University of Virginia, has developed this massive archive of primary sources that concern the experiences of Franklin County, Pennsylvania, and Augusta County, Virginia, in the years just preceding the Civil War. These two counties were "separated by several hundred miles and the Mason-Dixon line." The document archive includes newspapers, letters, diaries, photographs, maps, church records, population census, agricultural census, and military records. Students can research and write their own histories from the documents provided. The project is primarily intended for secondary schools, community colleges, libraries, and universities. This research is available in CD-ROM form from W.W. Norton Publishers (http://www.wwnorton.com).

War of 1812

http://www.army.mil/cmh-pg/books/amh/amh-06.htm

This is a discussion of the War of 1812, from *American Military History* (chapter 6). This e-text is sponsored by the Army Historical Series, Office of the Chief of Military History, U.S. Army. The war is presented as an outgrowth of the Napoleonic Wars. The major battles are narrated in detail as are comparisons of American and British military capabilities and strategies.

Documents and Images

"Across the Plains in 1844"

http://www.pbs.org/weta/thewest/resources/archives/two/sager1.htm

This account was written by Catherine Sager Pringle circa 1860. It is reprinted here from S.A. Clarke's *Pioneer Days in Oregon History,* vol. 2 (1905).

The *Amistad* Case

http://www.archives.gov/education/lessons/amistad/

The National Archives and Records Administration provides all relevant documents related to the *Amistad* slave mutiny. This site also includes teaching ideas that are based on the National Standards for History and the National Standards for Civics and Government.

The Annapolis Convention

http://www.yale.edu/lawweb/avalon/annapoli.htm

The Annapolis Convention assembled to discuss economic issues faced by the states under the Articles of Confederation. It resolved to explore alternatives to the Articles. This site contains the report of the commissioners from the states on September 14, 1786, and links to the Articles of Confederation, the Madison debates, the *Federalist Papers,* and the U.S. Constitution.

The Articles of Confederation

http://www.yale.edu/lawweb/avalon/artconf.htm

The Articles of Confederation established a central government for the thirteen colonies after the American Revolution. It was a weak system in which the separate states held the balance of power. This site contains a full-text copy of the Articles and links to the Annapolis Convention, the Madison debates, the *Federalist Papers,* and the U.S. Constitution.

The Bill of Rights

http://www.archives.gov/national_archives_experience/charters/bill_of_rights.html

The National Archives and Records Administration provides coverage of the Bill of Rights. Included here is a high-resolution image of the document.

Boundaries of the United States and the Several States

http://www.ac.wwu.edu/~stephan/48states.html

Ed Stephan of Western Washington University has created a charming animated map that depicts the territorial growth of the United States. This site allows students to visualize how national, territorial, and state boundaries changed over time.

Cherokee Nation v. Georgia

http://www.pbs.org/weta/thewest/resources/archives/two/cherokee.htm

This is a full-text copy of the decision handed down by Supreme Court chief justice John Marshall in 1831, which dealt with the forced removal of Native Americans from Georgia and other Southern states. The decision held that the Native Americans had rights and were "domestic dependent nations," a status between independent countries and tribes without rights.

The Confessions of Nat Turner

http://docsouth.unc.edu/turner/turner.html

This is the complete text of *The Confessions of Nat Turner* (1831). Nat Turner led a large slave revolt in 1831, and after his capture he allegedly made these confessions.

The Constitution of the United States

http://www.archives.gov/national-archives-experience/charters/constitution.html

This site is maintained by the National Archives and Records Administration. The Founding Fathers page features the biographies of the fifty-five delegates to the Constitutional Convention. Users can read a transcription of the complete text of the Constitution. This page also provides links to biographies of each of the thirty-nine delegates who signed the Constitution. The article "A More Perfect Union" is an in-depth look at the Constitutional Convention and the ratification process. A quiz section gives visitors the chance to test their knowledge.

The Federalist Papers

http://www.yale.edu/lawweb/avalon/federal/fed.htm

These essays were authored by John Jay, Alexander Hamilton, and James Madison, and argue in favor of constitutional ratification. The collection is searchable by keyword and linked to relevant documents such as the Articles of Confederation, the Annapolis Convention, the Madison debates, and the U.S. Constitution.

The Federalist Papers

http://www.law.emory.edu/FEDERAL/federalist/

These essays were authored by John Jay, Alexander Hamilton, and James Madison. First published in 1787–1788, they supported the Constitution. They serve as bold statements of American political theory, and this online version makes them more accessible than ever before, as it is keyword searchable and each essay is also individually available.

FindLaw: U.S. Constitution

http://www.findlaw.com/casecode/constitution/

This site contains all the articles and amendments to the U.S. Constitution. Each item is completely annotated with explanations and references. Through hyperlinks, users can access the full-text version of relevant Supreme Court decisions. Each decision is placed in its historical context along with pertinent theories of law and government. This is an invaluable resource for legal professionals.

First-Person Narratives of the American South

http://docsouth.unc.edu/fpn/index.html

This site contains an outstanding collection of electronic texts that document the American South. It includes diaries, autobiographies, memoirs, travel accounts, and ex-slave narratives. The focus is on first-person narratives of marginalized populations: women, African-Americans, enlisted men, laborers, and Native Americans.

"A Girl's Life in Virginia Before the War"

http://docsouth.unc.edu/burwell/menu.html

This memoir by Letitia M. Burwell describes Southern plantation life before the Civil War. It was originally published in 1895.

Godey's Lady's Book

http://www.history.rochester.edu/godeys/

Selections from the popular nineteenth-century women's magazine, *Godey's Lady's Book*. Issues from the 1850s include "For the Home," "Nor Just for Ladies," and "Fashion Corner" sections. Visitors to this site will find an informative glimpse into the daily life of the mid-nineteenth-century middle class.

"A Grandmother's Recollections of Dixie"

http://docsouth.unc.edu/bryan/menu.html

This is a collection of letters from Mary Norcott Bryan to her grandchildren. It was published in 1912. Her letters shed light on Southern plantations before the Civil War.

Historical Maps of the United States

http://www.lib.utexas.edu/maps/map_sites/hist_sites.html#US

The University of Texas at Austin has digitized the Perry-Castañeda Library Map Collection. This is an excellent source for digitized copies of rare maps.

"The Hypocrisy of American Slavery"

http://www.historyplace.com/speeches/douglass.htm

This speech was given by Frederick Douglass on July 4, 1852, in Rochester, New York. See elsewhere in this section Douglass's speech given the following day titled, "What to the Slave Is the Fourth of July?"

The Jay Treaty

http://odur.let.rug.nl/~usa/D/1776-1800/foreignpolicy/jay.htm

The Jay Treaty between Great Britain and the United States was the most controversial issue of George Washington's presidency. It was proclaimed in February 1796. Its real significance was that it represented Britain's recognition of American nationality.

Thomas Jefferson on Politics and Government: Quotations From the Writings of Thomas Jefferson

http://etext.virginia.edu/jefferson/quotations/

This site, sponsored by the University of Virginia, contains an extensive collection of Jefferson quotations. The stated goal of this site is to constitute a "fair statement of the complete political philosophy of Thomas Jefferson." Also included are a brief biography of Jefferson and links to related sites.

John Brown: An Address by Frederick Douglass

http://www.mdcbowen.org/p5/jb/douglass.htm

This speech by Frederick Douglass can be found at the Library of Congress Web site. It is a tribute to John Brown, a radical abolitionist who, in 1859, raided the federal arsenal at Harpers Ferry, Virginia, in a mad attempt to foment a slave revolt. Brown was hanged by the Virginia authorities. His last words were: "I, John Brown, am now quite certain that the crimes of this guilty land will never be purged away but with blood." Douglass memorialized Brown as a true hero of the abolitionist cause.

"A Journey to the Seaboard States" (1856)

http://odur.let.rug.nl/~usa/D/1851-1875/olmsted/jour01.htm

This essay by Frederick Law Olmsted focuses on slavery and the plantation system. It was written in 1856 while Olmsted was on a journalistic assignment for the *New York Daily Times*. Olmsted was critical of slavery as both cruel and inefficient.

Kentucky Resolution (1799)

http://odur.let.rug.nl/~usa/D/1776-1800/constitution/kent1799.htm

This was Thomas Jefferson's republican response to the Federalists' Alien and Sedition Acts. The resolution advanced the state compact theory and argued that states retained the right to notify Congress when it had exceeded its authority.

The Louisiana Purchase Treaty

http://www.archives.gov/exhibits/american_originals_iv/sections/louisiana_purchase_treaty.html

This online exhibit by the National Archives presents images of the document that was signed in Paris in 1803, along with a transcription of the text.

The Madison Debates

http://www.yale.edu/lawweb/avalon/debates/debcont.htm

The Debates in the Federal Convention of 1787 was created from notes taken by James Madison during the Constitutional Convention held in Philadelphia between May 14 and September 17, 1787. The debates are searchable by keyword or can be accessed according to specific dates. Also contained here are links to the Articles of Confederation, the Annapolis Convention, the *Federalist Papers,* and the U.S. Constitution.

John Marshall

http://odur.let.rug.nl/~usa/D/1801-1825/marshallcases/marxx.htm

Here are the major decisions written by Chief Justice John Marshall, including *Marbury v. Madison* and *Cherokee Nation v. Georgia.* Also included is a biography of Marshall.

The Monroe Doctrine

http://odur.let.rug.nl/~usa/D/1801-1825/jmdoc.htm

The Monroe Doctrine was an early statement on American foreign policy. It was taken from President James Monroe's annual message to Congress on December 2, 1823.

North American Slave Narratives

http://docsouth.unc.edu/neh/index.html

This large collection of American slave narratives is part of the Documenting the American South project sponsored by the University of North Carolina at Chapel Hill. This is an excellent resource for better understanding the slaves' world in the antebellum South.

The Prairie Traveler: A Hand-book for Overland Expeditions

http://www.kancoll.org/books/marcy/

This survival guide and handbook, written by Captain Randolph B. Marcy, U.S. Army, was published in 1859.

The Proclamation of Neutrality (1793)

http://odur.let.rug.nl/~usa/D/1776-1800/foreignpolicy/neutr.htm

President George Washington proclaimed American neutrality during the wars of the French Revolution.

Scanned Originals of Early American Documents

http://www.law.emory.edu/FEDERAL/conpict.html

Scanned originals of the Constitution, the Bill of Rights, and the Declaration of Independence.

The Sedition Act of July 14, 1798

http://www.yale.edu/lawweb/avalon/statutes/sedact.htm

This act, passed by Congress on July 14, 1798, made it a federal crime to speak against the U.S. government. It is perhaps the most repressive law in American history.

"Slavery a Positive Good"

http://douglassarchives.org/calh_a59.htm

This speech was given on the floor of the U.S. Senate by John C. Calhoun in 1837.

Treaty of Greenville (1795)

http://odur.let.rug.nl/~usa/D/1776-1800/indians/green.htm

This is the complete text of the American Indian treaty that formally opened the Northwest Territory for settlement.

Uncle Tom's Cabin

http://xroads.virginia.edu/~HYPER/STOWE/stowe.html

The American Studies program at the University of Virginia provides an e-text of Harriet Beecher Stowe's 1852 novel.

Virginia Resolution (1798)

http://www.yale.edu/lawweb/avalon/virres.htm

This was James Madison's republican response to the Federalist's Alien and Sedition Acts. It advanced the state compact theory, which argued that the federal government could operate only within its constitutionally defined limits.

Virginia Statute for Religious Freedom (1786)

http://religiousfreedom.lib.virginia.edu/sacred/vaact.html

This act was drafted by Thomas Jefferson in 1777. An amended version passed the Virginia legislature in 1786. It served as the precedent for the religious freedom article in the Bill of Rights.

"What to the Slave Is the Fourth of July?"

http://douglassarchives.org/doug_a10.htm

This speech was delivered by Frederick Douglass on July 5, 1852. See, elsewhere in this section, Douglass's speech given the day before in Rochester, New York, titled "The Hypocrisy of American Slavery."

Chapter 17

American Civil War History

Jeffrey W. McClurken

Metasites

The American Civil War Home Page

http://sunsite.utk.edu/civil-war/

Started in 1994, this is one of the oldest Civil War link sites, yet it remains useful because of its helpful categories and the sheer number of links.

Civil War and Reconstruction: Jensen's Guide to WWW Resources

http://tigger.uic.edu/~rjensen/civwar.htm

Built by an academic historian, this guide is a good place to start, given its topical and chronological categories of links to scholarly sites and primary source documents.

The Civil War Index Page

http://www.homepages.dsu.edu/jankej/civilwar/civilwar.htm

This site contains more specific subcategories, and more commercial links, than other metasites.

United States Civil War Center

http://www.cwc.lsu.edu/

Based at LSU, the Civil War Center has indexed over 9,000 Civil War Web sites, from scholarly sites to popular sites covering movies, quotes, reenactors, and vendors.

Library of Congress

This institution has worked to make accessible online numerous primary documents from its extensive collections, many of which relate to the Civil War.

Library of Congress: African American Odyssey

http://lcweb2.loc.gov/ammem/aaohtml/exhibit/aointro.html

The Web companion to an exhibit of materials from the Library of Congress. The sections on slavery, abolition, the Civil War, and Reconstruction are particularly useful.

Library of Congress: Civil War Maps

http://lcweb2.loc.gov/ammem/collections/civil_war_maps/

This impressive site includes an essay on the history of Civil War mapping and over 2,000 images of Civil War–era maps, atlases, and charts.

Library of Congress: Civil War Treasures From the New York Historical Society

http://memory.loc.gov/ammem/ndlpcoop/nhihtml/cwnyhshome.html

This site houses a broad selection of manuscripts, sketches, posters, and photographs that includes, but goes beyond, the New York area in its focus.

Library of Congress: Abraham Lincoln Papers

http://memory.loc.gov/ammem/alhtml/malhome.html

Heavy on research and light on context, this site contains over 20,000 documents, including letters, speeches, and notes from Lincoln.

Library of Congress: Selected Civil War Photographs

http://memory.loc.gov/ammem/cwphtml/cwphome.html

This collection includes over a thousand original pictures from the Civil War, many of them linked to a war chronology, and some historical context on photography.

National Park Service (NPS)

As part of its educational mission, the NPS and its many parks and historic places have made many primary documents and scholarly articles available to Web researchers.

Camp Life: Civil War Collections

http://www.cr.nps.gov/museum/exhibits/gettex/index.htm

Based on an exhibit at the Gettysburg Park, the site is an interesting virtual tour of the material culture of Civil War soldiers' daily life.

Civil War Archaeology

http://www.cr.nps.gov/seac/civilwar/index.htm

This site details NPS efforts at excavations at Fort Pulaski, Shiloh, and Andersonville, the notorious Confederate prison, giving a brief history of each location.

Civil War Soldiers and Sailors System (CWSS)

http://www.itd.nps.gov/cwss/

The CWSS is one of the most important research sites for the Civil War. It contains the names and basic information for over 6 million soldiers and sailors from both sides. The site also has many regimental histories, summaries of 364 battles, listings of Medal of Honor winners and prisoners of war, and a section on the key roles played by black soldiers.

NPS Battlefields and Historic Sites

Each NPS park or historic location has its own Web site, many of which are useful for Civil War researchers. Many of these Web sites include maps, battle summaries, scholarly articles, educational opportunities, and excerpts from letters, diaries, and memoirs. The following are some of the best.

Antietam National Park–http://www.nps.gov/anti/home.htm

Appomattox Courthouse National Historic Park—http://www.nps.gov/apco/index1.htm

Clara Barton National Historic Site—http://www.nps.gov/clba/

Fredericksburg and Spotsylvania National Military Park—http://www.nps.gov/frsp/vc.htm

Gettysburg National Military Park—http://www.nps.gov/gett/home.htm

Lincoln Home National Historic Site—http://www.nps.gov/liho/index.htm

Petersburg National Battlefield Park—http://www.nps.gov/pete/mahan/PNBhome.html

Vicksburg National Military Park—http://www.nps.gov/vick/home.htm

General Sites

American Civil War

http://spec.lib.vt.edu/civwar/

Virginia Tech's Special Collections has transcribed small collections of letters from several Union and Confederate soldiers.

American Civil War Collection

http://etext.virginia.edu/civilwar/

Constituting one segment of the University of Virginia's Electronic Text Center, this site includes several large diaries and hundreds of letters from and to ordinary soldiers, as well as Civil War–related fiction and poetry.

Captain Richard W. Burt: Civil War Letters From the 76th Ohio Volunteer Infantry

http://my.ohio.voyager.net/~lstevens/burt/

This bare-bones site offers transcriptions of letters, poems, and materials related to this Ohio soldier's wartime experience.

Civil War Diaries at Augustana College Library

http://www.augustana.edu/library/SpecialCollections/civil1.html

Two diaries of Illinois soldiers were scanned and transcribed for this site.

Civil War Diary of Bingham Findley Junkin

http://www.frontierfamilies.net/family/junkin/

This site is a transcription of a brief diary from a Pennsylvania enlisted soldier.

Civil War Letters of Samuel S. Dunton

http://home.pacbell.net/dunton/SSDletters.html

Plainly presented, these transcriptions of a New York soldier's letters home discuss his time in Baltimore, Washington, and Louisiana.

Civil War Resources From the Virginia Military Institute Archives

http://www.vmi.edu/archives/cwsource.html

The staff of VMI's archives has produced an excellent site combining various primary documents from more than sixty of their collections with secondary narratives on a variety of topics, including Stonewall Jackson, the Battle of New Market, and life in the Shenandoah Valley.

Civil War Women

http://scriptorium.lib.duke.edu/collections/civil-war-women.html

http://scriptorium.lib.duke.edu/collections/african-american-women.html

These Web sites present Duke University's three transcribed collections about women during the war, featuring the papers of Rose Greenhow, the Confederate spy and propagandist (first site), and three collections of Duke's material on African-American women from the Civil War era, including letters from slave women to their slaveholders and family members (second site).

Dwight Henry Cory Letters

http://homepages.rootsweb.com/~lovelace/cory.htm

Posted by a descendant of Cory, the site includes transcriptions of letters between the Ohio cavalry officer and his future wife.

Documenting the American South

http://docsouth.unc.edu/

This site showcases the impressive records of the University of North Carolina's Southern Historical Collection. Click on "Collections" to see digitized primary sources including autobiographies, slave narratives, and material on the Southern home front during the Civil War. (See also a collection of soldiers' letters at http://www.lib.unc.edu/mss/exhibits/civilwar/.)

Freedmen and Southern Society Project

http://www.history.umd.edu/Freedmen/

This site, part of a multivolume series publishing records in the National Archives relating to African-Americans during the war, contains examples of dozens of transcribed documents.

Ulysses S. Grant Association

http://www.lib.siu.edu/projects/usgrant/

The association has published twenty-six volumes of Union general Ulysses S. Grant's papers. The site includes a very useful chronology, linked to excerpts from his memoirs and other primary documents.

H-CivWar

http://www.h-net.org/~civwar/

This site is the Web presence for the H-CivWar discussion list. The site includes archived posts, subscription information, and related book reviews by scholars.

HarpWeek

http://www.harpweek.com/

This subscription site presenting *Harper's Weekly* (1857–1912) has an extensive free section on nineteenth-century topics, including articles on political cartoons, literature, race relations, and Constitutional amendments.

Robert E. Lee Papers

http://miley.wlu.edu/LeePapers/

Washington and Lee University makes available images of nearly fifty letters written by the school's most famous president and Confederate general. The site also includes a link to hundreds more transcribed letters from Lee.

Letters From an Iowa Soldier in the Civil War

http://www.civilwarletters.com/home.html

This attractively presented site contains fifteen letters from Private Newton Scott to his future wife, Hannah Cone.

Overall Family Civil War Letters

http://www.geocities.com/Heartland/Acres/1574/

This site presents transcribed and scanned letters from an Ohio family whose husband and father served and died of disease. Unlike many other online collections of letters, the site includes lots of context, including short biographies for nearly all of the people mentioned in the letters.

The Papers of Jefferson Davis

http://jeffersondavis.rice.edu/

The fifty documents selected from the fifteen-volume publication of the works of the Confederacy's president include his letters and speeches, as well as pictures and scholarly information on Davis and his family.

Pearce Civil War Documents Collection

http://www.nav.cc.tx.us/library/civilwar/full_text.htm

This small, well-organized, online collection is a sample of documents available at Navarro College in Texas. The site is very usable; however, other than letters from Captain L.D. Bradley of Texas, there is only one letter each from various other soldiers.

Secession Era Editorials Project

http://history.furman.edu/~benson/docs/

Sponsored by Furman University, this site includes transcriptions of newspaper editorials from all over the nation, representing all political parties, on four topics key to the coming of the Civil War: the Kansas-Nebraska Act, the caning of Charles Sumner, the Dred Scott case, and John Brown's raid.

Shotgun's Home of the American Civil War

http://www.civilwarhome.com/

This large, sweeping site, created by a passionate amateur, includes extensive secondary material from various articles, as well as extensive primary source records, including large excerpts from the Official Records of the War of the Rebellion.

Valley of the Shadow Project

http://jefferson.village.virginia.edu/vshadow2/

Based at the University of Virginia's Center for Digital History and started by historian Edward Ayers in 1993, the Valley Project brings together all available information on one Northern county (Franklin County, Pennsylvania) and one Southern county (Augusta County, Virginia) up to and during the Civil War years. The documents assembled by a team of scholars include searchable transcriptions of diaries, letters, newspapers, images, military records, and maps.

Women Soldiers of the Civil War

http://www.archives.gov/publications/prologue/1993/spring/
women-in-the-civil-war-1.html

This is an online version of an article by scholar DeAnne Blanton that explores the role of women who fought as men in the two armies. The site also contains photographs and records from the National Archives.

Chapter 18

Gilded Age and Progressive Era History

Jeremy Boggs

Metasites and Directories

American Memory

http://memory.loc.gov/ammem/

One of the preeminent history sites available, American Memory provides access to a plethora of materials held by the Library of Congress. Users can browse the content by topic or collection, or search all collections by keyword. The site also provides guides to help teachers incorporate the American Memory project into classroom learning. The site is currently undergoing an extensive but elegant redesign.

Gilded Age and Progressive Era Resources

http://www2.tntech.edu/history/gilprog.html

Maintained by the Department of History at Tennessee Tech, this site contains a growing list of sites useful to those interested in the history of the Gilded Age and Progressive Era.

History Matters

http://historymatters.gmu.edu/

This site is a joint project of the Center for History and New Media at George Mason University and the American Social History Project and Center for Media and Learning at the City University of New York. It contains invaluable resources for history teachers at the secondary and collegiate levels. Visitors can learn how to interpret documents, search various primary sources available on the site, and search reviews of other history-related sites.

Presidents

Ulysses S. Grant, 1869–1877

http://www.mscomm.com/~ulysses/

Webmaster Candace Scott has collected and made available numerous documents written by Ulysses S. Grant and his family and friends. Photos, letters, and interviews with various members of Grant's family are available.

Rutherford B. Hayes, 1877–1881

http://www.americanpresident.org/history/rutherfordbhayes/

This site contains a brief biography of Hayes's life, as well as links to images and other Web resources.

James A. Garfield, 1881

http://www.americanpresident.org/history/jamesgarfield/

A detailed biography of Garfield, who served only one hundred days as president before being assassinated.

Chester A. Arthur, 1881–1885

http://www.americanpresident.org/history/chesterccrthur/

A solid biography that details Arthur's life and links to his papers, images of him, and articles about him.

Grover Cleveland, 1885–1889 and 1893–1897

http://www.americanpresident.org/history/grovercleveland2/

Cleveland was deemed the "Guardian President" for his then record use of the veto power. This site provides a thorough overview of his life before and during his presidency.

Benjamin Harrison, 1889–1893

http://www.americanpresident.org/history/benjaminharrison/

Harrison's legacy continues to be debated, and the reasons for this are detailed in this short biography. The site also links to images of him, including a cartoon, and related articles.

William McKinley, 1897–1901

http://www.americanpresident.org/history/williammckinley/

McKinley served as president during the Spanish-American War. During his presidency he also sent over 2,000 soldiers to China to help suppress the Boxer Rebellion. McKinley won a second term in 1900, but he was assassinated a year later. This biography details his time in office and the historical contexts in which he served as president.

Theodore Roosevelt, 1901–1909

http://www.americanpresident.org/history/theodoreroosevelt/

Author, politician, and "Rough Rider," Roosevelt became William McKinley's vice president in 1901 and later took office after McKinley's assassination. This site provides an interesting discussion of the life of Roosevelt.

William Howard Taft, 1909–1913

http://www.americanpresident.org/history/williamhowardtaft/

This site provides a detailed biography of the twenty-seventh president, covering his life before and after his term in office.

Activists, Authors, Businessmen, and Inventors

Alexander Graham Bell Family Papers

http://memory.loc.gov/ammem/bellhtml/bellhome.html

Another splendid project in the American Memory collection, this site provides visitors access to the papers of Alexander Graham Bell and his family. Among the materials presented are family papers, written correspondence, laboratory notebooks, and various articles written by Bell. This is a rich resource for anyone interested in learning more about this influential inventor.

Andrew Carnegie

http://www.pbs.org/wgbh/amex/carnegie/

A companion to PBS's documentary titled *The Richest Man in the World*, this site contains insightful material related to Andrew Carnegie. A time line traces events during Carnegie's life. The gallery provides images and commentary, and the People and Events section gives detailed biographical information on Carnegie as well as a discussion of the Homestead Strike in 1892.

Eugene V. Debs

http://www.eugenevdebs.com

This site, created by the Eugene V. Debs Foundation, details the life and work of Debs, an ardent Socialist and supporter of labor rights, who was arrested for his involvement in organizing the 1893 strike against the Pullman Company.

Thomas A. Edison Papers

http://edison.rutgers.edu

A joint project of Rutgers University, the National Park Service, the New Jersey Historical Society, and the Smithsonian Institution, this site contains an impressive searchable database of Edison's papers and drawings. Access to newspapers and patents is also available, as well as biographic information on Edison.

Emma Goldman Papers

http://sunsite.berkeley.edu/Goldman/

This site provides access to a number of primary sources related to this political and social activist.

The Jack London Collection

http://sunsite.berkeley.edu/London/

This site, a project of the library at the University of California, Berkeley, gives visitors access to a variety of materials related to Jack London. Materials include audio clips, letters and postcards, and pictures. A brief biography of London, written by Dr. Clarice Stasz, is also available.

Poet at Work: Recovered Notebooks From the Thomas Biggs Harned Walt Whitman Collection

http://memory.loc.gov/ammem/wwhtml/wwhome.html

Visitors to this site can access four notebooks and a cardboard butterfly kept by Walt Whitman. These materials disappeared from the Library of Congress in 1942, but were recovered in 1995.

John D. Rockefeller Biographical Sketch

http://archive.rockefeller.edu/bio/jdrsr.php

Maintained by the Rockefeller Archive Center, this site provides a brief biography of Rockefeller. Other links on the site take users to a detailed bibliography of published material on Rockefeller as well as a section titled In Their Own Words, where visitors can read materials published by Rockefeller at the turn of the century. An interactive family tree traces the Rockefeller family from 1897 to the present.

Mark Twain in His Times

http://etext.lib.virginia.edu/railton/

Using resources available in the Barrett Collection of American Literature at the University of Virginia Library, Steven Railton has created an engaging site that explores the life and writing of Mark Twain. Railton has gathered a number of manuscripts, contemporary reviews, images, and exhibits related to Mark Twain. The site is maintained by the Electronic Text Center at the University of Virginia.

Booker T. Washington Papers

http://www.historycooperative.org/btw/

Created by History Cooperative and the University of Illinois Press, this site contains images as well as access to the published version of the *Booker T. Washington Papers*, published by the University of Illinois Press. The papers are searchable and can be printed.

Consumerism and Popular Culture

America at Work, America at Leisure: Motion Pictures From 1894–1915

http://memory.loc.gov/ammem/awlhtml/

This American Memory site contains 150 motion pictures that show various leisurely and sporting activities, including calisthenics, boxing, football games, and parades.

American Variety Stage: Vaudeville and Popular Entertainment, 1870–1920

http://memory.loc.gov/ammem/vshtml/vshome.html

Over 600 scripts, programs, and photos make up this American Memory collection on the early history of vaudeville.

Baseball Cards, 1887–1914

http://memory.loc.gov/ammem/bbhtml/bbhome.html

Part of the American Memory collection, this site contains over 2,100 baseball cards from 1887 to 1914.

Cartoons of the Gilded Age and Progressive Era

http://history.osu.edu/Projects/USCartoons/GAPECartoons.htm

This site, which is part of The Ohio State University Department of History's Cartoon Collections, features a number of cartoons about such topics as the antitrust movement, imperialism and its opponents, and the 1900 presidential campaign.

Emergence of Advertising in America, 1850–1920

http://scriptorium.lib.duke.edu/eaa

This is a rich resource of nearly 9,000 advertisements from the 1850s to the 1920s. Created and maintained by the John W. Hartman Center and Digital Scriptorium at Duke University. Users can search or browse the advertisements by topic or keyword.

Red Hot Jazz Archive: A History of Jazz Before 1930

http://www.redhotjazz.com

Webmaster Scott Alexander has gathered a number of documents that detail the development of jazz music. Several films of musical performances are available, as well as a number of essays on the historical development of jazz and biographical sketches of influential musicians of the time.

Industrialization and Urbanization

Child Labor in America, 1908–1912: Photographs of Lewis W. Hine

http://www.historyplace.com/unitedstates/childlabor/

Lewis W. Hine became an investigative photographer for the National Child Labor Committee in 1908, after a career as a teacher. The more than sixty photographs contained in this site are part of his work documenting working conditions of children across the United States.

City Sites: Multimedia Essays on New York and Chicago, 1870s–1930s

http://www.artsweb.bham.ac.uk/citysites/

A project by the University of Birmingham and the University of Nottingham in the United Kingdom, this site contains interactive essays on the history of New York and Chicago. The site is an interesting use of the Web for publication, offering readers a refreshing view of the urban histories of these two cities.

Panoramic Maps, 1847–1929

http://memory.loc.gov/ammem/pmhtml/panhome.html

This American Memory project provides access to a variety of panoramic maps of U.S. cities. Visitors can access the maps by subject, keyword, or geographic location. The maps offer an interesting view of how Americans perceived their urban landscapes.

San Francisco Historical Photograph Collection

http://sfpl.lib.ca.us/librarylocations/sfhistory/sfphoto.htm

The San Francisco Public Library has made available photographs and printed material related to San Francisco from 1850 to the present. Users can search for photographs, browse by subject, or locate images using an interactive map of the city.

Urban Experience in Chicago: Hull-House and Its Neighbors, 1889–1963

http://www.uic.edu/jaddams/hull/urbanexp/index.htm

This site by the University of Illinois at Chicago and the Jane Addams Hull-House Museum gives visitors access to valuable primary source documents, photographs, and essays pertaining to the history of Hull-House. Elegantly designed, this site includes a historical narrative, a time line, maps of the neighborhood, and resources for teachers.

Politics and Government

Finding Precedent: *Hayes v. Tilden*, the Electoral College Controversy of 1876–1877

http://elections.harpweek.com/controversy.htm

HarpWeek created this site to inform students and the public about the controversy surrounding the election in 1876–1877. The site contains images and cartoons from *Harper's Weekly* as well as an overview of the controversy, biographies on important figures, and a discussion of its resolution.

Foreign Relations of the United States

http://libtext.library.wisc.edu/FRUS/

A project of the University of Wisconsin Libraries, this site gives readers access to digital copies of *Foreign Relations of the United States,* a publication by the State Department's Office of the Historian. The collection can be searched or browsed, and an index is available for volumes covering the years 1861 to 1899 and 1900 to 1918.

The Presidential Election, 1860–1912

http://elections.harpweek.com/

This site, also created by HarpWeek, provides a concise overview of each presidential election between 1860 and 1912. Along with the overview, the site contains political cartoons from each election with explanations of the cartoons.

Uniting Mugwumps and the Masses: *Puck's* Role in Gilded Age Politics

http://xroads.virginia.edu/~MA96/PUCK/home.html

An online master's thesis by Daniel Henry Backer, this site explores the history of the mugwumps. The mugwumps were Republicans who, in the 1884 presidential election, supported Democrat Grover Cleveland instead of the Republican candidate, James Gillespie Blaine. Backer's site provides analysis of the magazine *Puck* and the political cartoons it contained. A cartoon archive provides access to twenty images that are used throughout the site.

Race, Class, and Gender Issues

African American Perspectives: Pamphlets From the Daniel A.P. Murray Collection, 1818–1907

http://memory.loc.gov/ammem/aap/aaphome.html

This American Memory collection provides access to published material written in the nineteenth century. Most of the publications were printed between 1875 and 1900. Authors of the materials include, among others, Booker T. Washington and Frederick Douglass.

By Popular Demand: "Votes for Women" Suffrage Pictures, 1850–1920

http://memory.loc.gov/ammem/vfwhtml/vfwhome.html

Thirty-eight pictures, including photographs of picketers and protesters, are available in this American Memory collection. Also included in the collection are cartoons commenting on the suffrage movement, antisuffrage demonstrations, and portraits of influential people during the movement.

A Coal Miner's Work

http://people.cohums.ohio-state.edu/kerr6/courses/History563/A%20Coal%20Miner's%20Work.htm

Written by K. Austin Kerr and sponsored by The Ohio State University, this site explores the life and times of late nineteenth-century coal miners.

The Dramas of Haymarket

http://www.chicagohistory.org/dramas/index.htm

A project by the Chicago Historical Society and Northwestern University, this site explores the Chicago Historical Society's Haymarket Affair Digital Collection. Organized like a drama—with a prologue, five acts, and an epilogue—the Dramas of Haymarket interprets documents available on the Haymarket affair in engaging fashion. The site is rich in multimedia, and hyperlinks to other relevant resources allow visitors to engage the material from different perspectives.

Images of African Americans From the Nineteenth Century

http://digital.nypl.org/schomburg/writers_aa19/

Sponsored by the Schomburg Center for Research in Black Culture at the New York Public Library, this site contains hundreds of images that reveal the lives of African-Americans in the nineteenth century.

Votes for Women: Selections From the National American Woman Suffrage Association, 1848–1921

http://memory.loc.gov/ammem/naw/nawshome.html

This American Memory collection contains 167 pamphlets, books, and other resources that contribute to the history of the suffrage movement. Papers of prominent suffragists, including Susan B. Anthony, Elizabeth Cady Stanton, and Alice Stone Blackwell, are available.

Women Working, 1870–1930

http://ocp.hul.harvard.edu/ww/

A project by Harvard University Libraries, this site provides a detailed account of the lives of women workers. Pamphlets, diaries, letters, and images are available so users can explore the lives of working women, including teachers, actresses, secretaries, farm laborers, and factory workers.

War and Imperialism

Anti-Imperialism in the United States, 1895–1935

http://www.boondocksnet.com/ai/index.html

If readers can ignore the moving advertisements on this site, they can take advantage of the hundreds of documents available on the anti-imperialism movement. The site contains speeches, essays, and cartoons from the era, as well as current discussion of the materials.

The Crucible of Empire: The Spanish-American War

http://www.pbs.org/crucible/

Created by the Public Broadcasting Company, this site provides related resources for a film produced by PBS also called *The Crucible of Empire*. The site includes a time line as well as discussion of various aspects of the Spanish-American War, including yellow journalism and music of the 1890s.

Events—Spanish-American War

http://www.history.navy.mil/photos/events/spanam/eve-pge.htm

This site, created by the Navy Historical Center, contains a number of images from the Spanish-American War.

The Spanish-American War in Motion Pictures

http://memory.loc.gov/ammem/sawhtml/sawhome.html

This American Memory site contains a searchable and browsable index of various films that depict the Spanish-American War. The films were produced by the Edison Manufacturing Company and the American Mutoscope and Biography Company.

A War in Perspective, 1898–1998

http://www.nypl.org/research/chss/epo/spanexhib/index.html

Created and maintained by the New York Public Library, this site contains a brief but thorough summary of various aspects of the Spanish-American War.

The World of 1898: The Spanish-American War

http://www.loc.gov/rr/hispanic/1898/

Part of the American Memory collection, this site houses various documents and resources pertaining to the Spanish-American War and the people involved. Users can browse the material through the subject index or look at specific resources, such as maps, literary commentary, and personal narratives.

Chapter 19

The Age of
Franklin D. Roosevelt

Anne Rothfeld

Metasites

American Memory

http://lcweb2.loc.gov/ammem

American Memory, maintained by the Library of Congress, is ideal for anyone interested in American history, and researchers may want to visit this Web page first. The Web site contains Age of Roosevelt topics including New Deal programs, election and inauguration, and correspondence and ephemera. Researchers can browse by collection names and search by all collections.

New Deal Network

http://newdeal.feri.org

The Franklin and Eleanor Roosevelt Institute sponsors this Web site, which is the starting point for historical figures and events of the Age of Roosevelt. New Deal Network offers primary source materials and photographs, both of which are searchable by topics and dates. This site hosts the H-US 1918–45, a moderated H-Net discussion list for teachers and historians.

Historical Figures

Herbert C. Hoover

Herbert C. Hoover Presidential Library and Museum

http://www.hoover.nara.gov

The Hoover Presidential Library and Museum constructed this Web site, which contains information on his presidency, education modules, and research guides to both the Hoover presidential papers and the papers of Rose Wilder Land and her mother, children's author Laura Ingalls Wilder. Rose Wilder wrote one of the first biographies of Hoover, published in 1919. This Web site, which is the best place to start for topics on Hoover, is updated weekly and has links to related sites.

White House—Herbert Hoover

http://www.whitehouse.gov/history/presidents/hh31.html

Maintained by the White House staff, this page has biographies of President Hoover and the first lady, Lou Henry Hoover, with links to the text of the president's inaugural address and to the Hoover Presidential Library.

Huey P. Long

Every Man a King: Excerpts From Huey Long's Autobiography

http://www.ssa.gov./history/huey.html

Constructed by the Social Security Administration, this Web site contains excerpts from Huey Long's autobiography, *Every Man a King,* published in 1933. Long was a showy politician, popular in the early 1930s, who advocated reallocation of wealth.

My First Days in the White House: Excerpts From Huey Long's "Second Autobiography"

http://www.ssa.gov./history/hueywhouse.html

The Social Security Administration also maintains this page, which includes excerpts from all eight chapters of Long's 1935 book, *My First Days in the White House.*

Anna Eleanor Roosevelt

Eleanor Roosevelt Center at Val-Kill

http://www.ervk.org

Val-Kill was Eleanor Roosevelt's cottage along the Hudson River. The Val-Kill Center's purpose is "to preserve Eleanor Roosevelt's home as a vibrant living memorial, a center for the exchange of significant ideas and a catalyst for change and for the betterment of the human condition." The Center maintains this page to provide information on Roosevelt and some photographs of her. There is an extensive list of useful links to topics and issues concerning her.

Eleanor Roosevelt Resource Page

http://personalweb.smcvt.edu/smahady/ercover.htm

This is a wonderful place to start any Internet search relating to Eleanor Roosevelt. The site, authored by Sherry S. Mahady, contains biographical and bibliographical information, quotes from scholars and peers, documents from Roosevelt's column, newspaper articles, letters from her papers and the National Archives, video clips, and links to other sites with information, pictures, and documents pertaining to the first lady.

Franklin D. Roosevelt

FDR Cartoon Collection database

http://www.nisk.k12.ny.us/fdr

This award-winning site, constructed by Paul Bachorz of Niskayuna High School in Niskayuna, New York, contains an extensive collection of over 30,000 FDR cartoons taken from newspapers and magazines during the 1930s and 1940s. There are also links to other Web sites, suggestions for school teachers, and Roosevelt's inaugural addresses.

Franklin D. Roosevelt Library and Museum

http://www.fdrlibrary.marist.edu

Created by the staff of the Roosevelt Presidential Library, this site provides short biographies of the president and the first lady. Additionally, the site contains several guides to the collections at the Roosevelt Presidential Library. Increasingly, the library is putting documents online. Now accessible is a collection of several thousand documents from the White House safe files during the Roosevelt years. Finally, there is an exceptional, copyright-free, online photograph database.

White House—Franklin D. Roosevelt

http://www.whitehouse.gov/history/presidents/fr32.html

The White House staff maintains this site, which contains short biographies of Franklin and Eleanor Roosevelt. There are links to the texts of FDR's inaugural addresses.

The Great Depression

African Americans and the New Deal

http://newdeal.feri.org/texts/subject.htm

This location, part of the New Deal Network, contains dozens of documents relating to blacks and the New Deal.

American Memory: FSA-OWI Photographs

http://lcweb2.loc.gov/ammem/fsowhome.html

American Memory, maintained by the Library of Congress, is a wonderful Web site for all topics in American history. It has thousands of primary sources that relate to the Age of Roosevelt. This particular location contains over 160,000 (including 1,600 in color) Farm Security Administration and Office of War Information photographs covering the years 1935 to 1945.

Dust Bowl Refugees in California

http://www.sfmuseum.org/hist8/ok.html

The Museum of the City of San Francisco maintains a Web site on California history, which has this section on dust bowl refugees. It contains primary sources and photographs.

A New Deal for the Arts

http://www.archives.gov/exhibits/new_deal_for_the_arts/index.html

The National Archives and Records Administration maintains an online version of this exhibit. The page has several good examples of New Deal art in various forms, including paintings, photographs, and posters.

The Trials of the Scottsboro Boys

http://www.law.umkc.edu/faculty/projects/FTrials/scottsboro/scottsb.htm

This location is part of the larger Famous American Trials Web site created by Doug Linder. The page on the Scottsboro boys contains a short history, biographical and bibliographical information, photographs, and trial documents.

Social Security Administration Online History

http://www.ssa.gov/history

The U.S. Social Security Administration built this page, which contains oral histories, video and audio clips, documents, photographs, brief biographies, and guides to the Social Security Administration archives.

Supreme Court Decisions (Legal Information Institute)

http://www.law.cornell.edu/supct/index.html

The Legal Information Institute and Cornell University sponsor this U.S. Supreme Court decisions Web site, which is an excellent place to gain quick access to decisions from the Wagner Act to Japanese relocation. This Web site contains an "Archives of Decisions" searchable by topic, author, or party. The site also contains general information on the U.S. Supreme Court.

The Voices From the Dust Bowl: The Charles L. Todd and Robert Sonkin Migrant Worker Collection, 1940–1941

http://memory.loc.gov/ammem/afctshtml/tshome.html

This page, part of American Memory, contains oral histories, photographs, and dozens of other primary documents relating to the dust bowl.

Works Progress (later Projects) Administration (WPA) Folklore Project and Federal Writers' Project

http://lcweb.loc.gov/ammem/wpaintro/

This American Memory site has several thousand WPA Folklore Project and Federal Writers' Project documents representing over 300 authors from twenty-four states from 1936 to 1940. The Library of Congress collection includes 2,900 documents. Searchable by keywords or by state.

WPA Murals and Artwork From Lane Technical High School Collection

http://www.lanetech.org

Maintained by Flora Doody, the director of Lane Technical High School's Artwork Restoration Project, this site has lots of WPA artwork, including eleven frescoes, two oil on canvas murals, an oil on steel fire curtain, two mahogany carved murals, and two concrete cast fountain statues. The site also contains artwork created for the General Motors Exhibition at the Century of Progress, Chicago's World Fair (1933–1934). Click on "Murals" at the above site to find the murals and artwork.

WPA's California Gold Northern California Folk Music From the Thirties

http://memory.loc.gov/ammem/afccchtml/cowhome.html

This American Memory Web site "includes sound recordings, still photographs, drawings, and written documents from a variety of European ethnic and English- and Spanish-speaking communities in Northern California. The collection comprises thirty-five hours of folk music recorded in twelve languages representing numerous ethnic groups and 185 musicians." This collection is well documented and easy to use. Search by musical instruments, ethnic groups, or performers.

Chapter 20

World War II

Alexander Zukas

Home Front

German Prisoners of War in Clinton, Mississippi

http://www2.netdoor.com/~allardma/powcamp2.html

Mike Allard's site has minimal text but some interesting pictures of German prisoners at the POW camp in Clinton, Mississippi.

The Homefront During World War II

http://www.gettysburg.edu/~mbirkner/fys120/homefront.html

Professor Michael Birkner of Gettysburg College created this Web site for his first-year seminar class. The site hosts oral histories of the residents of Adams County, Pennsylvania, a photo gallery of Gettysburg College during the war, advertising from the war years, and excerpts from the *Gettysburg Times* concerning everyday life on the home front. The site clarifies how the war affected small-town America.

The Japanese American Internment

http://www.geocities.com/Athens/8420/main.html

This is a rich and very developed site concerning the internment of Japanese-Americans during World War II. Included are sections on prewar intelligence reports on the loyalty of Japanese-Americans, the politics of internment, the state of mind and intentions of policy makers, life in the camps, the impact of the camps on those detained, and firsthand accounts by survivors. The site, maintained and regularly updated by C. John Yu, contains a large number of links to other Web sites exploring issues surrounding the internment of Japanese-Americans.

Japanese-American Internment and San Francisco

http://www.sfmuseum.org/war/evactxt.html

This site, maintained by the Museum of the City of San Francisco, contains dozens of newspaper articles about Japanese-American removal, photographs (including those by Dorothea Lange), contemporary accounts, and related information about internment.

Japanese American Internment at Harmony

http://www.lib.washington.edu/exhibits/harmony/

The University of Washington Libraries created this Web page about the internment camp in Puyallup, Washington, which contains primary source material including letters, the camp newspaper, drawings, pictures, and other documents. It is a useful place to begin an Internet search about internment.

Japanese American Internment in Arizona

http://jeff.scott.tripod.com/japanese.html

Jeffrey Scott, a specialist in Arizona history, maintains this page on the Gila River and Poston internment camps in Arizona. The site briefly describes the circumstances of Japanese internment and provides links to sites dedicated to the pictorial representation of these two camps, to books dealing with the camps, and to sites of photographic collections. The site also provides a list of manuscript sources and ephemera relating to the Arizona internment camps. The site is hosted on the Tripod.com domain.

Japanese American Internment (Resource Page for Teachers)

http://www.umass.edu/history/institute_dir/internment.html

The History Institute at the University of Massachusetts at Amherst sponsors this site, which is perhaps the best place to start searching for material on the internment of Japanese-Americans. Well organized and with dozens of Web links to documents, pictures, and related camp information, this site, designed for K–12 teachers, provides rich primary sources for classroom curricula.

Japanese Internment Camps During the Second World War

http://www.lib.utah.edu/spc/photo/9066/9066.htm

This online photograph exhibit, sponsored by the University of Utah Special Collections Department, displays a sampling of the library's collections concerning the internment of Japanese-Americans, particularly at the Topaz and Tule Lake camps.

The Lions' History: Researching World War II Images of African Americans

http://www.archives.gov/research/african-americans/ww2-pictures/index.html

Barbara Lewis Burger of the National Archives gathered this remarkable series of photos after immersing herself in African-American military history and researching life on the home front in the 1940s. Her intent was to produce a publication that fills a visual documentation void while at the same time stimulates interest in both black history and the holdings of the National Archives. This Web site does achieve both goals.

OWI Photographs

http://lcweb2.loc.gov/ammem/fsowhome.html

This site contains thousands of photographs of the home front taken for the Office of War Information during the war years. It is part of the American Memory project maintained by the Library of Congress.

Pictures of World War II

http://www.archives.gov/research/ww2/photos/images/thumbnails/index.html

The National Archives has a treasure trove of images from World War II. The war was documented on a huge scale by thousands of photographers and artists who created millions of pictures. American military photographers representing all the armed services covered the battlefronts around the world. Every activity of the war was photographed. On the home front, the many federal war agencies produced and collected pictures, posters, and cartoons on such subjects as war production, rationing, and civilian relocation. Among the areas covered in this photo ensemble are leaders, the home front, supply and support, rest and relaxation, aid and comfort, and victory and peace. If a picture is worth a thousand words, then little more needs to be said.

Rosie the Riveter and Other Women World War II Heroes

http://www.lezbeout.com/Rosietheriveter.htm

This site contains short vignettes about women's roles in World War II. Women worked as factory laborers, nurses and doctors, soldiers, journalists, prostitutes, and subjects of propaganda art. The site provides a different perspective on the war and some little-known information. A number of World War II propaganda posters illustrate the points in the texts.

Rutgers Oral History Archives of World War II

http://oralhistory.rutgers.edu/

The Rutgers World War II oral history project was funded by the Rutgers class of 1942 and directed by G. Kurt Piehler. The Web site has several dozen oral histories from veterans and civilians available for download (in Adobe Acrobat format).

San Francisco During World War II

http://www.sfmuseum.org/1906/ww2.html

This site maintained by the Museum of the City of San Francisco has information about San Francisco during the war years. Most of the primary sources on this site come from the *San Francisco News.*

Topaz Camp

http://www.greatbasinheritage.org/topaz.htm

Millard County, Utah, hosts this site, which provides a brief overview of Topaz, a Japanese-American relocation camp located in Millard County during World War II. The site explains the background to the relocation of Japanese-Americans, life in the camp, and conditions in the desert. The site also boasts picture postcards of the camp.

What Did You Do in the War, Grandma? Rhode Island Women During World War II

http://www.stg.brown.edu/projects/WWII_Women/tocCS.html

An oral history of Rhode Island women during World War II, written by students in the Honors English Program at South Kingstown High School, this site provides not only information about lesser-known aspects of the war, but also a good model of action for teachers interested in using the Internet for class projects.

World War II Posters: Powers of Persuasion

http://www.archives.gov/education/lessons/wwii-posters

The National Archives and Records Administration maintains this page, which has thirty-three war posters and one sound file. The page is divided into two categories representing the two psychological approaches used in rallying public support for the war.

WWII Propaganda Poster Collection From Northwestern University Library

http://www.library.northwestern.edu/govpub/collections/wwii-posters/

The Northwestern University Library's Government Publications division maintains this site, which has a searchable database of 300 wartime posters.

Military History

504th World War II HomePage

http://www.ww2-airborne.us/units/504/504.html

An example of the many sites dedicated to military units, this one chronicles the experiences of the 504th Parachute Infantry Regiment during World War II.

Achtung Panzer

http://www.achtungpanzer.com/panzer.htm

One of the many enthusiast sites dedicated to German armor. This one features many illustrations, tables of technical data, and a large number of links to other World War II sites.

A-Bomb WWW Museum

http://www.csi.ad.jp/ABOMB/

This online project is a Japanese-hosted Web site designed to inform visitors about the effects of atomic weapons on Hiroshima and Nagasaki and to encourage discussions about world peace. The Hiroshima City University Department of Computer Science produced the site that gives a different perspective on the dropping of atomic weapons on Japan from that usually found in the United States. The creators of the Web site state that "The Web site is neither meant to condemn nor condone the bombing, but is meant as a way for people to express their views on how to achieve peace, on what peace is, and other thoughts about peace." Although the site is a somewhat random collection of material, it provides a useful entry for teachers to present the issues surrounding the use of atomic weapons at the end of World War II for student discussion and to discuss the cultural legacy of the bomb.

Armies of the Second World War

http://books.stonebooks.com/armies/

A rich online database of day-by-day orders of battle and information about hundreds of division-, brigade-, and regiment-sized units in World War II, this database covers Commonwealth, Dominion, Colonial, and Exile armies, as well as minor Allied armies in Europe, Africa, and western Asia from September 1, 1939, through May 7, 1945. The site will be expanded to include further theaters of the war.

Atomic Bomb Decision

http://www.dannen.com/decision/index.html

This site contains full-text documents on the decision to use the atomic bomb. Most of the originals are in the U.S. National Archives. The documents contain the positions of those who argued for and against the use of atomic weapons on human targets in the months leading up to the dropping of the atomic bomb on Hiroshima.

The Battle of Britain

http://www.raf.mod.uk/bob1940/bobhome.html

This is a detailed, extensive Web site devoted to the aerial battle over Great Britain in 1940. It is hosted by the Royal Air Force and contains the official reports of the battle and a day-by-day account of the four-month battle.

BBC Online: World War Two

http://www.bbc.co.uk/history/war/wwtwo/index.shtml

This British Broadcasting Corporation Web site covers numerous topics on the war such as campaigns and battles, politics, the British home front, and the Holocaust. A multimedia zone offers interactive maps, photographs, and audio and video clips. WW2 People's War, linked to this site, is a new Web site from BBCi (BBC Interactive) History, aspiring to create a new national archive of personal and family stories from World War II.

China Defensive, 1942–1945: The China Theater of Operations

http://www.army.mil/cmh-pg/brochures/72-38/72-38.htm

This account of World War II in China was prepared in the U.S. Army Center of Military History by Mark D. Sherry. In it he explains the differences between the Chinese, European, and Pacific war fronts, what the United States hoped to achieve in China, and the ultimate result of U.S. interventions, supplies, and strategic intentions. The site helps fill out the picture of World War II in this major theatre of the war.

Codebreaking and Secret Weapons in World War II

http://home.earthlink.net/~nbrass1/enigma.htm

This site deals with some of the secret weapons developed by the combatants in World War II and how the Allies found out about the ones the Axis had developed. The site provides a window on the clandestine but militarily significant aspects of the war.

Dad's War: Finding and Telling Your Father's World War II Story

http://members.aol.com/dadswar/index.htm

If you can tolerate the small promotional effort for his works on writing personal history, Wes Johnson has done a service with this index of personal histories and initial instructions for writing the history of a family member who served in World War II (and, by extension, any war).

Feldgrau.com: A German Military History Research Site, 1919–1945

http://www.feldgrau.com/

A detailed Web site developed by an independent scholar working on a number of projects related to German World War II military history. It covers "the history of the units and formations of the various military, paramilitary, and auxiliary forces from 1933–45." Includes discussions of various battles and a bibliography of nearly 500 titles.

Guadalcanal Campaign

http://www.history.navy.mil/photos/events/wwii-pac/guadlcnl/guad-1.htm

This site is hosted by the Naval Historical Center of the U.S. Department of the Navy. It is the official U.S. Navy interpretation of the battle of Guadalcanal, with a large number of combat photographs and a brief narrative of the battle. This site is part of an extensive Web site commemorating the battle with links to other pages dealing with different aspects of the fighting.

Hyperwar: A Hypertext History of the Second World War

http://www.ibiblio.org/hyperwar/

A linked anthology of articles related to World War II, many of them discussing specific battles in detail, along with links to other sources.

Imperial Japanese Navy Page

http://www.combinedfleet.com/

Enthusiast Jon Parshall has created a detailed index to links about the Japanese navy during World War II, including detailed histories of individual vessels.

The Luftwaffe Home Page

http://www.ww2.dk/

This site provides data on the Luftwaffe and an index of links to Luftwaffe-related Web pages.

A Marine Diary: My Experiences on Guadalcanal

http://www.gnt.net/~jrube/index2.html

Entries from the diary of a Marine who served at Guadalcanal, with a large set of links to related World War II resources on the Internet.

Midway

http://www.history.navy.mil/photos/events/wwii-pac/midway/midway.htm

This is a Department of the Navy Naval Historical Center site. It contains a detailed narrative and excellent photographs of the battle. This is a good place to start gathering information about this important battle, often considered the turning point of the war in the Pacific. The site contains an FAQ section and a list of related resources.

Nanjing Massacre Archive

http://www.cnd.org/njmassacre/index.html

The *China News Digest* hosts this extensive site on the famous Nanjing Massacre in 1937–1938 in China, including the war crimes testimony and trial after the war.

Naval Air War in the Pacific

http://www.daveswarbirds.com/navalwar/

Photos and paintings of American air combat during World War II.

Normandy: 1944

http://normandy.eb.com/

Encyclopedia Britannica's multimedia examination of the Normandy invasion.

Open Directory Project: World War II

http://dmoz.org/Society/History/By_Time_Period/Twentieth_Century/
Wars_and_Conflicts/World_War_II/

This comprehensive directory contains over 1,030 Web sites on World War II including Air Forces (107), Arts and Literature (16), Atomic (62), Primary Sources (12), Education (5), Holocaust (382), Land Forces (62), Naval Forces (106), People (190), Regional (166), Theaters of Operations (183), War Crimes (5) and Weapons and Equipment (53).

The Pacific War: The U.S. Navy

http://www.microworks.net/pacific/

This page, which forms a conscious complement and counterpoint to the Imperial Japanese Navy page above, wants to inform visitors of the U.S. Navy's contribution to the overall victory that ended World War II with as much awesome detail as can be mustered. Comparing the information on both Web sites will give the student of World War II naval warfare an excellent overview of the military strength and tactics of these two major Pacific powers. The sites also contain short profiles of naval leaders and personal histories of veterans.

A People at War

http://www.archives.gov/exhibits/a_people_at_war/a_people_at_war.html

This site presents an online exhibition by the National Archives. It includes a brief discussion of events leading up to the war and links to related sites. Focuses on the people who served rather than providing a traditional history of the war.

Propaganda Leaflets of the Second World War

http://www.geocities.com/CapeCanaveral/4503

Most of the propaganda leaflets shown in these pages are anti-Nazi (airdropped by the UK/U.S. Allied Air Forces), although some Nazi leaflets are shown here also. The Web site author warns that some images and texts in the Nazi propaganda leaflets may be disturbing or offensive on religious, racial, or ethnic grounds. The material, which is produced exactly from the originals, provides visitors with good comparisons on the use of symbols and propaganda during the war.

Return to Midway

http://www.nationalgeographic.com/features/98/midway/

National Geographic has created this multimedia site featuring images and streaming video of the wrecks of the carriers sunk at the Battle of Midway.

The Russian Campaign, 1941–1945: A Photo Diary

http://www.geipelnet.com/war_albums/otto/ow_011.html

This site is a diary of a German soldier along with pictures he took of his experiences with an antitank battalion on the Russian front. It covers the whole span of the Russian campaign and provides an on-the-ground look at the fortunes of German troops and rare scenes of the fighting between German and Russian forces.

Second World War Encyclopedia

http://www.spartacus.schoolnet.co.uk/2WW.htm

This online encyclopedia is a Spartacus Educational Web site that enables research on individual people and events of the war in detail. The individual sections include Background to the War, Nazi Germany, Chronology of the War, Political Leaders, European Diplomacy, Major Offensives, the Home Front, British Military Leaders, U.S. Military Leaders, German Military Leaders, Japanese Military Leaders, Russian Military Leaders, French Military Leaders, the Armed Forces, the Air War, the Sea War, the Resistance, Scientists and Inventors, Resistance in Nazi Germany, French Resistance, the Holocaust, War Artists, Weapons and Tactics, Women in the War, Secret Agents, and Soldiers, Sailors and Pilots.

U-Boat Net

http://uboat.net/

A comprehensive study of the German U-boat, including maps, technology, and profiles of more than 1,100 German submarines employed during World War II.

What Did You Do in the War, Grandma?: Rhode Island Women During World War II

http://www.stg.brown.edu/projects/WWII_Women/tocCS.html

An oral history of Rhode Island women during World War II, written by students in the Honors English Program at South Kingstown High School, this site provides not only information about lesser-known aspects of the war, but also a good model of action for teachers interested in using the Internet for class projects.

Women Come to the Front: Journalists, Photographers, and Broadcasters During World War II

http://lcweb.loc.gov/exhibits/wcf/wcf0001.html

This Library of Congress site documents the work of eight female war correspondents, most of whom worked overseas while a few covered the home front. The site provides some corrective to the male-dominated discussions of World War II life at the front while documenting continued male prerogative in the periodical business.

The Women's Army Corps

http://www.army.mil/cmh-pg/brochures/wac/wac.htm

The U.S. Army has developed this online article about the Women's Army Corps during World War II.

The World at War

http://www.euronet.nl/users/wilfried/ww2/ww2.htm

Wilfried Braakhuis has created an extremely detailed time line of the war, with illustrations, statistics, and a very large number of links, organized by relevant dates. This graphic-intensive site takes a while to load, but is worth looking at.

World War Two in Europe

http://www.historyplace.com/worldwar2/timeline/ww2time.htm

Part of the History Place, a large Web site dedicated to assisting students and educators, this is a World War II time line with links to illustrations and short articles on specific events.

World War II on the Web

http://www.geocities.com/Athens/Oracle/2691/welcome.htm

An index to more than 400 Web sites concerned with World War II, many of them highly specialized.

World War II Poster Collection

http://www.library.northwestern.edu/govpub/collections/wwii-posters/

This collection of hundreds of World War II posters from the U.S. government is hosted by Northwestern University. The posters range from the mundane to the shocking, from recruiting posters to those exhorting greater patriotism and sacrifice as well as secrecy. Taken together, the posters provide an excellent window on wartime culture, at least as officially propagated by the U.S. government.

World War II Resources

http://www.ibiblio.org/pha/index.html

An extensive collection of historical documents from World War II based at the University of North Carolina-Chapel Hill.

World War II Seminar

http://history.sandiego.edu/gen/classes/ww2/175.html

Class materials for a World War II history course from the University of San Diego, including an extended bibliography and several time lines created by students.

The World War II Sounds and Pictures Page

http://www.earthstation1.com/wwii.html

Sounds, video, and images of many items related to World War II. The site includes aircraft, warships, propaganda posters, and other assorted images.

The World War II Study: North Africa

http://www.topedge.com/panels/ww2/na/index.html

In this site, many issues regarding the North Africa campaign of the Allies from 1940 to 1943 receive a fresh look. The author examines the importance of North Africa to the Allies and Axis and dispels myths about the campaigns and personalities of the North African theater. He provides a time line of the conflict and considers supply issues, troop levels, weaponry, commanders, tactics, and high-command disputes.

World War II Timeline

http://history.acusd.edu/gen/WW2Timeline/start.html

A fairly good and general time line for World War II. Includes a very valuable list of additional links. Also has a number of interesting pictures, maps, documents, and a good bibliography. Includes some student pages. A first-rate site by Steve Schoenherr of the University of San Diego's History Department.

World War II Web Sites

http://connections.smsd.org/veterans/wwii_sites.htm

This site serves as a gateway to World War II sites appropriate for students and teachers. Links revolve around the following topics: The Rise of Fascism—Germany, Italy and Japan, Holocaust, Pearl Harbor and America's Response, D-Day and the War in the Pacific, The Home Front, Plans for Peace and the Atomic Bomb, Personalities, Literature, Propaganda, Women in the War, and Miscellaneous. Updated regularly, the site leads users to movie clips, virtual tours, stories of the war, biographies, films, and photographs.

Chapter 21

The Cold War

Alexander Zukas

1948: The Alger Hiss Spy Case

http://www.thehistorynet.com/ah/blalgerhiss/index2.html

This links to a June 1998 *American History* article by James Thomas Grey that examines the Alger Hiss case and the issues that still remain unresolved fifty years later.

The 1956 Hungarian Revolution: A History in Documents

http://www2.gwu.edu/~nsarchiv/NSAEBB/NSAEBB76/

Hosted by the National Security Archive at The George Washington University, this site contains parts of this National Security Archive Electronic Briefing Book edited by Malcolm Byrne. The book is a compilation of new government documents from Hungarian, Russian, and U.S. archives, which shed light on the Soviet decision to invade Hungary in 1956 and the U.S. responses to that invasion. Twelve of the 120 documents in the book are reproduced on this Web site.

The Alger Hiss Story

http://homepages.nyu.edu/~th15/

Hosted at New York University and dedicated to students, scholars, archivists, teachers, and a general audience, this is an engaging, comprehensive site that re-creates one of the most important legal cases in U.S. history during the Cold War—a case that helped launch McCarthyism. The site strives to be an authorita-

203

tive portal to primary information about Alger Hiss, the Hiss case, and the early Cold War years, including new scholarship, newly released official documents from various governments and government agencies, and archival material, such as trial testimony, court and government records, and commentary, collected in many libraries and online repositories. It also functions as the digitized and online counterpart to the Alger Hiss Papers at the Harvard Law School Library. Acting in tandem with the Harvard collection, this Web site posts a complete summary of the charges against Hiss and takes a comprehensive look at the case for the defense. Among the many interesting leads to explore through the site are exclusive new interviews with eyewitnesses and others, Freedom of Information Act releases of government documents, grand jury secret testimony, and House Un-American Activities Committee files released in 2001.

American Experience: Race for the Superbomb

http://www.pbs.org/wgbh/pages/amex/bomb

This PBS companion site explores a top secret U.S. Cold War program to build a weapon more powerful than the atomic bomb dropped on Japan. The site includes audio clips, a time line, primary documents, and other educational materials.

The Avalon Project: Documents in Law, History, and Diplomacy

http://www.yale.edu/lawweb/avalon/coldwar.htm

Maintained by the Yale University Law School, this site contains basic documents under the following headings, among others: American Foreign Policy 1941–49; the United States Atomic Energy Commission proceedings in the Matter of J. Robert Oppenheimer; The Warsaw Security Pact: May 14, 1955; State Department Papers Relating to the Foreign Relations of the United States, Vol. X, Part 1, 1958–60; the U-2 Incident: 1960; the RB-47 Airplane Incident: July–September 1960; and the Cuban Missile Crisis.

The Berlin Airlift

http://www.wpafb.af.mil/museum/history/postwwii/ba.htm

This Web site is part of the larger online exhibit titled "U.S. Air Force Museum, Post–World War II History Gallery 1946–50s." The focus is primarily military. The site is a good source of information and images of the aircraft used to airlift provisions to the inhabitants of Berlin.

Berlin Wall Online

http://www.dailysoft.com/berlinwall/

Heiko Burkhardt developed this site chronicling the history of the Berlin Wall from a (West) German point of view. Replete with interesting facts, maps, photographs, stories of escape attempts, and an archive of related documents and material, the site places the Berlin Wall into the context of Cold War politics and German history. Some East German documents and resources are available on the site as are links to the British National Archives and the German Propaganda Archive (which highlights only Nazi and East German propaganda).

Chronology of Russian History: The Soviet Period

http://www.pbs.org/weta/faceofrussia/timeline-index.html

Part of a PBS Web site on the history of the Russian people called the *Face of Russia*, this interactive time line details major cultural, political, military, and social events of twentieth-century Russia and the Soviet Union. Clicking on the highlighted images and text brings up expanded content and images. Users can scroll through the time line chronologically or jump to a specific period using the key at the top of the page. The complete time line chronicles Russian culture since about 850 CE and includes streaming audio and video clips, still images, and text.

CIA and Assassinations: The Guatemala 1954 Documents

http://www.gwu.edu/~nsarchiv/NSAEBB/NSAEBB4/index.html

The National Security Archive is an independent, nongovernmental research institute and library located at The George Washington University in Washington, DC. The archive collects and publishes declassified documents acquired through the Freedom of Information Act. On May 23, 1997, the CIA released several hundred records that verified the CIA's involvement in the infamous 1954 coup in Guatemala at the height of the Cold War politics of "brinkmanship." Some of these documents, including an instructional guide on assassination found among the training files of the CIA's covert Operation PBSUCCESS, are stored on this site.

CNN—*Cold War*

http://cnn.com/SPECIALS/cold.war/

This Web site was created to accompany the twelve-part series on the Cold War airing on CNN in the winter and spring of 1998–1999. The Web site is a valuable resource because it provides an extraordinary diversity of materials, including multimedia and audio clips, interactive maps, primary documents, newspaper and journal coverage of the events, and transcripts of interviews that formed the basis for the series.

Cold War Guide

http://www.cold-war.info/

The Cold War Guide is a project of Roman Studenic of Bratislava, Slovakia, which provides a centralized database about the events of the Cold War and about the roles people, states, and government agencies played in it. It is a metasite that provides basic information and links to other sources that provide more detail. The Cold War Guide offers an index of all entries in an encyclopedia format, a time line of events, and an archive of texts, essays, and various data that includes more encyclopedia entries.

Cold War Hot Links: Web Resources Relating to the Cold War

http://homepages.stmartin.edu/fac_staff/dprice/cold.war.htm

David Price, an anthropologist at St. Martin's College in Lacey, Washington, has compiled an impressive list of links to Web sites that contain primary sources, essays, and analyses examining the impact of the Cold War on American culture.

Cold War International History Project

http://www.wilsoncenter.org/index.cfm?topic_id=1409&fuseaction=topics.home

The Cold War International History Project (CWIHP) Web site was established at the Woodrow Wilson International Center for Scholars in Washington, DC, in 1991. The project supports the full and prompt release of historical materials by governments on all sides of the Cold War. In addition to Western sources, the project has provided translations of documents from Eastern European archives that have been released since the collapse of communism in the late 1980s. Users may join discussion groups and download issues of the *Bulletin* issued by CWIHP.

The Cold War Museum

http://www.coldwar.org/

In 1996, Francis Gary Powers Jr. and John C. Welch founded the Cold War Museum to preserve Cold War history and honor Cold War veterans. The Cold War Museum, a Smithsonian Affiliate Museum, endeavors to maintain a historically accurate record of the people, places, and events of the Cold War that will enable visitors to reflect upon the global geopolitical climate of that period (1940s to 1990s). On its Web site, the museum displays artifacts and memorabilia associated with various Cold War–related events such as the Marshall Plan, the Berlin Air Lift, the Korean War, the building of the Berlin Wall, the U-2 Incident, the Cuban Missile Crisis, the Vietnam War, President Mikhail Gorbachev's glasnost, the fall of the Berlin Wall, and the collapse of the Soviet Union.

A Concrete Curtain: The Life and Death of the Berlin Wall

http://www.wall-berlin.org/gb/berlin.htm

This site contains a detailed history of the Berlin Wall from its creation to its destruction. Part of an exhibition comprising around a hundred photographs for the Deutsches Historisches Museum in Berlin, the site is a good place to start examining the historical and cultural significance of "The Wall."

The Costs of the Manhattan Project

http://www.brook.edu/FP/PROJECTS/NUCWCOST/MANHATTN.HTM

These estimates were prepared by the Brookings Institute and are part of the larger U.S. Nuclear Weapons Cost Study Project.

Cuba

http://bubl.ac.uk/link/c/cuba.htm

This metasite on Cuba is hosted and maintained by the Centre for Digital Library Research at Strathclyde University in Scotland under the acronym BUBL. The site has links to a Castro speech database, maps, political resources, and material on tourism and the economic impact of U.S. sanctions on Cuba.

The Cuban Missile Crisis, 1962

http://www.state.gov/www/about_state/history/frusXI/index.html

This is the site for volume 11 of *Foreign Relations of the United States,* which is the official U.S. Department of State volume of documents dealing with the Cuban Missile Crisis. The entire volume or excerpts can be read online. A very important source for the official documents dealing with this crisis.

The Cuban Missile Crisis, 1962

http://www.fas.org/irp/imint/cuba.htm

The Federation of American Scientists maintains this metasite. It contains links to online State Department documentation, analysis of President John Kennedy's advisers, transcripts of ExComm (Executive Committee) deliberations, and photographic evidence of the Soviet presence in Cuba until the 1980s.

The Cuban Missile Crisis, October 18–29, 1962

http://www.hpol.org/jfk/cuban/

This Web site contains audio files of a set of tape recordings released by the John F. Kennedy Library in October 1996. These recordings were made in the Oval Office. They include President Kennedy's personal recollections of discussions, conversations with his advisers, and meetings with the Joint Chiefs of Staff and members of the president's executive committee. Transcripts of the audio files are included. A rich source of information on the American perspective of the crisis.

Documents Relating to American Foreign Policy: The Cold War

http://www.mtholyoke.edu/acad/intrel/coldwar.htm

The International Relations Program at Mount Holyoke College maintains this Web site. Organized by years from pre-1945 to recent retrospectives on the meaning and significance of the Cold War, this site contains hundreds of links to both primary and secondary source material—especially useful to students and researchers because of the variety of sources available.

Documents Relating to American Foreign Policy: Cuban Missile Crisis

http://www.mtholyoke.edu/acad/intrel/cuba.htm

This collection of links allows researchers and students access to newspaper coverage of the crisis. The Web site contains important links to information relating to Soviet and Cuban perspectives on the crisis. Links to essays and books by the most influential historians of this crisis are also provided.

Famous American Trials: Rosenbergs Trial, 1951

http://www.law.umkc.edu/faculty/projects/ftrials/rosenb/ROSENB.HTM

Professor Douglas Linder of the University of Missouri-Kansas City School of Law created this site. The Web site contains links to a wealth of firsthand materials, including excerpts from the trial transcript, the judge's sentencing statement, excerpts from appellate court decisions, images, the Rosenbergs' final letter to their sons, and a link to the Perlin Papers, a collection of about 250,000 pages that relates to the investigation, trial, and execution of Julius and Ethel Rosenberg. The papers were declassified in the 1970s.

Fifty Years From Trinity

http://www.seattletimes.com/trinity/supplement/internet.html

The *Seattle Times* compiled this list of Internet resources relating to the development of the atomic bomb and nuclear energy.

For European Recovery: The Fiftieth Anniversary of the Marshall Plan

http://www.loc.gov/exhibits/marshall/marsintr.html

This Library of Congress Web page accompanied an exhibit on the fiftieth anniversary of the Marshall Plan in 1997. Besides an overview of the plan and a time line, the site has links developed by the National Library of the Netherlands and other European libraries: the rationale for the Marshall Plan, communist critiques of the plan, Soviet opposition, a negative view of aid to Europe, a Dutch view, and benefits for the U.S. economy, among others. There are also the complete texts of books on the Marshall Plan: *The Marshall Plan and the Future of U.S. European Relations, The Marshall Plan and You* (a Dutch book from 1949), *Kiplinger's Magazine's How to Do Business Under the Marshall Plan,* and W. Averill Harriman's album, *The Marshall Plan at the Mid-Mark.*

Harvard Project on Cold War Studies

http://www.fas.harvard.edu/~hpcws/

This annotated set of links relating to the study of the Cold War is prepared and maintained by the Davis Center for Russian Studies at Harvard University. The project intends to build on the achievements of the Cold War International History Project and the National Security Archive. The site also contains links to Harvard University's new *Journal of Cold War Studies.*

Institute for the History of the 1956 Hungarian Revolution

http://www.rev.hu/index_en.html

Dedicated to the study of the 1956 uprising in Hungary, the institute's Web site contains links to numerous aspects of the uprising. The institute, located in Budapest, has produced a multimedia CD-ROM on the history of the 1956 revolt and the site contains links to studies on Hungarian history since World War II, an oral history archive, a photo-documentary archive, and a database (in Hungarian) of biographies, oral history interviews and extracts from trial records, bibliographical data (books, articles, and audiovisual documents), and accounts of events and institutions. The institute considers itself the successor of the Imre Nagy Institute of Sociology and Politics, which operated in Brussels between 1959 and 1963, and other Western émigré organizations, and its purpose is to establish a genuine account of the events in Hungary from the point of view of those who participated in the revolt.

An Introduction to National Archives Records Relating to the Cold War

http://www.archives.gov/research/cold-war/

Hosted by the National Archives, this metasite was compiled primarily by Tim Wehrkamp. It "identifies several representative series and data sets of textual, electronic, still picture, and motion picture records that document U.S. government policies, programs, and actions during the Cold War. The compilers have chosen a selection of records that illustrate the range and content of National Archives and Records Administration (NARA) holdings relating to this period. These records by no means represent all NARA-held documentation concerning the topic. The intended audience for this publication is graduate students and other researchers new to the field of Cold War history who may be unfamiliar with NARA records relating to the era." It would be a good place for them to begin their research.

The National Security Archive Homepage

http://www.gwu.edu/~nsarchiv/

The National Security Archive is an independent, nongovernmental research institute and library located at The George Washington University in Washington, DC. The archive collects and publishes declassified documents gathered through the Freedom of Information Act (FOIA). The archive boasts the world's largest nongovernmental library of declassified documents, including thousands of documents relating to nuclear history, U.S.-Japanese relations, the Cuban Missile Crisis, and other crises of the 1960s and 1970s.

The Real Thirteen Days: The Hidden History of the Cuban Missile Crisis

http://www.gwu.edu/~nsarchiv/nsa/cuba_mis_cri/

The National Security Archive has created an extensive Web site on the Cuban Missile Crisis. It includes essays titled "Turning History on Its Head" by Philip Brenner, "The Declassified Documents" by Peter Kornbluh and Laurence Chang, "The Most Dangerous Moment in the Crisis" by Jim Hershberg, and "Annals of Blinksmanship" by Thomas Blanton. Visitors can hear audio clips of White House meetings, read the documents exchanged between the White

House and the Kremlin, see the U-2 surveillance photos of the Russian missile installations, and read a detailed chronology of events relating to the Cuban Missile Crisis from 1959 to 1992. This revisionist site is dedicated to dispelling myths about the crisis, especially the myth of calibrated brinkmanship—the belief that if you stand tough you win and that nuclear superiority made the difference in moments of crisis.

Secrets of War

http://www.secretsofwar.com/

This is the companion site to the History Channel's twenty-six-part documentary series titled *Sworn to Secrecy: Secrets of War,* which was aired in 1998. The site contains transcripts and links to maps, images, and other information relating to the history of espionage.

A Select Bibliography of the U-2 Incident

http://www.eisenhower.utexas.edu/u2.htm

This brief bibliography is located at the Dwight D. Eisenhower Presidential Library.

Senator Joseph McCarthy: A Modern Tragedy

http://www.foxvalleyhistory.org/mccarthy/

This archive contains film and audio clips from Senator Joseph McCarthy's speeches and appearances on television.

Soviet Archives Exhibit

http://metalab.unc.edu/expo/soviet.exhibit/entrance.html#tour

The Library of Congress developed this online exhibit where visitors can browse images of documents from the Soviet archives. The two main sections of this exhibit are the Internal Workings of the Soviet System and The Soviet Union and the United States. The section on postwar estrangement includes commentary on Soviet perspectives on the Cold War and the Cuban Missile Crisis.

Space Race

http://www.nasm.si.edu/exhibitions/gal114/gal114.htm

The space race was a high-profile area of the Cold War competition between the United States and the Soviet Union, the most powerful nations in the world after World War II. For a half-century, the two superpowers competed for supremacy in a global struggle on the earth, in air, at sea, and in space that was tied to an arms race and a drive for military primacy. This U.S. National Air and Space

Museum site contains links to the military origins of the space race, the Soviet challenge in space, the race to the moon, espionage from space, and building a permanent U.S. presence in space.

The U-2 Incident 1960

http://www.yale.edu/lawweb/avalon/u2.htm

The Avalon Project at Yale University developed this Web site on the U-2 incident in 1960. It is a useful starting place to find the basic diplomatic documents, including the exchange of notes between the United States and Soviet governments, public statements by State Department officials, and the documentation maintained by the State Department in the *Foreign Relations of the United States* series.

The Venona Project

http://www.nsa.gov/venona/index.cfm

VENONA was the code name used for the U.S. Signals Intelligence effort to collect and decrypt the text of Soviet KGB and GRU messages from the 1940s. These messages provided extraordinary insight into Soviet attempts to infiltrate the highest levels of the U.S. government. The National Security Agency has declassified over 3,000 messages related to VENONA and made them available at its home page.

The Wars for Vietnam

http://vietnam.vassar.edu/

This site, produced by students at Vassar College, provides an overview of the Vietnam War, primary documents and photos from the American and Vietnamese sides, detailed accounts of the battles of Ia Drang Valley, and links to other related sites. Many of the documents are from Vietnamese archives in Hanoi.

Chapter 22

General Twentieth-Century United States History

John Barnhill

Metasites

Digital History/Could You Have Passed the 8th Grade in 1895?

http://www.digitalhistory.uh.edu/

This American history site has time lines, videos, interactive time lines, graphics, standard bibliographies, links, and written content. The test from 1895 is in the multimedia section. It even has an "ask a historian" section—one of the best new sites.

Economic History

http://www.tntech.edu/history/economic.html

This site combines associations, archives, journals, and specialized sites in business and economic history and contemporary issues. Plus, it has historical price calculators. This page is part of the broader Tennessee Tech site that is old but still solid.

Google: U.S. History 20th Century

http://directory.google.com/Top/Society/History/By_Time_Period/
Twentieth_Century/

Nothing fancy—just many links by decade and by topic.

History Matters: The U.S. History Survey on the Web

http://historymatters.gmu.edu/

Everything anyone could ever need to teach the American History survey—making history relevant to current events, using primary documents, secrets of teachers, using the Web, and the reference desk.

Librarians Index to the Internet

http://lii.org/

Nothing fancy, just good solid search capability for just about any topic—and it stays current—good starting point.

U.S. Diplomatic History Resources Index

http://faculty.tamu-commerce.edu/sarantakes/stuff.html

This site ties to associations, archives, bibliographies, book reviews, journals, funding—a great starting point for the vast topic of American diplomatic history. It also has an index from "archive" to "White House."

WWW Virtual Library—History: Internet & W3 (World Wide Web)

http://vlib.iue.it/history/internet/index.html

This site includes an atlas, biographies, and bibliographies and is organized topically and chronologically by decade (including the eighteenth century). It is current as of 2004 and the starting point for history of the Net. It is, after all, a subset of the WWW Virtual Library, which has been growing and improving for more than a decade, a millennium by Net standards.

General Sites

America 1900

http://www.pbs.org/wgbh/pages/amex/1900/index.html

PBS sites based on the *American Experience* programs are generally well put together. This program features life in 1900, and the site describes the film and includes a searchable database.

The American Experience

http://www.pbs.org/wgbh/amex/index.html

The PBS program *American Experience* deals with arts, politics, technology, and culture through use of time lines, maps, and illustrations. Chronological, alphabetical, and thematic indexes allow easy access to materials supporting the films. Topics cover a range from the racehorse Seabiscuit through the Golden Gate Bridge to aviator Charles Lindbergh. Teacher's guides and bibliographies are also included.

American Memory Collection

http://memory.loc.gov/ammem/ammemhome.html

Collections range from photographer Ansel Adams to the Wright Brothers, with over a million documents, photos, and recordings. "Ask a librarian" has links to other Library of Congress sources as well as the National Archives, Virtual Reference, and much more. Inquiries get a reply in five days the site promises.

American Temperance and Prohibition

http://prohibition.osu.edu/default.htm

Nice variety of materials on the rise of the American prohibition movement. Material includes cartoons and photos and lots of text on events and major figures. The Ohio State University also has sites pertaining to immigration, lynching, and Ohio-specific topics, mostly dating to 1997 but still with live links.

Anti-Imperialism in the United States, 1898–1935

http://www.boondocksnet.com/ai/index.html

For teachers and interested persons alike this is the best anti-imperialism site, with cartoons and an extensive array of documents, including full-length works. It presents one side of the issue, and not even the side that won out—it needs to be used in conjunction with a good site on imperialism, such as the Age of Imperialism (http://www.smplanet.com/imperialism/toc.html).

Apollo Lunar Surface Journal

http://www.hq.nasa.gov/office/pao/History/alsj/frame.html

Although this site on the Apollo missions dates from 1995, updates continue, and it works well. No bad links, and as the site has grown it remains a good source for mission summaries, crew information, and photos.

CIA and Assassinations: The Guatemala 1954 Documents

http://www.gwu.edu/~nsarchiv/NSAEBB/NSAEBB4/index.html

Because this is a representative sample of the National Security Archive, it deserves examination. The NSA digs the documents out and puts them online in a straightforward array. Mostly, as in the case of the CIA and the 1954 coup, the material addresses matters unflattering to America's self-image.

Civil Rights Coalition for the 21st Century

http://www.civilrights.org/index.html

This site has a solid history of civil rights with links to many legal cases, a comprehensive set of links to civil rights organizations' sites, and an extensive issues section. It is a bit untidy, but that seems to be where civil rights is today. See especially the "Research Center."

Detroit Photos Home Page From the Library of Congress

http://memory.loc.gov/ammem/detroit/

With a bit more text, the 25,000 transparencies and glass negatives on this Library of Congress American Memory site could be invaluable. As it is, the Detroit Photographic Company photos give a good impression of turn-of-the-century life.

Digger Archives

http://www.diggers.org/

The diggers were a short-lived San Francisco commune that tried to provide street theater and free stores in the late 1960s. The site tries to preserve that history while linking to current groups clinging to those days and those values. Interesting.

The Digital Classroom

http://www.archives.gov/digital_classroom/index.html

The National Archives helps educators to teach using primary documents. This site includes a set of ten units on the twentieth century. The site also provides lesson plans, links to additional sources, a documentary analysis worksheet, and information about summer workshops for educators and electronics workshops for their classes.

The *Enola Gay* Controversy

http://www.lehigh.edu/~ineng/enola/

Originally designed for a university course at Lehigh University, Pennsylvania, the site remains valuable for its thorough treatment of the controversy over the Smithsonian's *Enola Gay* display, now removed. It shows clearly what can go wrong when historians and the public disagree on the meaning of an event. Extensive bibliography and links to other sites.

Famous Trials of the Twentieth Century

http://www.umkc.edu/famoustrials

This site looks at many famous trials from Socrates to O.J. Simpson, and its twentieth-century trials range from Bill Haywood to the Scopes "monkey" trial and from Charles Manson to President William Jefferson Clinton. Included are crime scene maps, evidence, transcripts, and verdicts. The site contains links to Linder's Constitutional Law pages, which are also well done—even a page of Supreme Court humor and a provocative section on evil—and to other famous trials such as those of Fatty Arbuckle and Patty Hearst.

The Forest History Society

http://www.lib.duke.edu/forest/index.html

Niche history taken seriously becomes an organization such as this, with an oral history program, publications, a searchable photograph database, a bibliography with 33,000 citations, and even a suggested middle school curriculum. The Forest History Society library and archives are at Duke University.

For European Recovery: The Fiftieth Anniversary of the Marshall Plan

http://lcweb.loc.gov/exhibits/marshall/

This site shows how the Library of Congress uses its resources to present a historical event, in this case the anniversary of the Marshall Plan. The site contains extracts from *The Marshall Plan and the Future of U.S.-European Relations,* the twenty-fifth anniversary document. The site also provides a fairly extensive explanation of the plan's rationale and chronology. It lacks audio and video, but it is a good representative exhibit of the Library of Congress and the plan, and it links to the Marshall Foundation (http://www.marshallfoundation.org/), which includes a filmography, annotated bibliography, and more.

The Emma Goldman Papers

http://sunsite.Berkeley.EDU/Goldman/

An online exhibit based on the 20,000 documents, images, and moving pictures in the Emma Goldman Papers Project housed at the University of California-Berkeley, is the entry point to a site that also includes a recommended curriculum for teaching the life of the radical Goldman as well as the issues that formed her times—women's rights, immigration, and other issues still unresolved. The site exemplifies what is best in archive sites—eye appeal and good content. Of course, it also has a page of "Emmarabilia" for sale, as well as a solicitation for money to fund the continuation of the site.

Kennedy Assassination Home Page

http://mcadams.posc.mu.edu/home.htm

This page remains the best balanced of the online sources on the Kennedy assassination, and its links are to the best materials. The owner does note that most of the assassination links are to conspiracy sites and that the books he recommends are not necessarily the best, just those necessary for a balanced understanding before digging further.

Kingwood College Library American Cultural History: The Twentieth Century

http://kclibrary.nhmccd.edu/decades.html

A component of a site designed for easy access by students to research a broad range of topics, the cultural history section is arranged by decade, with a historical overview and essays on fads and fashions, technology, the arts, and literature and music. The overall page at http://kclibrary.nhmccd.edu/research.htm has music site links, including the Rock and Roll Hall of Fame and lots of rock 'n' roll sites.

Mining History, Museums and Disasters

http://www.msha.gov/history.htm

The material is mostly text and photos on mining history. Tidily arranged discussions deal with canaries, emergency vehicles, African-Americans, Asian and children workers, and more. Links to state museums and memorials are extensive, but some links are bad. Take a minute to read "'Oh God, For One More Breath': Early 20th Century Tennessee Coal Miners' Last Words" at http://historymatters.gmu.edu/d/62/.

National Archives

http://www.nara.gov/

The National Archives and Records Administration has a good search capability, an online exhibit with samples of its records, and information on its services—records management, archives, and training at locations throughout the United States. The Web site barely scratches the surface of the 4 billion records NARA has in its custody, but it is the starting point for finding material and finding out how to find more.

National Civil Rights Museum

http://www.civilrightsmuseum.org/about/about.asp

The Lorraine Motel in Memphis, Tennessee, where Martin Luther King was assassinated, is now part of the National Civil Rights Museum. When the motel property experienced a succession of failures, the Martin Luther King, Jr. Memorial Foundation saved it. The museum includes archives and exhibits on the broad history of civil rights, not just King and his assassination. It is a good example of how sometimes it is necessary to change in order to preserve.

New Deal Network

http://newdeal.feri.org/index.htm

Coverage of the 1930s on this site includes documents, photos, good links, and, of course, lesson plans and such. It includes the H-Net discussion list, H-US 1918–45, which includes current news, teaching resources, and opportunities for teachers and historians to talk about the period.

Oyez: U.S. Supreme Court Multimedia

http://www.oyez.org/oyez/frontpage

The audiophile will really enjoy the hours of arguments before the Supreme Court of the United States. Others might find more of interest in the photos and biographies of current and former justices. Further information for some, but not all, justices is in the links to transcripts, lists of cases, and other material. The virtual tour of the court is interesting as well.

Presidential Elections, 1860–1996

http://fisher.lib.virginia.edu/elections/maps/

This site maps popular vote totals for every presidential election between 1860 and 1996 and electoral results from 1900 through 1996. It also includes a detailed look at the 2000 election and links to related sites. Hopefully, 2004 will get that treatment too. Includes links to related sites.

Presidential Libraries

http://www.archives.gov/presidential_libraries/presidential_records/
presidential_records.html

This site lists presidential libraries from Hoover to Clinton, with an overview of the libraries and links to the library sites. Address, fax, and e-mail information helps too.

Presidential Speeches

http://odur.let.rug.nl/~usa/P/

This Groningen, Netherlands, project is a good example of a European American studies site, and it even includes an extended discussion of the genesis and methodology of the project. It includes mostly State of the Union and inaugural addresses, presidential biographies, and links to other sources.

Redstone Arsenal Historical Information

http://www.redstone.army.mil/history/welcome.html

This is an exceptionally good government military history (as in done by historians hired by the military) site using photos and videos and a range of textual materials to cover the U.S. Army's aviation and missile command. Contents include oral histories, chronologies, and information about specific types of weapons. Pluses include the links and the lightly humorous touch within the text.

Jonas Salk

http://www.achievement.org/autodoc/page/sal0int-1

Salk developed the polio vaccine. This site is more than strictly a biography though. It is part of the Academy of Achievement site, which seeks to use historical figures as role models. Another use for history: "Achievement TV is an electronic forum that allows students to learn from outstanding individuals of our time while, at the same time, satisfying core curriculum requirements."

Skylighters

http://www.skylighters.org/

This site is the official home of the 225th AAA Searchlight Battalion Veterans. As well as being a good place to learn about World War II, it is a good example of the military reunion genre. It has a chronology, links, and oral histories. And, if you do not like this one, go to the World War II Web ring linked at the bottom of the page.

United States Entry into World War I: A Documentary Chronology

http://edsitement.neh.gov/view_lesson_plan.asp?id=471

EDSITEment provides a lesson plan for teaching high school students the topic while giving them practice in using Web resources to make historical judgments. This site includes course objectives, complementary lessons, and more.

Veterans History Project

http://www.loc.gov/folklife/vets/vets-home.html

This project is attempting to capture the stories of America's 25 million living veterans, or a fair sample thereof. The site includes audio, visual, and text material, a searchable database, a short course, student guide, and links to other oral history projects.

Watergate

http://www.washingtonpost.com/wp-srv/national/longterm/watergate/splash1a.htm

Where else but at the *Washington Post* would a user look for the Watergate scandal? Bob Woodward and Carl Bernstein, who broke the case and brought down President Richard Nixon, were *Post* reporters. The site has a time line, a Where Are They Now? section, and a May 2005 article on the disclosure of the identity of "Deep Throat" that ended a two-decades-long mystery.

White House Historical Association

http://www.whitehousehistory.org/

This site is a good example of the charitable nonprofit approach to history. The WHHA site mixes education and entertainment and a bit of fund-raising. It includes recommended lessons as well as a tour. There is also music and animation—and the obligatory gift shop. But the content is quite extensive too—with multipage time lines of topics ranging from African-Americans to the West Wing of the White House, to music.

Chapter 23

Women's History

Melissa Ooten

African-American Women: Online Archival Collections at Duke

http://scriptorium.lib.duke.edu/collections/african-american-women.html

The Digital Scriptorium from the Special Collections Library of Duke University offers the rare opportunity for users to access and read letters written by slave women online. It also offers links to other materials on African-American women's history.

Agents of Social Change

http://www.smith.edu/libraries/libs/ssc/curriculum/index.html

This document collection from the Sophia Smith Collection at Smith College seeks to reach middle and high school students. It contains some information online and offers a guide to the collections housed at Smith. These collections include the papers of attorney Constance Baker Motley, attorney Mary Kaufman, pacifist Jessie Lloyd O'Connor, and feminist Gloria Steinem as well as the records of the Women's Action Alliance and the National Congress of Neighborhood Women.

American Women's History: A Resource Guide

http://www.mtsu.edu/~kmiddlet/history/women.html

This site, from Middle Tennessee State University, offers a variety of indexed and linked material. It includes both a subject index and a state index of sources on topics ranging from advice literature and public speaking to material culture and quilts. The site also offers advice on how to find both primary and secondary sources, available both on- and offline.

Elizabeth Blackwell: "That Girl There Is a Doctor in Medicine"

http://www.nlm.nih.gov/hmd/blackwell/index.html

This site chronicles the life of Elizabeth Blackwell, the first American woman to receive the MD degree. It is the online version of a 1999 exhibit held at the National Library of Medicine in Bethesda, Maryland. The Web site is divided into four different periods of Blackwell's life: admission into medical school, college life, graduation, and career.

The Chinese in California, 1850–1925

http://lcweb2.loc.gov/ammem/award99/cubhtml/cichome.html

While this Library of Congress American Memory site is not devoted specifically to women, it does contain significant amounts of material on women. A subject search of "women" calls up a variety of source material, in particular images of both white women and Chinese women in various settings, most notably San Francisco's Chinatown.

Civil Rights in Mississippi Digital Archive

http://avatar.lib.usm.edu/%7Espcol/crda/index.html

This archive from the McCain Library and Archives at the University of Southern Mississippi contains several oral interviews of women who worked in the civil rights movement. Selected manuscripts and photographs can also be found through the site, along with a history of the civil rights movement in Hattiesburg and a civil rights time line. At present, the site is best used for listening to the oral histories of women activists and in finding useful links to other civil rights Web sites.

Civil War Women: Primary Sources on the Internet

http://scriptorium.lib.duke.edu/women/cwdocs.html

This bibliography from Duke University provides a starting point for researching women during the Civil War era. Users can find links to scanned letters, diaries, and documents, and a list of photographs that include women in the Library of Congress and National Archives.

Documenting the American South

http://docsouth.unc.edu/

Documenting the American South, from the University of North Carolina, houses an extensive collection of primary resources for the study of Southern history and Southern women. Searchable by collection, title, author, or subject, this database contains a number of works by women.

Documents From the Women's Liberation Movement— Duke Special Collections

http://scriptorium.lib.duke.edu/wlm/

This online archival collection from Duke University's Special Collections can be searched by keyword or by subject. A diverse set of documents include "Women Rap About Sex," the Radicalesbians' "The Woman-Identified Women," a photo essay on "What Sort of Man Reads Playboy," and Anne Koedt's "The Myth of the Vaginal Orgasm." Unlike other sites, Duke includes a significant number of documents that address women's sexualities.

Feeding America: The Historic American Cookbook Project

http://digital.lib.msu.edu/projects/cookbooks/

Michigan State University Libraries and the Institute of Museum and Library Services present the Feeding America project. This project provides an online collection of some of the most important American cookbooks from the late 1700s to the early 1900s. Full text exists for dozens of the cookbooks, and they are fully searchable.

The Emma Goldman Papers

http://sunsite.berkeley.edu/Goldman/

This site contains anarchist Emma Goldman's papers. Goldman was deported from the United States following imprisonment for protesting the draft during World War I. It includes links to two exhibitions introducing Goldman, including one at the Jewish Women's Archive, another important site for women's history (http://www.jwa.org/index.html). Accessible online primary sources include selections from her several books, her published essays and speeches, and third-person accounts of Goldman's life and work.

A Historical Investigation into the Past: Lizzie Borden/Fall River Project

http://ccbit.cs.umass.edu/lizzie/

This project, developed by the History Department and the Center for Computer-Based Instructional Technology at the University of Massachusetts-Amherst, encourages users to examine the evidence of the Lizzie Borden axe murder trial and to draw their own conclusions about Borden's life. The digital archive contains documents and illustrations from Borden's trial, material on the surrounding community of Fall River (including the 1880 census, a visitor's guide, poll tax payment, and a city directory), and late nineteenth-century newspaper articles and literature to give students a broad context in which to interpret the components of class, gender, race, and region that may have affected Borden's trial.

Internet Women's History Sourcebook

http://www.fordham.edu/halsall/women/womensbook.html

Derived from three major online sourcebooks, this site, from Paul Halsall of Fordham University, offers information specific to women's history in ancient, medieval, and modern times. Included regions range from ancient Egypt to North America, Latin America, and southeast Asia, just to name a few. Links are also provided to articles and materials that provide a context for the historical study of women.

Japanese American Relocation Digital Archives

http://jarda.cdlib.org/

This site, from the Online Archive of California, provides a historical overview of the World War II relocation of Japanese-Americans in the United States. Materials relevant to women constitute a large part of the database, including hundreds of photographs and artistic works. In all, the archive contains over 10,000 images and over 20,000 pages of electronic transcripts, all searchable.

Jewish Women's Archive

http://www.jwa.org/index.html

The Jewish Women's Archive divides its information into "discover," "teach," and "research." The teaching section of the site offers suggestions on integrating Jewish women's histories into the curriculum and the research area contains a virtual archive, searchable by a person's name, subject, occupation, or location.

The Lesbian History Project

http://www-lib.usc.edu/~retter/main.html

The Lesbian History Project is most useful for the large number of links it provides, including links to current and archived journals, dissertations and theses, course syllabi, images, and one to a history of Southern Californian lesbians, including a chronology.

Making It Their Own: Women in the West

http://scholar.library.csi.cuny.edu/westweb/pages/women.html

This section of Catherine Lavender's WestWeb focuses exclusively on Western women. It contains several primary sources, including journals, diaries, letters, and autobiographies from individuals such as Willa Cather and Leslie Marmon Silko. The primary texts are evenly divided between Native American and white women. Life history manuscripts from the Folklore Project of the WPA Federal Writers' project are also included.

Mother Jones Collection

http://libraries.cua.edu/MotherJones/

This site contains information on the life and work of labor activist and union organizer Mary Harris Jones, known popularly as Mother Jones, from the Terence Powderly and John Mitchell collections at Catholic University. Separate letter, picture, and subject indexes guide users through the available sources.

National Women's History Project

http://www.nwhp.org/

This Web site, from the nonprofit educational corporation the National Women's History Project, seeks to both celebrate and educate about women's historical accomplishments. The site's Biography Center lists dozens of women whose accomplishments the project believes deserve recognition. For each woman, the site lists an outline of her life as well as further resources on her both in print and online. The site is also dedicated to promoting Women's History Month each March.

New York Triangle Shirtwaist Fire

http://www.ilr.cornell.edu/trianglefire/

This site is devoted to the Triangle Shirtwaist fire of New York City, which took the lives of 146 immigrant workers in 1911. The user-friendly site contains the story and its aftermath, including links that introduce the topic, discuss sweatshop and strike conditions in garment factories before the 1911 fire, and detail funerals, protests, investigations, and reform attempts. Primary sources available through the site include testimonials from factory workers, letters written to factory owners and managers, songs of labor activists, and numerous newspaper and magazine accounts. The site also includes excerpts from the Factory Investigating Commission of New York State in 1912 that was established as a result of the fire to investigate factory conditions throughout the state.

The Pill: American Experience

http://www.pbs.org/wgbh/amex/pill

The Pill, the PBS Web site accompanying the film of the same name, contains a synopsis and transcript of the film, along with primary sources, especially concerning the 1960 approval of the birth control pill. Further Reading provides contemporary books and Web sites. Website Features allows users to vote on issues concerning medical insurance and the pill and to submit their own personal comments and questions about the pill and birth control in general. Questions about the pill will be answered by Harvard Medical School professor Dr. Daniela Carusi.

The Eleanor Roosevelt Papers, The Human Rights Years, 1945–1962

http://www.gwu.edu/~erpapers/index.html

The Eleanor Roosevelt Papers, a research center associated with The George Washington University, presents this project focusing on Roosevelt's human rights advocacy spanning the years after she left the White House. Users can access information on her life and works written both by and about her. Sources include letters, speeches, newspaper columns, book excerpts, and articles. Separate sections are devoted to information on how to teach Eleanor Roosevelt and on human rights advocacy.

Salem Witch Trials: Documentary Archive and Transcription Project

http://etext.virginia.edu/salem/witchcraft/home.html

This documentary archive, from the University of Virginia and the Danvers Archival Center, is one of the most sophisticated on the subject. Available documents include three volumes of transcribed court records. Interactive maps of the village allow users to track the locale of both the accused and their accusers across the spring of 1692. Holdings from several archives including the Boston Public Library, the Massachusetts Historical Society, and the Peabody Essex Museum have also been scanned and are available in their original form for users' perusal. Contemporary books supplement the documents to set the documents in their historical context.

Tejano Voices

http://libraries.uta.edu/tejanovoices/

The Center for Mexican American Studies Oral History Project at the University of Texas at Arlington presents seventy-seven Tejano and Tejana voices speaking about racial discrimination in Texas during the post–World War II era. The site offers brief biographies, interview summaries and transcripts, photographs of the interviewees, and the opportunity to listen to the recorded interviews. About two dozen of the interviews were conducted with women.

The Ten O'Clock News

http://main.wgbh.org/ton/

This Web site houses 532 tapes from the WGBH-Boston Media Archives and Preservation Center. This collection focuses on stories related to African-Americans aired on the news from 1974 to 1991. The site can be searched by keyword and browsed by category, and video clips are available for many of the featured stories. While not devoted specifically to women, the site does include several stories about women and gender in Boston's African-American communities.

Urban Experience in Chicago: Hull House and Its Neighborhoods

http://www.uic.edu/jaddams/hull/urbanexp/contents.htm

This interpretive site from the University of Illinois at Chicago seeks to situate the history of Hull House into the broader context of its surrounding urban environs. Six major sections constitute the site: Historical Narrative, Timeline, Images, Geography, Teacher's Resources, and Search. In the historical narrative, each chapter has its own subsections including relevant newspaper articles, letters, memoirs, images, and unpublished manuscripts. Users can search for specific material either by author, title, or word or phrase, or they can browse document keywords.

Votes for Women: Selections From the National American Woman Suffrage Association Collection, 1848–1921

http://memory.loc.gov/ammem/naw/nawshome.html

http://memory.loc.gov/ammem/vfwhtml/vfwhome.html

The first site's collection consists of over 160 items from NAWSA. It includes a variety of materials including diaries and book-length studies of suffrage movements and postcards. The second site includes thirty-eight photographs, including portraits, some parades, and pictures of women voting.

WASP (Women Airforce Service Pilots)

http://www.twu.edu/wasp/

This site, maintained by Texas Woman's University, offers information on Women Airforce Service Pilots (WASPs) from the World War II era. It includes information on related archival collections, photographs, and news updates. Of particular interest is the online Oral History Project containing WASPs' oral history transcripts and an "Ask an Archivist" option for asking a question via e-mail.

Who Was Martha Ballard?

http://www.dohistory.org/martha/

This site, from DoHistory, centers on the invaluable eighteenth-century diary of midwife Martha Ballard, who resided in Maine. The time line keeps track of notable events in Ballard's life and her community, along with notable events in the fields of science and medicine and in the history of Maine and the United States.

Women Come to the Front: Journalists, Photographers, and Broadcasters in WW II

http://www.loc.gov/exhibits/wcf/wcf0001.html

This Library of Congress site highlights the careers of eight women during World War II. The site features the work of photographer Therese Bonney, photographer Toni Frissell, photojournalist Marvin Breckinridge Patterson, journalist Clare Boothe Luce, columnist and radio broadcaster Janet Flanner, photographer Esther Bubley, photographer Dorothea Lange, and correspondent May Craig. Extensive displays of the work of each individual are accessible.

Women and Social Movements in the United States, 1600–2000

http://womhist.binghamton.edu

This site contains over four dozen document projects revolving around more than a thousand primary source documents. About half of the projects are available for free; the other half are only accessible through subscription. Available for free, projects range in time from the American Revolution to the present and include a wide range of women. The expanded subscription version of the Web site, jointly published by the Center for the Historical Study of Women and Gender at the State University of New York at Binghamton and Alexander Street Press (both of these also collaborate on the site as a whole), contains an invaluable database of books, pamphlets, and additional primary source projects, although access to the database requires subscription.

Women in World History

http://www.womeninworldhistory.com

This site provides resources for learning about women globally. "Lessons" offer thirteen curriculum initiatives for exploring women's history in the classroom, and "essays" contextualize the histories of women from different historical time periods and areas of the world.

Women's Diaries

http://oldsite.library.upenn.edu/etext/collections/diaries/?

From the Schoenberg Center for Electronic Text and Image at the University of Pennsylvania Library, this site offers online access to the manuscripts of six women's diaries dating from the mid-nineteenth to the mid-twentieth century.

Women Working: 1870–1930

http://ocp.hul.harvard.edu/ww/

This site from Harvard University provides online access to manuscripts and images related to working women's histories. The collection contains over 2,000 books and pamphlets, 1,000 images, and 5,000 scanned pages. Users can both browse and search the collections.

WWW Virtual Library Women's History

http://www.iisg.nl/w3vlwomenshistory/

Maintained by the International Institute of Social History, this site lists institutions, organizations, archives, library collections, and online resources related to women's history. Conference announcements related to women's history themes are also included.

Chapter 24

Modern Military History

S. Mike Pavelec

Here are a few modern military history (defined as from 1898 to 2005) Web
sites for initial research into the field of academic military history. These Web
sites are slanted toward the technology side of military history. There are many
more; these are some of the most reliable and helpful sites for beginning (and
continuing) researchers.

The Best of the List

Air and Space Power Chronicles

http://www.airpower.maxwell.af.mil/

The U.S. Air Force's journal site. A good place for information on the scholarly
pursuits at the Air University at Maxwell Air Force Base, Alabama.

BUBL LINK: A Catalogue of Internet Resources

http://www.bubl.ac.uk/link/m/militaryhistory.htm

A British site of compiled military history Web sites by one of Britain's best
search networks.

eHistory.com

http://ehistory.osu.edu/

A Web site dedicated to electronic history (history on the Web). Formerly independent, it is now being run through The Ohio State University's Department of History. Look for vast improvements in the content of this great site for research and images.

Eye Witness to History

http://www.eyewitnesstohistory.com/

A collection of firsthand accounts of historical events. The Web site covers a variety of topics; see specifically the valuable military history entries and information.

Federation of American Scientists

http://www.fas.org/main/home.jsp

A collection of the latest analyses on current U.S. military capabilities. Further information is provided on world military systems and capabilities.

Globalsecurity.org

http://www.globalsecurity.org

An informative Web site dedicated to historical and current military operations and analysis. Includes interesting and informative military history documents and articles.

The Historical Text Archive

http://www.historicaltextarchive.com/

An independent Web site dedicated to articles, texts, and books on history and historical research. Good content on military history.

The History Guy

http://www.historyguy.com/

A history Web site with good information and resources. See especially the military history section.

The History Net

http://www.historynet.com

A clearinghouse for history on the Web; especially rich in resources and articles on military history.

Military History

http://www.militaryhistory.about.com/

An informative Web site dedicated to all aspects of military history. Site contains good articles and information from a number of sources.

Military History Online

http://www.militaryhistoryonline.com/

Another well-built Web site dedicated to all aspects of military history. Of particular interest are well-written articles with references on a number of military history topics.

OnWar.com

http://www.onwar.com/

A starting place for research on individual wars, rebellions, and uprisings across time. Especially helpful time lines and chronologies of human conflict.

The Society for Military History

http://www.smh-hq.org/

The main Web site for the academic organization dedicated to the scholarly pursuit of military history. Also a useful place to start when looking for academic historians, their conferences, and academic military history articles and research.

University of North Texas Department of History, Center for the Study of Military History

http://www.hist.unt.edu/military.htm

An excellent academic-sponsored Web site with multiple links for military history research and documentation.

The War Times Journal

http://wtj.com/

An online journal full of information and resources on military history.

The West Point Atlas Home Page

http://www.dean.usma.edu/history/web03/atlases/atlas%20table%20of%20contents.htm

This Web site of the U.S. Army school at West Point provides atlases for all American wars; see especially the extensive coverage of World War II and Vietnam.

The Women's Army Corps Veterans Association

http://www.armywomen.org/

This WAC Web site, dedicated to women in uniform, is a valuable historical research tool with images and links.

Archives, Documents, and Primary Research

The Avalon Project at Yale Law School

http://www.yale.edu/lawweb/avalon/20th.htm

A great place for online documents, specifically twentieth-century documents. The Yale Law School has dedicated extensive time and effort to making primary documents available online.

EuroDocs: Primary Historical Documents From Western Europe

http://eudocs.lib.byu.edu/index.php/Main_Page

A Brigham Young University library project presenting primary historical documents from Europe, including a great wealth of treaties in translation for English research.

The National Archives (formerly the Public Record Office), England

http://www.nationalarchives.gov.uk/default.htm

The Web site dedicated to the British counterpart of the American National Archives and Records Administration. This site is the gateway for research in Britain.

National Archives and Records Administration (NARA)

http://www.archives.gov/index.html

The Web site dedicated to the National Archives of the United States. A starting place for online research and contact information for the holdings and archivists at the National Archives in Washington, DC.

National Museum of the U.S. Air Force

http://www.wpafb.af.mil/museum/

The best site for the beginner and advanced researcher on American airpower.

Smithsonian National Air and Space Museum

http://www.nasm.si.edu/

The main Web site for the Smithsonian's excellent collection of archives and artifacts.

The World War I Document Archive

http://www.lib.byu.edu/~rdh/wwi/

An excellent research guide and Web site dedicated to World War I documents and archives. See especially the Maritime War subsection.

Spanish American War (1898–1902)

The Spanish American War Centennial Web Site

http://www.spanamwar.com/

A Spanish American War Web site with extensive information and images. The best Web site for information devoted to this war.

The World of 1898: The Spanish-American War

http://www.loc.gov/rr/hispanic/1898/

The Library of Congress Hispanic Division's Web site on Hispanic perceptions of the Spanish-American War. Good time lines, images, articles, and references.

Boer War (1899–1902)

Anglo Boer War Museum

http://www.anglo-boer.co.za/

A Web site dedicated to the Boer War from the South African (white) perspective. The Anglo Boer War Museum sponsors the Web site.

The Boer War: South Africa (1899–1902)

http://www.geocities.com/Athens/Acropolis/8141/boerwar.html

A personal Web site with valuable information and research on the Boer War.

Russo-Japanese War (1904–1905)

The Russo-Japanese War Research Society

http://www.russojapanesewar.com/

A Web site dedicated to the Russo-Japanese War of 1904–1905. A very interesting and informative site for important information on an underinvestigated war.

World War I (1914–1918)

The Aerodrome

http://www.theaerodrome.com/

An excellent starter site for World War I aviation research.

The Great War and the Shaping of the Twentieth Century

http://www.pbs.org/greatwar/

The PBS site dedicated to World War I and its aftermath.

Over the Front: The League of WWI Aviation Historians

http://overthefront.com/main/index.html

A group dedicated to World War I Aviation scholarship and research. The league publishes the journal *Over the Front* and is the sister organization of *Cross and Cockade* in England.

The War at Sea (WWI)

http://www.gwpda.org/naval/n0000000.htm

World War I naval warfare Web site with wonderful research and information. There are extensive bibliographies on World War I naval history. Part of the excellent World War I Document Archive.

World War One: Trenches on the Web

http://www.worldwar1.com/

One of the best sites for research and finding aids on World War One. See especially The Great War Society Within Trenches on the Web.

Russian Civil War (1917–1922)

Allied Intervention in the Russian Civil War

http://www.regiments.org/wars/20ww1/russia.htm

An English site dedicated to lists and bibliography of Allied intervention in the Russian Civil War. Also presents time lines and biographies.

Russian Civil War

http://www.spartacus.schoolnet.co.uk/RUScivilwar.htm

An encyclopedic reference tool on the Russian Civil War.

Chaco Wars (1927–1929, 1932–1935)

The Chaco War

http://www.american.edu/TED/ice/chaco.htm

The American University's case study on the Chaco war and its relevance in history.

The Gran Chaco War

http://worldatwar.net/chandelle/v1/v1n3/chaco.html

A useful Web site—with images and maps—on the Gran Chaco War between Bolivia and Paraguay. Useful information on this overlooked conflict.

Spanish Civil War (1936–1939)

History of the Spanish Civil War

http://dwardmac.pitzer.edu/Anarchist_Archives/spancivwar/spancivwarhis.html

A Pitzer College (Claremont, California) Web site dedicated to the history of the Spanish Civil War. See especially the information on the American volunteers in the war, the Abraham Lincoln Brigade.

Spanish Civil War

http://www.spartacus.schoolnet.co.uk/Spanish-Civil-War.htm

A student-sponsored Web site full of encyclopedic resources and information.

The Spanish Revolution and Civil War, 1936–1939

http://www.geocities.com/capitolhill/9820/

A Spanish Civil War site from the leftist perspective. Within the site there are numerous links to other Spanish Civil War sites and resources. Of particular interest is a digital reproduction of the music for "L'Internationale" available to play on the Web site.

World War II in Europe (1939–1945)

Achtung Panzer

http://www.achtungpanzer.com/panzer.htm

Extensive resources and links on World War II German tank and armored warfare.

Axis History Factbook

http://www.axishistory.com/

An amateur Web site dedicated to Germany and the Axis in World War II. Useful information and images presented by a dedicated amateur historian and academic political scientist.

The Battle of Britain Historical Society

http://www.battleofbritain.net/

The introductory Web site for both the Royal Air Force Fighter Command Battle of Britain and the Battle of Britain Historical Society. Both have excellent resource material on the famous aerial struggle over England in World War II.

Feldgrau.com—The German Armed Forces, 1919–1945

http://www.feldgrau.com/

An informative site on research materials and topics on the German armed forces leading up to and during World War II.

Hyperwar: A Hypertext History of the Second World War

http://www.ibiblio.org/hyperwar/

An individual attempt to link multiple resources on World War II. There is a good bibliography as well as valuable information and resources on the war.

The Luftwaffe, 1933–1945

http://www.ww2.dk/

This Luftwaffe site has good information and useful links for Luftwaffe research and discussion groups.

Sword of the Motherland

http://www.russianwarrior.com/

An excellent Web site dedicated to Russian and Soviet military history. See especially the World War II pages, resources, and links under the "Great Patriotic War."

UBoat.net

http://uboat.net/

Extensive resources and links on German World War II submarines and their operations.

The Warbirds Resource Group

http://www.warbirdsresourcegroup.org/

A resource site for all manner of World War II aircraft and aviation research.

World War II in the Pacific (1939–1945)

The Hiroshima Archive

http://www.lclark.edu/~history/HIROSHIMA/

Lewis and Clark College's (Portland, Oregon) site dedicated to the documents and controversy surrounding the atomic bomb dropped on Hiroshima in August 1945.

Imperial Japanese Navy

http://homepage2.nifty.com/nishidah/e/index.htm

A Web site dedicated to the Imperial Japanese Navy (IJN). It is maintained by an individual whose credentials cannot be verified, but the site has very interesting and authentic nuts-and-bolts data on the IJN.

Imperial Japanese Navy Page

http://www.combinedfleet.com/

A Web site dedicated to the Imperial Japanese Navy of World War II.

A Marine Diary: My Experiences on Guadalcanal

http://www.gnt.net/~jrube/indx2.html

An American marine's recollection of his ordeal at Guadalcanal complete with images and information on this important Pacific battlefield.

National Atomic Museum—The Manhattan Project Display

http://www.atomicmuseum.com/tour/manhattanproject.cfm

The National Atomic Museum in Albuquerque, New Mexico, and the Web site dedicated to the history of the American Manhattan Project and the development of the atomic bomb during World War II.

The Pacific War: The U.S. Navy

http://www.microworks.net/pacific/

A helpful resource guide to World War II U.S. Navy Pacific theater campaigns and information.

Chinese Civil War (1945–1949)

The Chinese Civil War at Eduseek.com

http://www.eduseek.com/navigate.php?ID=497

An encyclopedic reference to the Chinese Civil War with good links, including an animated map of the war.

Handbook for the Chinese Civil War

http://www.nwc.navy.mil/chinesecs/

Professor Andrew Wilson of the Naval War College's Strategy and Policy Department presents a basic reader and good source of information on the Chinese Civil War.

Cold War—U.S. Versus USSR

Cold War Bibliography

http://www.cmu.edu/coldwar/bibl.html

Carnegie Mellon University's Web site (somewhat dated—from 2000—but watch for updates) on the Cold War. A lot of good information directly garnered from the Cold War Science and Technology Colloquium.

Cold War Hot Links

http://homepages.stmartin.edu/fac_staff/dprice/cold.war.htm

A Web site dedicated to links on Cold War information by Professor David Price of St. Martin's College in Lacey, Washington.

The Cold War Museum

http://www.coldwar.org/

The Web site of the museum dedicated to the Cold War. Informative time lines, documents, and images.

Documents Relating to American Foreign Policy: The Cold War

http://www.mtholyoke.edu/acad/intrel/coldwar.htm

Within Professor Vincent Ferraro's personal Web site, he has posted this Cold War documents page. See his other documents pages for even more important information.

Journal of Cold War Studies

http://www.fas.harvard.edu/~hpcws/journal.htm

Harvard's academic journal dedicated to Cold War studies helps researchers stay updated on the latest research on the Cold War.

The Korean War (1950–1953)

The Korean War

http://www.korean-war.com/

A Web site with excellent resources and links on Korean War history. See especially the extensive bibliography.

The Korean War Project

http://koreanwar.org/

The starting place for Korean War research and information.

The Korean War Veterans Association

http://www.kwva.org/

A valuable resource for locating and contacting veterans of the Korean War.

French Indochina (1945–1954)

Air War Over French Indochina

http://hedgehoghollow.com/awoic/

A good Web site devoted to the French phase of the Indochinese War (to 1954) and all the air forces involved. Good images, links, and source references.

Dien Bien Phu

http://www.dienbienphu.org/english/

A Web site dedicated to the preservation of the French perspective of the battle of Dien Bien Phu.

Cuban Missile Crisis (1962)

The Cuban Missile Crisis, 1962

http://www2.gwu.edu/~nsarchiv/nsa/cuba_mis_cri/

George Washington University's Cuban Missile Crisis Web site. Complete with documents, photos, and analysis of the crisis.

The United States in Vietnam (1954–1975)

The Lyndon Baines Johnson Library and Museum— University of Texas

http://www.lbjlib.utexas.edu/

The Gerald R. Ford Library and Museum— University of Texas

http://www.ford.utexas.edu/

These two excellent Web sites focus on the American presidencies during and immediately after the American involvement in the Vietnam War. The University of Texas is also sponsoring its Vietnam War Declassification Project at http://www.ford.utexas.edu/library/exhibits/vietnam/vietnam.htm, which will offer more documents, resources, and images in the near future.

The Vietnam Project

http://www.vietnam.ttu.edu/

Texas Tech University's Vietnam Project, complete with resources, document archives, and extensive oral interviews.

Vietnam War Bibliography

http://www.clemson.edu/caah/history/FacultyPages/EdMoise/
bibliography.html

Dr. Edwin Moise of Clemson University in South Carolina provides a bibliography and detailed links relating to his Vietnam Wars classes and a history of the Vietnam Wars in general. An excellent research tool on the conflicts in Southeast Asia.

The VietnamWar.net

http://www.vietnamwar.net/

A nonacademic site dedicated to the Vietnam War, with documents and resources.

Vietnam: Yesterday and Today

http://servercc.oakton.edu/~wittman/

Professor Sandra Wittman of Oakton Community College in Skokie, Illinois, presents this Web site dedicated to online Vietnam resources.

The Wars for Vietnam, 1945–1975

http://vietnam.vassar.edu/

Vassar College's Vietnam Wars Web site, complete with documents and images.

The Arab-Israeli Wars (1948–1981)

The Arab-Israeli Conflicts in Maps

http://www.jafi.org.il/education/100/maps/

Well-illustrated maps pertaining to the history of Israel and Palestine.

The Arab-Israeli Wars

http://english.aljazeera.net/NR/exeres/
A5179275-0F1D-40A2-A3AB-3745424C6EFC.htm

Content and links on the Arab-Israeli Wars from the Arab perspective.

Army Area Handbook

http://lcweb2.loc.gov/frd/cs/iltoc.html

The U.S. Army Area Handbook on Palestine and the conflict in the Middle East, published by the Library of Congress, Federal Research Division.

The Israeli Defense Force Homepage

http://www1.idf.il/DOVER/site/
homepage.asp?clr=1&sl=EN&id=-8888&force=1

The IDF Homepage with detailed information on the history of the IDF and conflicts in the area since 1948.

The Jewish Virtual Library

http://www.jewishvirtuallibrary.org/

An informative Web site with a number of documents and articles relating to the Arab-Israeli Wars from the Israeli perspective.

The Falklands War (1982)

The Falkland Islands Conflict, 1982

http://www.falklandswar.org.uk/

An excellent site for initial research on the British Falklands campaigns of 1982.

Grenada (Operation Urgent Fury) (1983)

Special Operations: Grenada, 1983

http://www.specialoperations.com/Operations/grenada.html

An interesting Web site dedicated to Operation Urgent Fury in Grenada as well as additional information on Operation Just Cause in Panama in 1989. Good bibliographical references.

The Persian Gulf War I (1990–1991)

Desert Storm.com
http://www.desert-storm.com/

A Web site dedicated to the history and documentation of the Desert Storm campaign.

Fog of War—The 1991 Air Battle for Baghdad
http://www.washingtonpost.com/wp-srv/inatl/longterm/fogofwar/fogofwar.htm

An in-depth analysis of the air war during Desert Storm.

Operation Desert Storm: 10 Years After
http://www2.gwu.edu/~nsarchiv/NSAEBB/NSAEBB39/

The George Washington University's National Security Archive collection on the documents relating to the postwar analyses of the 1991 Persian Gulf War.

Operation Desert Storm/Desert Shield
http://www.gulflink.osd.mil/timeline/

Good information on the dual campaigns in the Persian Gulf War of 1991.

Gulf War II—Operation Iraqi Freedom (2003–present)

Defend America
http://www.defendamerica.mil/

The U.S. Department of Defense Web site with ongoing coverage of the Iraq War.

Iraq War Information
http://www.iraqwar.info/

A Web site dedicated to current information on the Iraq War.

Operation Iraqi Freedom
http://www.mnf-iraq.com/

Central Command's Web site devoted to current information on the war in Iraq.

Operation Iraqi Freedom

http://www.jfsc.ndu.edu/library/publications/bibliography/
operation_iraqi_freedom.asp

The National Defense University's first look at the publications, articles, and resources on the Iraq War.

Overviews: Air Power

The Aerial Reconnaissance Archives

http://www.evidenceincamera.co.uk/index.htm

A useful place to start for aerial reconnaissance information, history, and images.

Redstone Arsenal Historical Information

http://www.redstone.army.mil/history/

A Web site dedicated to the history of the U.S. missile program. Interesting documents, images, articles, and monographs on missile history.

U.S. Air Force Historical Research Agency

http://www.au.af.mil/au/afhra/

The U.S. Air Force's office for historical research. A wonderful and reliable site to start researching U.S. airpower history.

U.S. Air Force Historical Studies

https://www.airforcehistory.hq.af.mil/

A starting place for U.S. Air Force historical research.

Overviews: Army

U.S. Army Center of Military History

http://www.army.mil/cmh-pg/

A starting place for U.S. Army historical research.

Overviews: Defense

The U.S. Department of Defense

http://www.defenselink.mil/

The U.S. Department of Defense Web site, dedicated to information and news.

Overviews: Navy

American Merchant Marine at War

http://www.usmm.org/

A starting place for U.S. Merchant Marine historical research.

The Battleship Page

http://www.battleship.org/

A site dedicated to extensive information on U.S. Naval battleship history and information.

Haze and Gray and Underway—Naval History and Photography

http://www.hazegray.org/

A Web site dedicated to world naval history. It covers most of the world's navies and is particularly interesting to researchers on American naval history. This Web site has *The Dictionary of American Fighting Ships* online as well as a list of all U.S. warships of all time.

The Naval Institute

http://www.usni.org/

A self-titled Independent Forum on National Defense that provides information and images on naval technology and capabilities as well as naval history. The Naval Institute maintains the Web site and publishes through the Naval Institute Press and the journals *Proceedings* and *Naval History.*

The Naval Vessel Register

http://www.nvr.navy.mil/

The U.S. Department of Defense register of U.S. Navy warships provides information on all the current U.S. Navy ships.

Naval Weapons of the World

http://www.navweaps.com/

A Web site on historical as well as modern naval weapons from around the world. Loaded with helpful information on naval (shipboard) weapons with good images.

U.S. Marine Corps History and Museum Division

http://hqinet001.hqmc.usmc.mil/HD/

A starting place for U.S. Marine Corps historical research.

U.S. Naval Historical Center

http://www.history.navy.mil/

A starting place for U.S. Navy historical research. See especially (and for starters) the navy's excellent resources and images on the Battle of Midway at the "Midway Night" link.

Museum Locators

There are far too many museums to list separately—this Web site is a great museum locator:

Yahoo Index of Military History Museums and Memorials

http://dir.yahoo.com/Arts/Humanities/History/By_Subject/Military_History/Museums_and_Memorials/

A comprehensive guide to museum and memorial listings and Web sites. Hosted by Yahoo.com.

Chapter 25

Historiography

Ranin Kazemi

Metasites

Bibliographies in the Google Directory

http://directory.google.com/Top/Reference/Bibliography/History/

Bibliographies on specific themes, regions, and periods. It may also prove useful to check "Bibliographies in the Yahoo! Directory" (http://dir.yahoo.com/Arts/Humanities/History/Bibliographies/) .

Historians in the Google Directory

http://directory.google.com/Top/Society/History/Historians/

This is certainly not an exhaustive list of important historians, but it provides a good starting point. Parallel and additional categories may also be found in the Yahoo! Directory (http://dir.yahoo.com/Arts/Humanities/History/Historiology/Historians/).

Internet History Sourcebooks Project

http://www.fordham.edu/halsall/

Collections of documents and links to texts on various themes, regions, and periods. This Web site is edited by Paul Halsall of Fordham University. For materials on historiography see Studying Ancient History, (http://www.fordham.

edu/halsall/ancient/asbook01.html), Studying [Medieval] History, (http://www.fordham.edu/halsall/sbook1a.html), and Studying [Modern] History. Some of the materials might in fact be identical.

Internet Public Library

http://www.ipl.org/

The Internet Public Library is maintained by the School of Information at the University of Michigan. It provides links to digital libraries and important resources and institutions in various fields, including history. See entries under History, Philosophy, History of Arts and Humanities, History of Social Sciences, and Books.

Philosophy of History in the Google Directory

http://directory.google.com/Top/Society/Philosophy/Philosophy_of_History/

Of the two categories listed on the Web site, "Philosophers" is the more important since it gives links to a number of philosophers whose works are extremely important in historical studies. There are also specific Web pages on aspects of the philosophy of history. The parallel category in the Yahoo! Directory is "Historiology" (http://dir.yahoo.com/Arts/Humanities/History/Historiology/). See particularly "Historiography in the Yahoo! Directory" (http://dir.yahoo.com/Arts/Humanities/History/Historiology/Historiography/).

Voice of the Shuttle

http://vos.ucsb.edu/index.asp

This database, managed by the University of California, Santa Barbara, has a section on history. The materials under the subsection Historiography are organized under three main rubrics: General History Resources (by far the most important of the three), Paradigm-Setting Works of History Writing, and Theoretical or Methodological Works. The materials under General History Resources will also prove beneficial for the links to databases that provide annotated links, archives, electronic documents, maps, and other historical resources.

WWW Virtual Library History—Central Catalogue

http://vlib.iue.it/history/index.html

This index, maintained by the European University Institute, provides links on various aspects of historical studies. Pertinent materials to historiography may be found under the category titled Research: Methods and Materials.

General Web Sites

EServer.org: History and Historiography

http://eserver.org/history/

This site includes original works published online by the EServer and links to historical and historiographical materials. The EServer is based at Iowa State University.

Historians and Philosophers: A Collated Web Index

http://www.scholiast.org/history/histphil.html

This Web site, created and maintained by a history student at the University of Copenhagen, has a list of historians and philosophers whose works have been consequential to historical inquiries. The materials are organized under four periods: Classical Period, Medieval and Renaissance Period, Early Modern Period, and Modern Period. The Modern Period is broken up into three different sub-periods. Some of the links might not work, and the entries are of uneven value.

Labyrinth

http://labyrinth.georgetown.edu/

This Web site provides links to numerous electronic resources in medieval studies. Users need to know what types of historiographical questions and texts or else what intellectuals they seek information on in order to utilize this index effectively.

Philosophy of History Archive

http://www.nsu.ru/filf/pha/

This Web site is maintained by Professor Nikolai Rozov of Novosibirsk State University. Contrary to its claim, it is not a comprehensive archive of materials on the philosophy of history and theoretical history. Nonetheless, it provides some additional points of departure for the student of historical method.

Digital Libraries

Archive for the History of the Economic Thought

http://socserv.socsci.mcmaster.ca/~econ/ugcm/3ll3/

Presented here are the full texts of works by important historians and intellectuals whose output is important to history writing, including Emile Durkheim, G.W.F. Hegel, David Hume, Karl Marx, Charles de Secondat Montesquieu, Thomas Paine, Jean-Jacques Rousseau, Arnold Toynbee, Max Weber, and Xenophon.

Electronic Texts for the Study of American Culture

http://xroads.virginia.edu/~HYPER/hypertex.html

Classical studies of American history and works of historiographical importance, for instance, by Francis Parkman, Alexis de Tocqueville, and Frederick Jackson Turner.

Eliohs: Electronic Library of Historiography

http://www.eliohs.unifi.it/

A virtual collection of texts that have particular historiographical value. Some of the authors represented here are Sir Thomas More, Sir Francis Bacon, Michel-Guillaume-Saint-Jean de Crèvecoeur, Edward Gibbon, David Hume, Jean-Jacques Rousseau, Adam Smith, Voltaire, Jacob Burckhardt, Charles Darwin, Alexis de Tocqueville, Lord Acton, Herbert Butterfield, and Frederick Jackson Turner.

Gallica: bibliothèque numérique de la Bibliothèque nationale de France

http://gallica.bnf.fr/

This digital library provides electronic texts of many important French works, including those of French historians.

Internet Classics Archive

http://classics.mit.edu/index.html

The English translations of the works of some Greco-Roman writers and six classical Iranian and Chinese authors. The Web site also gives links to the Perseus Digital Library.

Perseus Digital Library

http://www.perseus.tufts.edu/

An "evolving digital library" funded by a number of institutions including the Digital Libraries Initiative Phase 2 and Tufts University. Of particular historiographical importance are the texts under Classics, including works by Herodotus, Strabo, Thucydides, and Tacitus.

Major Figures

Fernand Braudel Center

http://fbc.binghamton.edu/

This is the Web site for the Fernand Braudel Center at Binghamton University, State University of New York. The Braudel Center was founded in 1976 "to engage in the analysis of large-scale social change over long periods of historical time." Because of their particular methodological approach, the scholarly activities sponsored by the center might be of interest to those who inquire about historical methodology in general.

Collingwood and British Idealism Centre

http://www.cf.ac.uk/euros/collingwood/

A starting point to inquire about R.G. Collingwood, a central figure in any inquiry about historical methodology. The center is housed at Cardiff University.

The Foucault Pages at CSUN

http://www.csun.edu/~hfspc002/foucault.home.html

Materials and links on this contemporary French thinker.

Institute for Vico Studies

http://www.vicoinstitute.org/

The only Giambattista Vico center in the English-speaking world, the institute was founded in 1974 at Emory University, and its Web site provides a starting point for studies of this Italian historian.

Marxists Internet Archives

http://www.marx.org/

A wealth of materials by and on Karl Marx and those who were influenced by his thought.

Voltaire Society of America

http://humanities.uchicago.edu/homes/VSA/

A good starting point for inquiries about this eighteenth-century French intellectual.

Aspects of Historiography

Aragonese Historiography

http://eserver.org/history/aragonese-historiography.txt

This essay, published by the EServer, pertains to the essentials of Aragonese historiography.

Classical Historiography for Chinese History

http://www.sscnet.ucla.edu/history/elman/ClassBib/

Bibliographies for classical Chinese historiography.

Iranian Historiography

http://www.iranica.com/articles/v12f3/v12f3036.html

A collection of articles in *Encyclopedia Iranica* on Iranian historiography before and after the advent of Islam.

National Center for History in the Schools

http://nchs.ucla.edu/

The NCHS has published over sixty teaching units on aspects of U.S. and world history. It promotes a standards-based approach to teaching history in schools, emphasizing the National Standards for History.

World History Archives

http://www.hartford-hwp.com/archives/index.html

A Web site that contains numerous documents to "support the study of world history from a working-class and non-Eurocentric perspective." Under World Historiography, users find a number of texts of uneven quality.

Writing Tips and Standards

http://personal.stthomas.edu/gwschlabach/courses/writing.htm

These practical tips and suggestions for undergraduates are edited by Gerald Schlabach of the University of St. Thomas, St. Paul, Minnesota. See particularly A Sense of History: Some Components and Ten Commandments of Good Historical Writing.

Journals

Cromohs: Cyber Review of Modern Historiography

http://www.cromohs.unifi.it/

There are many articles and full-text materials in this electronic journal. See particularly Useful Resources to find indexed links to relevant Web sites.

History and Theory

http://www.historyandtheory.org/

This is the Web site of the international journal *History and Theory*, "devoted to the theory and philosophy of history." It provides a link to H-History and Theory, an academic discussion network on the subject (http://www.h-net.org/~hist-thr/), which is also managed by this journal.

Histos: The Electronic Journal of Ancient Historiography

http://www.dur.ac.uk/Classics/histos/

This journal is administered at the University of Durham. It publishes all its materials both online and in "fully-edited and hard-copy format."

Storia della Storiografia: History of Historiography

http://www.cisi.unito.it/stor/home.htm

The Web site of the international journal *Storia della Storiografia*. The journal was founded in 1982 and is presently located at the University of Turin.

Teaching History: A Journal of Methods

http://www.emporia.edu/socsci/journal/

The Web site of the journal *Teaching History*, which was founded in 1976 and whose goal is to provide "history teachers at all levels with the best and newest teaching ideas for their classrooms." The journal is housed at Emporia State University.

Chapter 26

Historic Preservation and Conservation

Anne Rothfeld

Advisory Council on Historic Preservation

http://www.achp.gov

Created by the independent federal agency that advises the president and Congress on historic preservation issues, this Web site offers links to historic preservation officers throughout the United States and information about the National Historic Preservation Act of 1966.

American Institute for Conservation of Historic and Artistic Works

http://aic.stanford.edu/

This organization of professional conservators shares its expertise on how to care for prized possessions, from paintings and photographs to home videotape. AIC's Web site also offers literature discussing the care of materials, including paper and photographs, and advice on how to locate and select a professional conservator.

Built in America: Historic American Buildings Survey and Historic American Engineering Record, 1933–Present

http://memory.loc.gov/ammem/collections/habs_haer/

As part of its American Memory project, the Library of Congress has begun digitizing the vast documentation of American architecture, engineering, and design collected by the Historic American Buildings Survey and the Historic American Engineering Record. As the materials are made available online, they can be searched by keyword, subject, and geographic area.

CoOL: Conservation OnLine

http://palimpsest.stanford.edu

From Stanford University Libraries, information on a wide range of conservation topics of interest to libraries, archives, museums, and their user community, including digital imaging and the conservation and use of electronic records.

Council on Library and Information Resources

http://www.clir.org/

Offers online publications related to current issues in the preservation of library materials. Many full-text articles and reports are available.

Heritage Conservation and Historic Preservation

http://www.slv.vic.gov.au/services/conservation/guides/

The State Library of Victoria in Australia has assembled this online library about conservation issues. International in scope, the many topics addressed by articles and accompanying Web links include information about caring for cultural objects such as books and paper, film and photographs, and sound and magnetic materials.

Keeping Our Word: Preserving Information Across the Ages

http://www.lib.uiowa.edu/exhibits/keeping/contents.htm

This virtual version of an exhibit by the University of Iowa Libraries addresses the issues of preserving materials from cave paintings and clay tablets to electronic media. The exhibit includes links for doing further research on preservation issues.

Links to the Past: National Park Service Cultural Resources

http://www.cr.nps.gov

A site of great scope and depth, this project of the National Park Service is the place to start for information about visiting historic places throughout the national parks system, teaching with historic places, and working at historic locations as a national parks volunteer. Online exhibits cover topics such as the life of Frederick Douglass and camp life at Gettysburg, and virtual tours take Web visitors to historic places in Detroit, Seattle, and other regions of the country. The site also serves as the gateway to programs such as Tools for Teaching, the Historic American Buildings Survey and Historic American Engineering Record, and the National Register of Historic Places.

National Archives and Records Administration— Archives and Preservation Resources

http://www.archives.gov/preservation/index.html

From the experts at the National Archives, information about preserving documents and photographs. NARA's Web page includes guidance on general preservation, preparations for emergencies, and specifications for proper storage.

National Center for Preservation Technology and Training

http://www.ncptt.nps.gov

This project within the National Park Service includes an extensive, annotated database of online resources in archaeology, history, historic architecture and landscapes, and conservation of materials and objects. The database includes links for subscribing to listservs related to preservation and conservation.

National Preservation Institute

http://www.npi.org

This organization offers online registration for its numerous training seminars in historic preservation and cultural resources management.

National Trust for Historic Preservation

http://www.nthp.org

This private, nonprofit organization dedicated to saving historic buildings, neighborhoods, and landscapes offers a site with information about the group's mission and many projects, including its annual list of the nation's most endangered places. A link to its *Preservation* magazine offers tables of contents, book reviews, and excerpts from some other features of the magazine. This site links to the National Trust's Main Street Center, which works to revitalize historic and traditional commercial areas and provides information about the history and preservation of Main Street communities and advice for organizing a Main Street revitalization project.

Northern States Conservation Center

http://www.collectioncare.org

Northern States Conservation Center of Saint Paul, Minnesota, here offers numerous articles about the management and preservation of museum collections, including advice about museums' use of the World Wide Web.

PreserveNet

http://www.preservenet.cornell.edu

Incorporating the PreserveNet Information Service and the PreserveNet Law Service, this Web site at Cornell University includes extensive links to preservation organizations, education programs, conferences and events, and job and internship opportunities. The Law Service offers texts of major state and federal preservation legislation and models for preservation ordinances. This is also the host site for the Guide to the African-American Heritage Preservation Foundation Inc.

RLG DigiNews

http://www.rlg.org/preserv/diginews

RLG DigiNews, a bimonthly electronic newsletter by the Research Libraries Group in cooperation with the Cornell University Library Department of Preservation and Conservation, focuses on preservation through digital imaging. Back issues to 1997 are available and searchable.

The Society of Architectural Historians

http://www.sah.org

International in scope, this organization's collection of Internet resources promotes the study of historical architecture and includes links to collections of images of historic buildings. A searchable guide to master's programs and degrees in architecture history is available.

State Historic Preservation Legislation Database

http://www.ncsl.org/programs/arts/statehist_intro.htm

The National Conference of State Legislatures offers this database of state legislation and constitution articles governing historic places, archaeological locales and materials, and significant unmarked burial areas. The database is searchable through state name and topic area.

World Heritage

http://whc.unesco.org/pg.cfm

Home page for the UNESCO project that encourages the preservation of cultural and natural heritage locations around the world. This Web site includes information about more than 500 World Heritage places, including those considered endangered. The Web site, which appears in both English and French, comprises searchable links including news, reports, and events.

World Monuments Fund

http://www.wmf.org/

The Web site of this private, nonprofit organization working to safeguard works of art and architecture includes information about the fund's international list of the hundred most endangered monuments.

Chapter 27

Living History and Historic Reenactment

Bambi L. Dingman and
Jessie Bishop Powell, Merriman

Please note: This section only lists living history and historic reenactment sites that are related to American History—for a more complete listing, please see the chapter on this topic in the *21st Century History Highway.*

Metasites

The Costume Page

http://www.costumepage.org/tcpsupp.html

This is the definitive source for costuming information on the Web, conveniently sorted by period of interest. Links to costume suppliers, accessories, and patterns for every time period.

Histrenact: The Historical Reenactment Web Site

http://www.montacute.net/histrenact/welcome.htm

Links to general suppliers and craftsmen, historical information, online reenactment information, and societies that re-create different time periods.

Reconstructing History Patterns

http://www.reconstructinghistory.com/patterns/partners.html

Links to general suppliers for Celtic, medieval, and Victorian costuming.

General Sites

ALHFAM

http://www.alhfam.org/

Home of the Association for Living History, Farm and Agricultural Museums. The association's Web page has conference information, employment classifieds for living history specialists, planning tips for living history locations, and extensive links to living history organizations throughout the world.

American Longrifle Association

http://www.longrifle.org/

A period trekking group and umbrella organization spanning the years 1750 to 1850. A calendar of events can be found online, as well as photographs and a bibliography.

Buckskins and Black Powder

http://www.hogheavenmuzzleloaders.com

This excellent site has links to a variety of black powder and buckskinning sites on the Web. Also includes information about black powder clubs, the fur trade era, and re-creating history.

Butler's Rangers

http://iaw.on.ca/~awoolley/brang/brang.html

This corps of rangers served in the American Revolution and is re-created at living history events today. Information about the rangers, both past and present, can be found on this site, as well as historical source material and other information.

C & D Jarnagin Company

http://www.jarnaginco.com/

A provider of fine wares for the period 1750 through 1865, with a full complement of uniforms and equipment for American troops.

Camp Chase Gazette

http://www.campchase.com/

A well-known publication devoted to American Civil War re-creation. The online edition contains informative articles, a virtual roster of Civil War reenactors, upcoming events, and other relevant information.

Camp Life

http://www.cr.nps.gov/museum/exhibits/gettex/index.htm

Gettysburg National Park holds the largest Civil War collection in the National Park System, with more than 40,000 cataloged items. A unique aspect of the collection is that many of the pieces are common, everyday items that allow visitors a glimpse into the lives of the soldiers who owned them. Now a portion of the collection can be viewed online in this virtual museum of photographs and artifacts devoted to everyday camp life.

Castle Keep Ltd.

http://www.reenact.com/

Living history information and supplies for reenactors, categorized by period of interest, from medieval times to the twentieth century.

The Civil War Artillery Page

http://www.cwartillery.org/artillery.html

Information about organization and drill, weapons, ammunition, equipment, history, and reenactment of field and foot artillery units of the American Civil War.

Civil War Reenactors Home Page

http://www.cwreenactors.com/

This Web site offers photos, history, trivia, event reviews, and related links for reenactors and Civil War enthusiasts.

Coon 'n Crockett Muzzleloaders

http://www.coon-n-crockett.org/cnc~home.htm

This page is loaded with information about the club, the muzzleloading hobby, photos, and upcoming events.

Fall Creek Sutlery

http://fcsutler.com/

Supplies for Civil War reenactors and Victorian era enthusiasts.

Flintlock FAQ

http://members.aye.net/~bspen/flintlockfaq.html

A beginner's guide to flintlock shooting with a concise history of flintlock weapons and answers to questions about flintlock performance.

French and Indian War—Mohican History Links

http://www.mohicanpress.com/mo08000.html

The information provided here will be of interest to French and Indian War reenactors. Links to both Mohican and colonial history.

French and Indian War Webpage

http://web.syr.edu/~laroux/lists/alpha.html

Though the site itself appears not to have been updated since 2000, its lists of soldiers, companies, and battles will prove useful to the French and Indian War reenactor.

GI Journal

http://www.militaria.com

Articles of interest to World War I and World War II reenactors and links to division Web pages, reproduction uniforms, and military history magazines.

The Gunfighter Zone

http://www.gunfighter.com

A Web site for reenactors of the Old West and members of Cowboy Action Shooting groups, with links to discussion boards, suppliers, books, magazines, and informative articles.

Historic Enterprises

http://www.historicenterprises.com/

Specializes in highly accurate handmade replicas of museum examples. Although it is a commercial site, it includes a great deal of historical information and interesting photos of the company's work.

The Historical Maritime Society

http://www.hms.org.uk/

Re-creates British Navy life from 1793 to 1815 (Napoleonic War period).

19th Indiana Volunteer Infantry, Co. A

http://www.19thindiana.com/

Civil War reenactors and nineteenth-century civilian impressionists. This Web page has an event schedule, company newsletter and historical information.

Japanese Internment Camps

http://www.teacheroz.com/Japanese_Internment.htm

Links to various pieces of information regarding life in America's Japanese internment camps during World War II.

Jas. Townsend & Son

http://jas-townsend.com/

A mail-order company specializing in historic clothing, camp gear, tents, books, music, knives, tomahawks, oak kegs, and other assorted items for the period 1750 to 1840.

1st Kansas Volunteer Infantry and Kansas Women's Relief Corps

http://www.firstkansas.org/

Maintained by Jeremy Birket, this site was last updated in July 2004. It contains information about the company's participation in the Civil War.

King's Arms Press and Bindery

http://www.kingspress.com/

Specialized reprints of eighteenth-century books and pamphlets, including drill books and regulations, as well as military treatises.

Links to the Past

http://www.cr.nps.gov/colherit.htm

An extensive Web page from the National Park Service with online archives for many historic locations, as well as battle summaries, battlefield information, national landmarks, and online exhibits.

Longshot's Rendezvous

http://www.wizzywigweb.com/longshot/

A source of rendezvous information for mountain men, buckskinners, and muzzleloaders of Missouri and Illinois. Also includes a guide to getting started in rendezvous and links to other sources.

28th Massachusetts Volunteer Infantry, Co. A, C, & H

http://www.28thmass.org/

A well-designed Web page with information for historical research and reenacting.

Milieux: The Costume Site

http://www.milieux.com/costume/

A comprehensive list of links to costuming sites with diversified themes, such as medieval costuming, armor, Civil War uniforms, colonial garb, and modern accessories.

Morningside Books

http://www.morningsidebooks.com

Noted for its Civil War collection and as a recognized dealer of Don Troiani artwork.

Mountain Men and the Fur Trade

http://www.xmission.com/~drudy/amm.html

An online research center devoted to the history and traditions of trappers, explorers, and traders, with a digital collection, bibliography, an archive of trade records, and links to Web sites related to the fur trade era.

47th New York State Volunteers, "Washington Grays"

http://www.awod.com/gallery/probono/cwchas/47ny.html

A federal reenacting unit. The Web page has an extensive unit history and Civil War reenactment information.

5th New York Volunteer Infantry, Co. A, Duryée's Zouaves

http://www.zouave.org/

An excellent Civil War company Web page with a detailed history, roster, and extensive photo gallery.

Northeastern Primitive Rendezvous

http://www.frontiernet.net/~oakhill/

Guns, clothing, and accessories for the period 1640 to 1840.

North/South Alliance

http://www.nsalliance.org/

Information on the First Confederate and First Federal Divisions in the American Civil War and an event listing. Most documents are PDF.

The Northwest Territory Alliance

http://www.serve.com/rbriggs/main.html

This group strives to re-create the lifestyle, culture, and arts of the Revolutionary War era with an accurate representation of uniforms, weaponry, and battlefield tactics. This Web site offers forms and documents useful to reenactors, an event schedule, chronology of events in the War for Independence, pattern lists, and publications.

The Patriots of Fort McHenry

http://www.bcpl.net/~etowner/patriots.html

This organization hopes to preserve the historical legacy of the patriots who defended Baltimore in 1814. Fort McHenry is best known as the scene of the battle that Francis Scott Key witnessed and wrote about in the "Star Spangled Banner."

Plimoth Plantation

http://www.plimoth.org/

Plimoth Plantation's Pilgrim Village brings to life the Plymouth of 1627. This Web site has plenty of information about the village and also includes educational information for reenactors. This is a wonderful source of information for anyone who wishes to interpret in the first person.

Pre-1840's Buckskinning

http://www.living-history.net

Contains a lengthy list of rendezvous groups around the United States, publications, trader events, and buckskinning classifieds. Last updated in 2003.

Reenactor Net

http://www.reenactor.net/

A list of links to reenactor Web sites, categorized by time period. Regularly updated.

64th Regiment of Foot

http://freenet.vcu.edu/sigs/reg64/

Members of the 64th Regiment portray British infantry soldiers from the time of the Revolutionary War. Their Web page has information on the British army, regimental colors, the Brown Bess, women and the army, and plenty of primary reference material.

The 42nd Royal Highland Regiment, "The Black Watch"

http://www.42ndrhr.org/index.php

This well-designed site is a terrific source of information on period music, dancing, uniforms, and everything related to the "Black Watch" of the late 1700s in North America.

Shadows of the Past

http://www.sptddog.com/sotp/

This organization's guide to reenacting the Old West, with articles, historical resources, photographs, literature, and links to related sites.

1st South Carolina Artillery, C.S.A.

http://www.awod.com/gallery/probono/cwchas/1scart.html

Reenacts the history of the men who manned the artillery of the Confederate defenses of the South Carolina coast during the American Civil War. The Web site has history, photos, and a bibliography.

Trev's Rendezvous Down Under

http://www.geocities.com/Yosemite/Trails/1878/

This site has contact information for many groups that are accessible only through e-mail, as well as for organizations that are already on the Internet.

20th Century Fashion: Women's Fashion: 1940s

http://www.costumegallery.com/1940.htm

Fabric rationing in the 1940s affected the way people dressed. This Web site gives information about American women's fashion in this period.

U.S. Civil War Center

http://www.cwc.lsu.edu

The Civil War Center is an attempt to index all the Civil War sites on the Web. There are links to national parks, battlefields, roundtables, reenacting groups, events, and events. This should be one of the first stops for people interested in re-creating the American Civil War.

U.S. Regulars Civil War Archive

http://www.usregulars.com/

Library of key works on Civil War strategy, tactics, and drill used by the regular army and volunteers and at the U.S. Military Academy at West Point.

Welcome to Fort Erie and the War of 1812

http://www.iaw.on.ca/~jsek/

Helpful information about the Fort Erie siege and the War of 1812 reenactment units.

White Oak Society, Inc.

http://www.whiteoak.org/

This Web site has a wealth of information about rendezvous and the fur trade era, from interpreters who portray authentic characters of the eighteenth century.

World War I Trenches on the Web

http://www.worldwar1.com/

A compendium of information for the World War I reenactor. This history of the Great War has a reference library, war poster reproductions, interesting articles, and reenactor photographs. Last updated in 2004.

World War II Women and the Homefront

http://www.teacheroz.com/WWIIHomefront.htm

Site contains a multitude of links to help reenactors authentically create American women's experience of World War II.

Chapter 28

Genealogy

Samuel Dicks

Genealogists have created many Internet sites and other research tools that are also of use to biographers, social and military historians, and other scholars. Probate, military, census, immigration, naturalization, marriage, and land records are among the many kinds of materials genealogists have accumulated on the Internet. The Internet makes it easy to identify the kinds of materials available before a trip is planned, make contact with others working on the same family lines, and find other ways to obtain detailed information. Cyndi's List and RootsWeb (see below), as well as search engines and published reference works, provide additional research tools. The single most useful reference work is *The Source: A Guidebook of American Genealogy,* published by Ancestry. com (see below) and available at most public libraries.

Most Useful Sites

American Family Immigration History Center (Ellis Island Records)

http://www.ellisislandrecords.org

From 1892 to 1924 over 22 million people entered the United States through Ellis Island. The ships' manifest records ordinarily include the immigrant's given name and surname, ethnicity, last place of residence, name of ship and departure port, arrival date, age, gender, and marital status, along with the location of their name on the manifest. Numerous other Web sites, including Ancestry. com and RootsWeb.com, provide background on the Ellis Island experience. If you are searching for passenger records before 1892, the Immigrant Ships Transcribers Guild (http://www.immigrantships.net/) is compiling a list of earlier ship passengers.

Ancestry.com

http://ancestry.com

This is the best-known and most useful subscription Internet site for genealogists. On-screen indexed copies of federal censuses, military indexes, vital records, British records, a genealogy periodical index of the Allen County Public Library in Fort Wayne, Indiana, with over a million articles, and many other sources for people not easily found elsewhere are here. Some materials are also available without membership or with free trial memberships. Some libraries also subscribe to this site and make it free to their patrons. There is an interesting free daily Internet genealogy newsletter.

Cyndi's List of Genealogy Sites on the Internet

http://cyndislist.com/

Cyndi Howell's Web site is the best-known and most comprehensive genealogy site, with over 200,000 links to states, counties, provinces, nations, military records, ethnic, religious, and other sites too numerous to note. Users who browse through Cyndi's List slowly over several days will discover many other helpful sites that are little known.

Family History Library (LDS Church, Salt Lake City)

http://www.familysearch.org/

The Church of Jesus Christ of Latter-day Saints maintains the world's largest family history library, and a large amount of information from the library continues to be added to this Web site. Local Family History Centers, commonly operated by volunteers in Mormon churches in many cities, can provide additional information and arrange for the borrowing of microfilm. Church records from overseas and local government records are among the many holdings that may be accessed online or, in some cases, by visiting a local center. Holdings available for low cost on CD-ROM include the Freedmen's Bank Records (a major African-American database), the 1880 U.S. Federal Census, the 1881 Censuses for the British Isles and Canada, and Vital Records (Birth, Marriage, Death) for Mexico and the Scandinavian countries. There are forms, teaching aids, and a great deal more at this Web site. Check the various site subheadings, such as Research Guidance, Web Sites, and Family History Library Catalog.

Heritage Quest

http://heritagequest.com/

This is a commercial Web site that has items you may wish to purchase or consult, but more important, many state, local, and university libraries include this extensive collection among the Internet databases available free to their patrons. The Heritage Quest database includes the U.S. censuses, Revolutionary War pension files, early local histories and family genealogies, and many other materials, all of which can be accessed through a place or name word search. This site is often overlooked by novices, but is much too important to ignore, especially if you can gain free access with a library password. Check with your local library or genealogical society to see if it is available in your area.

The National Archives and Records Administration

http://www.archives.gov/research_room/genealogy/

The National Archives has one of the most useful sites provided by the federal government. Census schedules (1790–1930); alien, immigration, and naturalization records; ship passenger records; military and military pension records; and Native American records are among the sources most commonly used by genealogists. (Most naturalization records before November 27, 1906, are in county courthouse or state records. The "naturalization" section on this site explains how citizenship of wives, children, and veterans was handled differently in earlier periods.) Many of the microfilmed materials, including census schedules and military pension indexes, are also in the thirteen regional branches of NARA, which can be accessed from this site. Useful articles from the NARA journal, *Prologue,* may be found at "Genealogy Notes." The sites relating to the census schedules provide an explanation of the Soundex system, an index made in the 1930s for Social Security applicants who were born before birth certificates were common. Soundex takes into account different spellings and acts as an index for most censuses since 1880. A Soundex converter that allows users to list several surnames at once is http://www.bradandkathy.com/genealogy/yasc.html.

For casualty or other military records, see http://www.archives.gov/research_room/arc/topics/highlights.html.

RootsWeb

http://rootsweb.com/

Rootsweb is the oldest and largest free genealogy site. Its home page lists large numbers of other useful sites including the Social Security Death Index (SSDI), which provides information on individuals with death claims since the early 1950s. One of its best-known features is the Rootsweb Surname List (RSL), a sort of international bulletin board where users can connect with others pursuing the same surnames. There are connections to many other state and local sites and other resources, plus a free, informative weekly Internet newsletter.

State Historical Societies and Archives

http://www.ohiohistory.org/links/arch_hs.html

Most states have a state historical society and a state archives. The historical society will probably include microfilm copies of newspapers and census records, private papers donated to the society, early state and local histories, and other publications relating to the region. A state archive is ordinarily the custodian of official state papers, such as those of the governor or adjutant general (some states had censuses for years ending in 5, such as 1895, and adjutant general records are useful for military records for state militias in war time). Newspapers and other materials may also be in a state library or a state historical library. The Ohio Historical Society provides links to most state historical societies and archives; other state societies, archives, and libraries can be located at the Cyndi's List or RootsWeb sites (see above).

U.S. Bureau of Land Management: General Land Office Records

http://www.glorecords.blm.gov/

This is one of the most useful federal sites for genealogists and historians. The transfer of land titles from the federal government to individuals and much more can be found here. Surname searches may also bring forth maps and copies of the original documents.

USGenWeb

http://usgenweb.org./

The USGenWeb Project, manned by volunteers, is one of the most useful sites for quickly accessing states and counties. Users can click an individual state in the left margin to go to state and county sites for all fifty states, and many other links. Additional local sites, sometimes by private parties, may also be obtained by using a search engine and the name of the county and state or by searching for local historical or genealogical societies or public libraries.

U.S. Immigration and Naturalization Service

http://uscis.gov/graphics/aboutus/history/

Now part of the Department of Homeland Security and recently renamed U.S. Citizenship and Immigration Services, this site provides much detail on immigration and naturalization records, Chinese immigrant files, and other topics, as well as useful teaching aids.

U.S. Vital Records Information

http://vitalrec.com/index.html

Modern state and territory sites for finding birth, marriage, divorce, and death records are available here. Some records are available online and may be accessed at county or state links.

Additional Sites

The 10,000 Year Calendar

http://calendarhome.com/tyc/

Genealogists and historians are often stuck with incomplete dates expressed as "the Sunday after Christmas" or "Friday, November 23." This is the most elaborate of various sites that provide a calendar for any month of any year desired. There is also information on calendar changes, Mayan and Chinese calendars, and other related topics. For a simpler perpetual calendar, go to http://www.timeanddate.com/calendar/.

African-American Genealogy: Christine's Genealogy Website

http://ccharity.com/

This provides information and links to most other sites that deal with African-American genealogy. Also see the African-American page on Cyndi's List.

African-Native American Genealogy

http://www.african-nativeamerican.com/

Black Indian Slaves, Indian Territory Freedmen, and Frontier Slave Narratives are among the many resources included on this site.

AfriGeneas: African Genealogy in the Americas

http://www.afrigeneas.com/

AfriGeneas includes a guide for beginners, research sites, articles, message boards, and much more of interest to genealogists and historians. Many state and local historical societies also have extensive materials on African-American history, including early newspapers and manuscripts.

Amistad Research Center (Tulane University)

http://www.amistadresearchcenter.org/

This major research center includes extensive manuscripts, oral histories, photographs, and other materials from the Abolitionist era and the American Missionary Society to the Harlem Renaissance and beyond. It also includes material on Native Americans, Puerto Ricans, Appalachian whites, Asian-Americans, and Mexican-Americans, among others. Included in its collection are correspondence and other materials of many people involved in antislavery and civil rights movements.

Civil War Soldiers and Sailors

http://www.itd.nps.gov/cwss/

The National Park Service, in conjunction with the National Archives and Records Administration and various military and genealogy organizations, has developed this computerized database of Civil War soldiers and sailors, both Union and Confederate. Individuals not listed here may be located at various state or local Web sites, including state archives and historical societies. Union pension file indexes are also available at NARA branches and other locations with the use of Soundex, or at Ancestry.com (fee-based). Confederate records are in various state archives. Also see 1883 and 1890 U.S. veterans' censuses for Union veterans or dependents (only available for some states)—some of them are on the Internet at http://www.arealdomain.com/pensioners1883.html.

The Commonwealth War Graves Commission

http://www.cwgc.org/

This commemorative site provides personal and service details for the 1.7 million soldiers from throughout the British Commonwealth who died in World War I or World War II. Also includes civilian casualties and other information.

Family Tree Maker Online

http://familytreemaker.genealogy.com/

Family Tree Maker has one of the largest software programs for genealogists. It also provides much free information on its Web site.

The Federation of East European Family History Societies (FEEFHS)

http://feefhs.org/

This is a major Web site for Central and Eastern European countries, from Switzerland and Germany to eastern Russia, whose emigrants have ethnic links with those peoples currently in the United States and throughout the world.

Helm's Genealogy Toolbox

http://www.genealogytoolbox.com/

Matthew L. Helm's site is one of the oldest and best-known sites for a wide variety of information and links.

International Black Sheep Society of Genealogists

http://blacksheep.rootsweb.com/

An organization for those with horse thieves or other scoundrels among their ancestors; the site has many interesting stories and useful links.

JewishGen

http://www.jewishgen.org/

JewishGen is the primary Internet source for those engaged in Jewish genealogy. It connects with numerous databases, including JewishGen Family Finder, which connects people searching the same ancestral towns and surnames. For locating Holocaust survivors, see the Holocaust Global Registry at this site.

Native American Enumerations

http://www.us-census.org/native/

Because Indians on reservations were not considered citizens and therefore not counted in determining congressional districts until 1924, they were not included in the ten-year federal censuses, but were counted at various times in special enumerations. This site provides a detailed explanation and connections to the available sources. Also see http://www.accessgenealogy.com/native/.

For Native American mailing lists, see http://lists.rootsweb.com/index/other/Ethnic-Native/.

The Online Genealogical Database

http://gentree.com/gentree.html

This site contains links to all known databases on the Web. Family sites are included only if a database is available for searching.

Tracing Your Native American Genealogy (Carolyne's Genealogy Helper)

http://www.angelfire.com/tx/carolynegenealogy/

Tracing Native American family history presents unusual difficulties. Carolyne Gould provides help through the maze of confusing resources.

USGS National Mapping Information Query Form

http://geonames.usgs.gov/pls/gnis/web_query.gnis_web_query_form

For those doing genealogical research, this Geological Survey Query Form is useful for locating obscure population centers, cemeteries, and other sites in the United States. In most cases, users can obtain the coordinates and also maps indicating the locations. Many Canadian sites may be seen at http://atlas. gc.ca/site/english/sitemap/index.html. Maps for other places in the world are at http://uk2.multimap.com.

Chapter 29

Environmental History

David Calverley

Metasites

American Society for Environmental History

http://www.h-net.org/~environ/ASEH/welcome_IE4.html

ASEH is one of the most important environmental history organizations in North America. This site provides information about available academic positions in environmental history and upcoming conferences such as the annual conference sponsored by ASEH. The Resources link provides connections not only to additional Web sites, but also to online essays concerned with various historiographical themes in environmental history. Through the Publications link users can access a number of online versions of the society's quarterly journal *Environmental History.* The journal (available on the History Cooperative Web site) is useful not only for its articles, but for the extensive annotated bibliography in each issue of books, articles, and academic theses in environmental history.

Environmental History on the Internet

http://www.cnr.berkeley.edu/departments/espm/env-hist/eh-internet.html

Although this site provides a large collection of links, it is not well developed as the links are simply listed with the appropriate title and affiliation but no annotation. Furthermore, some of the links are no longer active. Researchers can use the broken links and Web site titles to search the Internet; patience and typing will lead to the updated Web sites and URLs. Despite these shortcomings, the variety of links provided (ranging from local to national to international environmental history) makes this a useful site for researchers and students.

H-Environment

http://www.h-net.org/~environ/

H-Environment is part of the larger H-Net (History Network) system, which is maintained to develop various Internet-based historical resources. This particular discussion chain on environmental history contains links to bibliographies, scholarly reviews of recent monographs, syllabi in environmental history universities from around the world, and various Web pages. It also provides a very useful discussion list to join for users interested in environmental history. List members can post requests for information and aid from other members, often receiving detailed responses in return. Online debates and discussions are also lively and at times entertaining. This is a scholarly site, but useful for students seeking bibliographic help from other listserv members.

General Sites

American Museum of Natural History

http://www.amnh.org/

This site offers links pertaining to various environmental historical issues. Of particular interest is the Resources to Learning link that highlights a number of the Web pages and resources maintained by the museum.

Association for Environmental Archaeology

http://www.envarch.net/

Very academic in its structure and content, this association's Web site contains links to archaeological and related sites that are concerned with the environment. The association lists upcoming conferences and provides its newsletter to download (as PDF files) and a listing of articles in its journal, *Environmental Archaeology: The Journal of Human Palaeoecology*.

Cultural Environmental Studies

http://www.wsu.edu/~amerstu/ce/ce.html

Maintained by Wisconsin State University, this site attempts to meld environmental history with other subfields of history: women's history, ethnic studies, regional studies, etc. It provides useful resources, including links to "learning modules" dealing with various elements of environmental history. There are also links to a variety of sites ranging from pop culture depictions of the environment to indigenous peoples, environmental art, justice, and writings. In addition, the site offers an excellent annotated bibliography of print resources.

Environmental History of Latin America: On-Line Bibliography

http://www.stanford.edu/group/LAEH/index.html

This site is useful for its extensive bibliography (over 600 references). The bibliography is divided by region (Amazon, Andes, Brazil, etc.). Regional bibliographies contain books (with some links to reviews) and articles. There are also several bibliographies providing information about video documentaries and Internet links pertaining to Latin America.

Environmental History Timeline

http://www.radford.edu/~wkovarik/envhist/

Bill Kovarik of Radford University, Virginia, maintains this site. The time line portion of the site is very detailed, providing a good overview of world environmental history. The site includes a useful bibliography of print resources and an interesting history of events in American environmental history, such as the addition of lead to gasoline and the resulting environmental and health problems that occurred.

The Evolution of the Conservation Movement, 1850–1920

http://lcweb2.loc.gov/ammem/amrvhtml/conshome.html

Maintained by the Library of Congress, this site offers an excellent overview of U.S. environmental history through its detailed chronology. The chronology has embedded links to various primary and secondary documents on the Web page. Of particular interest to senior researchers is the access provided to the Library of Congress's digitized environmental collection, complete with call numbers and links for each item to other archival materials. There are also streaming videos of the collection's films, such as the building of the Theodore Roosevelt Dam. This site should be supplemented with the library's Conservation and Environment map link (http://memory.loc.gov/ammem/gmdhtml/cnsvhome.html).

Nature Transformed: The Environment in American History

http://www.nhc.rtp.nc.us/tserve/nattrans/nattrans.htm

Operated by the National Humanities Center, this site offers useful short essays for teachers who want to incorporate environmental history into their classrooms. Leading U.S. historians and high school teachers worked to create the site, and senior U.S. scholars such as Shepard Krech III and Alfred Crosby wrote the essays. Each essay offers a strong general overview of key issues in American environmental history in addition to a number of useful links to various Web sites concerned with the same topic.

The Time Line of Waste

http://www.st-andrews.ac.uk/%7Ewaste/timeline/index.htm

Maintained by the Arts and Humanities Research Board Research Center for Environmental History at the University of Stirling in Scotland, this site is part of the center's research projects into waste management and wastelands. The site offers a basic chronological breakdown, starting in the year 500 CE and divided into sections continuing to the late twentieth century, of perceptions and policy treatment of wastewater and wastelands in Europe. The clear, straightforward writing provides a useful overview of this particular facet of environmental history. This Web site is very useful for senior high school and junior undergraduate students and for teachers who want to integrate environmental history into their classrooms.

U.S. Environmental History

http://www.mtsu.edu/~lnelson/Environmental-History.html

Dr. Lynn Nelson of Middle Tennessee State University maintains this site as part of his environmental history course. It is useful for its astounding number of links to various government, nongovernmental, academic, and professional organizations concerned with environmental history and environmental themes—links that some of the other Web sites listed in this chapter overlook. There are also links to biographies of important individuals in environmental history. While the site is designed simply, the first section provides page links to various sections on the Web page. These links are well maintained and direct the researcher to other online resources.

Chapter 30

Immigration History

Pamela Grey

Ancestors in the Americas

http://www.cetel.org/

http://www.pbs.org/kbyu/ancestors/resourceguide/

This Public Broadcasting Service video series, at the first site, focuses on the immigration of Asians to the Americas from the 1700s through the 1900s. The series uses a "documemoir" approach involving personal narrative. Narrated QuickTime video clips can be played without additional software. Primary documents, a time line, and viewer guides provide materials and questions that are appropriate for secondary or college-level courses. The site also has an extensive listing of snail mail addresses and links. The second site is a more extensive related research site, Ancestors: Resource Guide.

The Cabildo Online Project

http://lsm.crt.state.la.us/cabildo/cab8.htm

This site gives a brief overview of both forced immigration to New Orleans and the arrival of those who came as a less expensive alternative to entry at New York Harbor: New Orleans was the second leading port of entry between 1820 and 1860.

Center for Immigration Studies

http://www.cis.org/

This conservative think tank is devoted "exclusively to research and policy analysis of the economic, social, demographic, fiscal, and other impacts of immigration on the United States." The site is organized around topical themes and features timely immigration news and an interactive question and answer book. It is an excellent resource for the conservative protectionist viewpoint.

The Data and Program Library Service

http://dpls.dacc.wisc.edu/slavedata/index.html

The University of Wisconsin-Madison, through this site, offers an online data archive of the movement of forced labor during the eighteenth and nineteenth centuries. The site lists slave ship movements, raw data, and documentation of the slave ships and trade between England, Cuba, France, Brazil, and Virginia during the two centuries.

Digital History: Using New Technology to Enhance Teaching and Research

http://www.digitalhistory.uh.edu/historyonline/ethnic_am.cfm

Jointly sponsored by the History Department and the School of Education at the University of Houston, this site includes a searchable index of 1,500 links and more than 400 annotated documents, maps, speeches, and films. Linked primary print sources include African-American, Mexican-American, Native American, and Asian-American voices; a chronology of immigration history; and a featured online exhibit on Chinese immigrants and the Transcontinental Railroad. Separate links include stereopticon slides of Irish-American immigrants and readings on Italian-Americans. The Huddled Masses is a guided reading giving definitions, suggested study questions, and movies appropriate for secondary and college students.

The History Channel's Ellis Island Scrapbook

http://www.historychannel.com/ellisisland/index2.html

This interactive Ellis Island scrapbook provides photographs and narratives of immigrants' experiences on Ellis Island.

The Immigration History Research Center

http://www.ihrc.umn.edu/

This center, founded in 1965 at the University of Minnesota, aims to provide information about immigration. The goal of Collections Online: A Digital

Library of American Immigration and Ethnic History (COLLAGE) is to provide "public access to primary documents for K–12 education." Users can search with an online tool for photographs, documents, and text passages from sites including the International Institute of San Francisco, the National Park Service, and the National Trust for Historic Preservation. Over thirty ethnic groups are represented in the collections.

Immigration: Library of Congress

http://memory.loc.gov/learn/features/immig/alt/introduction.html

This project of the American Memory Collection of the Library of Congress links to a wide variety of immigrant experiences. Among those featured are Native American, African, German, Irish, Scandinavian, Italian, Japanese, Mexican, Chinese, Cuban, Puerto Rican, Polish, and Russian. Images can be used at any grade level. Text is appropriate for advanced upper elementary classes through college level. Each immigrant group is examined in detail through text, artifacts, and images. Topical lesson plans, resources, and bibliographies are linked from the site.

The Lower East Side Tenement Museum

http://www.tenement.org/

This virtual museum experience provides teaching materials, artifacts, and the tenement. The virtual tour takes visitors through the lives of the 10,000 residents who lived at 97 Orchard Street between 1870 and 1915 in an effort to promote understanding, historical perspective, and tolerance of the immigrant experience on Manhattan's Lower East Side. The site uses QuickTime panorama and RealPlayer applications in a video and audio tour illustrating the lives of the immigrants who called the rooms home. Excavation details and examination of individual artifacts are a highlight of the site. The museum is a founder of the International Coalition of Historic Site Museums of Conscience.

The Making of America (MoA)

http://moa.cit.cornell.edu/moa/ (Cornell)

http://www.hti.umich.edu/m/moagrp/ (Michigan)

This joint project of Cornell University and the University of Michigan was funded by the Andrew W. Mellon Foundation. MoA includes more than 70,000 digital images and 3.5 million pages covering the history of the United States from the antebellum period through Reconstruction. Cornell adds over 910,000 pages to this joint project. Images are appropriate for classes from middle school through college. Selected images can be used at the elementary levels.

The Migration Policy Institute

http://www.migrationpolicy.org/research/usimmigration.php

This is an independent think tank dedicated to the study of the worldwide movement of people. The page referenced above provides background papers for journalists and policy makers, links to statistics and analysis on refugee protection, immigration policy, and bibliographic materials.

Jacob Riis' *How the Other Half Lives*

http://www.cis.yale.edu/amstud/inforev/riis/title.html

Jacob Riis documented the immigrant experience in an early forerunner of the field of photojournalism. This site presents a hypertext edition of *How the Other Half Lives: Studies Among the Tenements of New York,* which was originally published in 1890.

Statue of Liberty—Ellis Island Foundation, Inc.

http://www.ellisisland.org/

This site provides a search of passenger arrival records. Users enter the name, gender, and approximate date of birth of an immigrant to call up records. The database includes over 25 million names. Links include secondary and college-level material about starting genealogical research. Free registration is necessary to view immigration records.

Statue of Liberty National Monument and Ellis Island

http://www.americanparknetwork.com/parkinfo/sl/index.html

This Web site provides facts about the Statue of Liberty and the Ellis Island immigrant station. It features a time line, statistics on immigration, and the newcomer photographs of Augustus Sherman. The site is an excellent introduction to basic photography that uses the Statue of Liberty as a focal point in asking students to tell their own family stories through photography.

The Story of Africa: Slavery

http://www.bbc.co.uk/worldservice/africa/features/storyofafrica/index_section9.shtml

In this radio series the BBC World Service gives a detailed history of peoples of the African continent, resistance movements, the Atlantic slave trade, the journey, and resettlement efforts.

Talking Walls: The Barracks on Angel Island

http://www.riverdeep.net/talkingwalls/angelisland/

Angel Island Immigration Station Foundation http://www.aiisf.org/

Angel Island Immigration Station http://people.lib.ucdavis.edu/tss/punjab/
angelisland.html

Angel Island was the Pacific gateway for West Coast immigration from 1910
until 1940.

The first site introduces Angel Island to elementary age visitors. The second
provides background material on the island and the immigrant experience. The
third site provides current photos of the island and an interactive link to island
arrival records. It is geared for high school or college readers.

UNESCO: Virtual Visit of Goree Island

http://webworld.unesco.org/goree/

This interactive video tour, with text, details the experiences of forced African
laborers who were taken from the prison called "The House of Slaves," constructed in 1776, in the present-day Republic of Senegal.

The University of California, Riverside, Keystone-Mast Collection, California Museum of Photography

http://photo.ucr.edu/projects/immigration

Stereoscopic photographic slides produced by the Keystone View Company,
Underwood and Underwood, and the H.C. White Company illustrate immigration from 1900 to 1920. The slides show Ellis Island and the immigrant
experience in New York City.

U.S. Citizenship and Immigration Services

http://uscis.gov/graphics/index.htm

This site offers a comprehensive overview of the government agency, required
forms, laws and regulations, and a glossary of terms. The site is presented at
a high school reading level. The Web page also offers links to immigration
statistics, U.S. Customs and Border Protection, and the Student Exchange and
Visitor information.

U.S. Citizenship and Immigration Services: History, Genealogy, and Education

http://uscis.gov/graphics/aboutus/history/

This site has specific links to the National Archives and catalogs immigration
points of entry by state and territory and includes Chinese Immigrant files.

U.S. Immigration on the Internet Modern History Sourcebook Project

http://www.fordham.edu/halsall/mod/modsbook28.html

This metasite includes arguments for and against immigration, links to sites arranged by ethnicity and race, and primary documents related to immigration.

Chapter 31

State and Provincial Historical Societies
Canada and United States

Thomas Saylor

Metasite

National Council on Public History
http://www.ncph.org/
Listing of publications, resources, activities, and useful links.

Canada

Canada's National History Society
http://www.historysociety.ca/
Extensive listing of archives, government departments, libraries, museums, organizations, and publications.

Historical Society of Alberta
http://www.albertahistory.org/

British Columbia Historical Federation
http://www.bchistory.ca/

Fédération des Sociétés d'histoire du Quebec
http://www.histoirequebec.qc.ca/

Manitoba Historical Society
http://www.mhs.mb.ca/

Newfoundland Historical Society
http://www.infonet.st-johns.nf.ca/providers/nfldhist/

The Ontario Historical Society
http://www.ontariohistoricalsociety.ca/

Prince Edward Island Museum and Heritage Foundation
http://www.gov.pe.ca/peimhf/

Royal Nova Scotia Historical Society
http://nsgna.ednet.ns.ca/rnshs/

Saskatchewan History and Folklore Society
http://www.shfs.ca/

Yukon Historical and Museums Association
http://www.yukonalaska.com/yhma/

United States

Alabama Department of Archives and History
http://www.archives.state.al.us/

Alaska Historical Society

http://www.alaskahistoricalsociety.org/

Arizona Historical Society

http://www.ahs.state.az.us/

http://www.arizonahistoricalsociety.org/

Arkansas Historical Association

http://www.uark.edu/depts/arkhist/home

California Historical Society

http://www.californiahistoricalsociety.org/

Colorado Historical Society

http://www.coloradohistory.org/

Connecticut Historical Society

http://www.chs.org/

The Historical Society of Delaware

http://www.hsd.org/

Florida Historical Society

http://www.florida-historical-soc.org/

Georgia Historical Society

http://www.georgiahistory.com/

The Hawaiian Historical Society

http://www.hawaiianhistory.org/

Idaho State Historical Society

http://www.idahohistory.net/

Illinois State Historical Society

http://www.historyillinois.org/

Indiana Historical Society

http://www.indianahistory.org/

State Historical Society of Iowa

http://www.iowahistory.org/

The Kansas State Historical Society

http://www.kshs.org/

Kentucky Historical Society

http://history.ky.gov/

Louisiana Historical Society

http://www.louisianahistoricalsociety.org/

Maine Historical Society

http://www.mainehistory.org/

Maryland Historical Society

http://www.mdhs.org/

Massachusetts Historical Society

http://www.masshist.org/

Michigan Historical Center

http://www.michigan.gov/hal/0,1607,7-160-17445_19273---,00.html

Minnesota Historical Society

http://www.mnhs.org/

Mississippi Department of Archives and History

http://www.mdah.state.ms.us/

Missouri Historical Society

http://www.mohistory.org/

Montana Historical Society

http://www.his.state.mt.us/

Nebraska State Historical Society

http://www.nebraskahistory.org/

Nevada Historical Society

http://dmla.clan.lib.nv.us/docs/museums/reno/his-soc.htm

New Hampshire Historical Society

http://www.nhhistory.org/

New Jersey Historical Society

http://www.jerseyhistory.org/

Historical Society of New Mexico

http://www.hsnm.org/

New York Historical Society

http://www.nyhistory.org/

North Carolina Office of Archives and History

http://www.ah.dcr.state.nc.us/

State Historical Society of North Dakota

http://www.state.nd.us/hist/

Ohio Historical Society

http://www.ohiohistory.org/

Oklahoma Historical Society

http://www.ok-history.mus.ok.us/

Oregon Historical Society

http://www.ohs.org/

The Historical Society of Pennsylvania

http://www.hsp.org/

Rhode Island Historical Society

http://www.rihs.org/

South Carolina Historical Society

http://www.schistory.org/

South Dakota State Historical Association

http://www.sdhistory.org/

Tennessee Historical Society

http://www.tennesseehistory.org/

Texas Historical Commission

http://www.thc.state.tx.us/

Texas State Historical Association

http://www.tsha.utexas.edu/

Utah State Historical Society/Division of State History

http://history.utah.gov/

Vermont Historical Society

http://www.vermonthistory.org/

Virginia Historical Society

http://www.vahistorical.org/

Washington State Historical Society

http://www.washingtonhistory.org/wshs/

West Virginia Division of Culture and History

http://www.wvculture.org/

Wisconsin Historical Society

http://www.wisconsinhistory.org/

Wyoming State Historical Society

http://wyshs.org/

Chapter 32

History Book Sources on the Internet

Mariah Hudson

Book Search Networks

In the past few years the trend in bookselling on the Internet has been the consolidation of independent sellers' book holdings onto large book search network sites. These search networks have greatly contributed to the ease of locating academic and popular books by minimizing search efforts. Another advantage of search networks is that many compare prices and offer multiple copies of the same title, allowing users to select the book condition. Many search sites also offer a quality guarantee and have standardized no-hassle return policies. Almost all Web sites now take credit cards or Paypal. When available, the listing will indicate the number of categories for browsing and the approximate number of titles currently available.

Advanced Book Exchange

http://www.abebooks.com

ABE claims to be the world's largest online bookseller, and the selection of history titles is truly impressive. ABE offers used and new, rare and out-of-print books and is one of the best sites for locating books published before 1900. It offers more than 365,000 titles on general history, 380,000 titles on military history, and 47,000 titles on medieval and Renaissance history. Unfortunately, ABE does not have subcategories by time period, which would make browsing easier.

Alibris

http://www.alibris.com

Alibris offers new and used books, only a small proportion of which are rare books. Alibris is well indexed with fifty-five geographic and topical search categories. Browsing is made easy by clearly indexed subtopics; there are fifteen topics under U.S. history and twenty under military history. A separate textbook search is available.

Amazon.com

http://www.amazon.com

Amazon is teamed up with Borders and offers mostly new books, though some used books are available through independent sellers who list books on the site. History books are organized by thirteen geographic and topical categories. There are eight searchable subcategories for U.S. history and sixteen for military history. One noteworthy feature is Amazon's searchable selection of historical journals, documentaries, software, and DVDs.

Antiqbook

http://www.antiqbook.com/

Antiqbook sells primarily used books and specializes in antiquarian works, making this a first stop for rare or out-of-print European works and a highly recommended site for antiquarian and rare book searches in general. This site includes selections from hundreds of individual sellers. Many of the sellers are in Europe; however, there are over a hundred history booksellers in the United States. The Antiqbook site is well organized and cross-indexed by geographic region, time period, and subspecialty.

Barnes and Noble

http://www.bn.com

Barnes and Noble features popular new works and a limited selection of used books provided by independent dealers. While its prices are not significantly lower than the cover price, fast shipping and local in-store searches are two features that make this site worthwhile if you need a book in a hurry. Two unique features are searches by Nobel Prize or National Book Award winners and finalists, and searches by price. The prereserve feature gives the option of preordering soon-to-be-released books.

Best Book Buys

http://www.bestwebbuys.com/books

Currently listing 195,584 history books on eighty-five topics, this well-categorized site has one of the largest selections of new books online. Best Book Buys searches and compares prices at several of the major book dealers on the Internet, including Alibris, Amazon, and Barnes and Noble. BBB is a recommended site for in-print books searches and price comparisons.

Biblio

http://www.biblio.com

Biblio sells from the inventories of hundreds of independent booksellers. It claims to have 14 million new and used books, of which 10 percent are history titles. Biblio has an extensive collection of African-American, military, regional and women's histories. A community bulletin board offers a forum to exchange ideas with other collectors.

Bibliology

http://www.bibliology.com

Though Bibliology has a poor interface for general searches, making browsing nearly impossible, it has a large selection of rare books from sellers around the globe and coordinates the sale of primary documents and manuscripts from private dealers. A recommended primary document source.

Bookfinder

http://www.bookfinder.com

Bookfinder searches all the major book networks, including Amazon, Powell's, and Alibris. Bookfinder is best for specific book searches. While the specificity of the search function makes browsing tedious, one useful feature is a search for books in different languages (mainly French, German, and Spanish).

Books and Book Collecting at Trussel

http://www.trussel.com/f_books.htm

Trussel does not sell books, but provides a wealth of information on local resources and dozens of independent dealers.

Half.com

http://half.ebay.com

Half offers new and used books at half off the cover price or less. Half, a subsidiary of eBay, displays books for sale through eBay on the bottom of the screen with price information, which is helpful for comparing prices and makes searching eBay unnecessary. This site allows individuals to list books and has an extensive selection of academic and popular books. History titles are listed with nonfiction works.

International League of Antiquarian Booksellers

http://www.ilab-lila.com

ILAB coordinates the sale of books and documents through its member sites, of which there are hundreds. ILAB has some of the most specific search features available and offers access to the inventories of small booksellers across the globe, making it one of the best book search networks for rare and antiquarian books.

Massachusetts and Rhode Island Antiquarian Booksellers

http://www.mariab.org

MARIAB, an organization for sellers of rare books in New England, has been in business for twenty-nine years. Though MARIAB does not sell books, it has detailed information on the holdings of over 150 booksellers, as well as dozens of online catalogs and search services. This site is a must stop for locating rare early American books and primary sources.

Tom Folio

http://www.tomfolio.com

Tom Folio is an extensive search network site, hosting more than a hundred American bookstores listed by region as well as many more international sellers. There are ten geographic search categories with tens of thousands of new and used titles available.

Independent Book Sellers

Although books search networks have improved the ease of finding fairly common books, individual booksellers are by no means an obsolete search source. Independent booksellers may provide a better selection of scholarly, rare, and antiquarian books, because networks often offer only a fraction of a seller's inventory and may exclude less common works. The list below represents a few of the many independent sellers that do not list inventory on search networks or those whose collections are not fully listed elsewhere. The location is listed for booksellers who have bookshops; the rest are online only. Specialized bookstores frequently offer a phone search for titles and documents that are not online. Many also offer book location services.

2ndHandBooks.com

http://www.2ndHandBooks.com

E-mail: books@2ndHandBooks.com

Used rare and out-of-print books. Specialties: U.S., Africa, Renaissance, medieval, European, natural history. Number of history titles: thousands. Location: Metairie, Louisiana.

Alden Books

http://www.aldenbooks.com/

E-mail: info@aldenbooks.com

New and used scholarly works. Specialties: North America, Asia. Number of history titles: 2,500+.

Asia Book Room

http://www.OldBookroom.com

E-mail: books@AsiaBookroom.com

Specialty: Asia, Middle East, Pacific, Africa. Number of history titles: 15,000+. Location: Australia.

Book Close Outs

http://www.bookcloseouts.com

E-mail: service@bookcloseouts.com

Popular new and used bargain books. Specialty: ancient, Asian, biography, world. Number of history titles: 10,300. Location: New York City; Ontario, Canada.

Books Unlimited

http://www.booksunlimited.com

E-mail: otierney@booksunlimited.com

New and used popular books, some scholarly works. Specialty: general, U.S. history. Number of history titles: 10,000+. Location: Denver.

Comenius-Antiquariat

http://www.comenius-antiquariat.com/english

E-mail: 2005@comenius-antiquariat.ch

Used and rare books, many of which are in German. Specialty: Swiss history. Number of history titles: 6,500+. Location: Switzerland.

Ed Conroy Bookseller

http://www.edconroybooks.com

E-mail: info@edconroybooks.com

Primarily used books. Specialties: military, modern European. Number of history titles: 35,000+.

D.K. Publishers Distributors Ltd.

https://www.dkpd.com/servlet/dkHome

E-mail: order@dkpd.com

New books. Specialty: India, Asia. Number of titles: 75,000, more than 10 percent in history. Location: India.

E-books

http://www.ebooks.com/

E-books offers recent academic and popular history books as digital selections on forty-four topics and regions. Selection is limited, but downloading makes purchasing convenient. Specialties: U.S., European, ancient history. Number of history titles: 1,000+.

Editions

http://www.nleditions.com

E-mail: info@nleditions.com

Primarily new or gently used; all hardback. Selections are updated weekly. Specialties: none, but 2,000 U.S. titles. Number of history titles: 20,000+ online, 70,000 not listed online, but accessible by phone. Location: Boiceville, New York.

Great Northwest Bookstore

http://www.greatnorthwestbooks.com

E-mail: gnworders@greatnorthwestbooks.com

Primarily used books; much of the extensive stock is not yet online. GNB offers phone searches for unusual or rare titles. Specialty: American, Western. Number of history titles: 40,000+. Location: Portland, Oregon.

Ground Zero Books Ltd.

http://www.groundzerobooksltd.com

E-mail: info@groundzerobooksltd.com

New, used, scholarly, rare, and out-of-print military history books. Specialties: military, the history of war. Number of history titles: 53,000+.

History Wiz Books

http://books.historywiz.org

E-mail: eeyore@books.historywiz.org

New and used books. The collections of eighteenth-century, African-American, and American Revolution titles make this a worthwhile site for Americanists. Specialties: European, U.S., world. Number of history titles: 1,000+.

Labyrinth Books

http://www.labyrinthbooks.com

E-mail: books@labyrinthbooks.com

New and used book selection dedicated to scholarly and university press works. Specialties: European, world, women's, U.S., New York City. Number of titles: 155,000, of which more than 25 percent are history. Location: New York City.

David M. Lesser, Fine Antiquarian Books LLC

http://www.lesserbooks.com

E-mail: dmlesser@lesserbooks.com

Dedicated to American history, David M. Lesser offers used and rare American books and documents. Specialties: American colonial and Revolution. Number of history titles: 10,000+. Location: online site also offers print catalogs.

Parmer Books

http://www.stairway.org/parmer/index.html

E-mail: ParmerBook@aol.com

Primarily used and academic; most of Parmer's stock is historical. Specialties: Western, Pacific, exploration. Number of history titles: 4,000. Location: San Diego.

The Personal Navigator

http://www1.shore.net/~persnav/

E-mail: persnav@shore.net

Used rare and antiquarian books and documents. Specialties: military, American, nineteenth-century. Number of history titles: 1,000+.

Mark Post, Bookseller

http://www.markpostbooks.com

E-mail: markpost1@earthlink.net

Primarily used antiquarian and rare books. Specialties: America, Europe, colonial Africa. Number of history titles: 3,300+. Location: San Francisco.

Powell's

http://www.powells.com/

E-mail: help@powells.com

Highly recommended site for new, used, rare, and out-of-print works with a large proportion of academic books. Specialties: U.S., European, military. Number of history titles: over 100,000. Location: Portland, Oregon.

Primary Source On-Line History Bookstore

http://www.historesearch.com/bookstore.html

E-mail: jmike@snowcrest.net

New and used scholarly monographs and textbooks. Specialties: ancient, Western. Number of history titles: 1,000+.

Serendipity Books

http://members.iinet.net.au/~serendip/

E-mail: books@serendipitybooks.com.au

New and used academic titles. Specialties: Australia, Southeast Asia. Number of history books: 11,000+. Location: Perth, Western Australia.

Xerxes Books

http://www.xerxesbooks.com

E-mail: catra@xerxesbooks.com

Offers used and out-of-print books. Highly recommended site for works published before 1900. Specialties: scholarly, general history. Number of history titles: 27,000. Location: Glen Head, New York.

Chapter 33

History and Social Studies Organizations

Stephen Kneeshaw

American Historical Association

http://www.historians.org/

The American Historical Association traditionally has served historians in all disciplines through a variety of member services. In recent years the AHA has given more time and attention to the needs of precollegiate teachers. The home page for the AHA provides information on the association and on more than a hundred affiliated societies, selected articles from the newsletter *Perspectives*, a calendar of historical events, and a "primer" on how the AHA serves K–12 teachers in history. Some sections of the Web site are available only to members.

The Historical Society

http://www.bu.edu/historic/index.html

By its self-description, the Historical Society wishes "to revitalize the study and teaching of history by reorienting the historical profession toward an accessible, integrated history free from fragmentation and over-specialization." The society offers historians an open forum for "frank debate" on issues critical to the historical profession. The Web site includes a table of contents for *The Journal of the Historical Society* and *Historically Speaking* (newsletter) and snippets of the published materials, but full access requires membership in the society.

The History Cooperative

http://www.historycooperative.org

Although technically not an "organization," the History Cooperative provides online connection to the journals of several professional associations, including the *American Historical Review* and the *Journal of American History.* This service began in 2000 as a cooperative venture of the American Historical Association, the Organization of American Historians, the University of Illinois Press, and the National Academy Press. Users can access electronic versions of articles in current issues and some past issues. Many of the journals are "ungated," but some, such as the *AHR* and *JAH,* require membership for full access.

History News Network

http://hnn.us/

Developed and run through the Center for History at George Mason University, the History News Network offers a daily listing of materials that should interest historians who teach and those who prefer research. In sections such as Hot Topics, Breaking News, and Culture Watch, readers can follow developing stories, read the thoughts of historians from a wide range of print and online sources, and get daily thoughts from historians-as-bloggers who respond to the contemporary events. The Teacher's Lounge provides a useful section on Memories and teaching suggestions for 9/11 and also discusses other notable events.

H-NCH—National Coalition for History

http://www.h-net.org/~nch/

H-NCH is "the official electronic voice" of the National Coalition for History (formerly the National Coordinating Committee for the Promotion of History), which supports history and historians in the political circles of Washington, DC, and the American states. The Web site provides a connection to past issues of *Washington Updates* (1997–present), describing the work of NCH and its lobbying successes.

National Council for History Education

http://www.history.org/nche

The NCHE Web site is more useful than many organizational sites because it goes well beyond descriptions of NCHE and its programs. For example, History Links sends a user to a diverse mix of sites: Web sites for historical organizations; history education sites; links of interest to social studies educators; and repositories of primary sources, promoted as "a listing of over 3000 websites . . . for the research scholar."

NCSS Online—National Council for the Social Studies

http://www.ncss.org

NCSS Online offers Web-based information services for the National Council for the Social Studies, the largest umbrella organization for social studies educators. This site promotes NCSS, which is to be expected, but it also provides links for professional development, standards and curriculum, and teaching resources.

Organization of American Historians

http://www.oah.org/

The Organization of American Historians is the premier professional association for United States history. But beyond its service to college and university teachers and researchers, OAH serves precollegiate history teachers through such means as the *OAH Magazine of History* and outreach programs described on this Web site. A link to History Teaching Units introduces lesson plans for grades 6–12 based on primary documents developed by the OAH in concert with the National Center for History in the Schools at the University of California at Los Angeles.

Society for History Education—*The History Teacher*

http://www.thehistoryteacher.org/

This Web site for the Society for History Education, which publishes *The History Teacher,* links the organization and the journal together through the Web server at California State University at Long Beach, where the journal is housed. The Web site provides a current table of contents for current and past issues of *The History Teacher,* links to related organizations, and contact information for the society and the journal.

Chapter 34

Maps and Images

Martin V. Minner

Maps—Metasites

Cartographic and Spatial Data on the Internet

http://www.lib.uchicago.edu/e/su/maps/mapweb.html

A collection of map links compiled at the University of Chicago. Emphasizes Chicago and Illinois.

Map History/History of Cartography

http://www.maphistory.info/index.html

A gateway site with thousands of map history links for professional historians and amateur researchers. A companion site provides links to many map images.

Odden's Bookmarks

http://oddens.geog.uu.nl/index.php

An extensive site at Utrecht University providing a searchable list of more than 22,000 links to cartographic sites, map collections, and other map resources.

Perry-Castañeda Map Collection— Historical Map Web Sites

http://www.lib.utexas.edu/maps/map_sites/hist_sites.html

Compiled by the Perry-Castañeda Library at the University of Texas, this site offers a wide-ranging list of links to historical map Web sites. The scope is global.

Selected Map Sites

Aiabama Maps

http://alabamamaps.ua.edu/

More than 6,000 digitized maps from the University of Alabama Map Library.

Cartographic Modeling Lab

http://cml.upenn.edu/

The University of Pennsylvania's Cartographic Modeling Lab provides re-sources for Geographic Information Systems (GIS) research and offers online versions of the lab's projects.

Civil War Maps

http://lcweb2.loc.gov/ammem/collections/civil_war_maps/

Offers digitized Civil War maps from the Library of Congress, the Virginia Historical Society, and the Library of Virginia.

Color Landform Atlas of the United States

http://fermi.jhuapl.edu/states/

Provides a variety of maps for each of the fifty states, including topographical maps, satellite images, county maps, and scans from an 1895 atlas.

Cultural Maps

http://xroads.virginia.edu/~MAP/map_hp.html

An American studies project at the University of Virginia, this site seeks to create an American historical atlas examining the physical landscape as well as mapmakers' mental and cultural terrain.

Early Washington Maps: A Digital Collection

http://www.wsulibs.wsu.edu/holland/masc/xmaps.html

A searchable collection of maps and bird's-eye views from Washington State University.

Earth Sciences and Map Library, University of California-Berkeley

http://library.berkeley.edu/EART/MapCollections.html

Several thousand digitized maps, including a strong California collection.

Harvard Map Collection

http://hcl.harvard.edu/maps/

Provides detailed online viewing of two sixteenth-century Mercator globes.

Historical City Maps

http://www.library.yale.edu/MapColl/cities.html

Yale University Library's online collection of American and European city maps.

Historic Cities

http://historic-cities.huji.ac.il/historic_cities.html

A project at the Hebrew University of Jerusalem featuring a worldwide collection of historical city maps.

IEG-Maps

http://www.ieg-maps.uni-mainz.de/

A collection of Central European maps since 1812 at the Institute for European History in Mainz.

John R. Borchert Map Library, University of Minnesota

http://www-map.lib.umn.edu/

Provides research tools and a substantial list of map library links.

Lewis & Clark: The Maps of Exploration 1507–1814

http://www.lib.virginia.edu/small/exhibits/lewis_clark/home.html

Based on an exhibit at the University of Virginia's Alderman Library, this site examines the Lewis and Clark expedition and the history of North American cartography from Columbus to Jefferson.

Library of Congress Geography and Maps: An Illustrated Guide

http://www.loc.gov/rr/geogmap/guide/

This site, an introduction to the Library of Congress's cartographic collections, features selected images in a variety of subject areas.

Making Sense of Maps

http://historymatters.gmu.edu/mse/maps/

An introduction to the use of maps as historical evidence. Includes interactive exercises and a bibliography.

Map Collections: 1500–2004

http://lcweb2.loc.gov/ammem/gmdhtml/gmdhome.html

Part of the Library of Congress's American Memory project, this site provides online images in the following subject areas: cities and towns, conservation and the environment, discovery and exploration, cultural landscapes, military battles and campaigns, transportation, and general maps.

Map Division, New York Public Library

http://www.nypl.org/research/chss/map/map.html

Provides sample images from the library's map collections.

MapHist

http://www.maphist.nl/

The MapHist e-mail discussion group for map historians maintains an online archive of maps that have been discussed on the list.

Maps of the Pimería: Early Cartography of the Southwest

http://dizzy.library.arizona.edu/branches/spc/set/pimeria/welcome.html

Based on maps from the University of Arizona Library Map Collection, this exhibit examines the cartographic history of the region of New Spain encompassing what is now southern Arizona and northern Sonora.

National Geographic: Maps and Geography

http://www.nationalgeographic.com/maps/

The online version of *National Geographic* provides a variety of map resources.

The Newberry Library

http://www.newberry.org/

The Newberry Library's site includes bibliographic material on the library's maps and history of cartography collections and sample images.

New York State Historical Maps

http://www.sunysb.edu/libmap/nymaps.htm

Offers annotated online maps of New York State from 1556 to 1895.

Osher Map Library

http://www.usm.maine.edu/~maps/

This site provides online versions of exhibits that have appeared at the Osher Map Library and Smith Center for Cartographic Education at the University of Southern Maine.

Philadelphia—Maps and Geographic Information

http://www.library.upenn.edu/datasets/philamaps.html

Provides a variety of historical and contemporary maps of Philadelphia.

The Ryhiner Map Collection

http://biblio.unibe.ch/stub/ryhiner/

Thousands of digitized maps, with an emphasis on Switzerland.

University of Georgia Rare Map Collection

http://scarlett.libs.uga.edu/darchive/hargrett/maps/maps.html

The University of Georgia's Hargrett Rare Book and Manuscript Library provides online images of many historical maps from its collection, with an emphasis on maps of Georgia.

University of Michigan Map Library

http://www.lib.umich.edu/maplib/

Online maps of Michigan and a collection of Web links.

The U.S. Civil War Center

http://www.cwc.lsu.edu/links/links3.htm#Maps

The U.S. Civil War Center, a division of Louisiana State University Libraries Special Collections, has compiled a list of links to Civil War maps. Other portions of the site provide links to images and multimedia.

The Walker Collection: Maps of Asia Minor and the Middle East, 1511–1774

http://www.lib.unimelb.edu.au/collections/maps/digital/walker.html

A completely digitized collection of 135 maps at the University of Melbourne.

Images—Metasites

ArtServe

http://rubens.anu.edu.au/

The Australian National University's ArtServe site provides links to worldwide art and architecture sites, primarily emphasizing the Mediterranean region, Japan, and India.

Images Canada: Picturing Canadian Culture

http://www.imagescanada.ca/index-e.html

A gateway site offering search capabilities in numerous Canadian image collections.

Mother of All Art and Art History Links Page

http://www.art-design.umich.edu/mother/

An annotated collection of links to visual resources, image collections, online exhibitions, and museums. Sections on Africa, Asia, and the Middle East, as well as on Europe and the Americas, make this metasite a valuable resource for world history.

Rotch Visual Collections

http://libraries.mit.edu/rvc/index.html

The Rotch Visual Collections at the Massachusetts Institute of Technology offer a useful page of links to image collections on the Web, organized by subject area.

Selected Image Sites

American Memory

http://memory.loc.gov/ammem/amtitle.html

The American Memory site, produced by the National Digital Library Project of the Library of Congress, provides access to more than 9 million digitized primary source items on U.S. history and culture. Some of the best image collections are "Suffering Under a Great Injustice": Ansel Adams's Photographs of Japanese-American Internment at Manzanar; Edward S. Curtis's The North American Indian; Daguerreotype Portraits and Views, 1839–1864; America from the Great Depression to World War II: Photographs from the FSA-OWI, 1935–1945; Panoramic Photographs: Taking the Long View, 1851–1991; Small-Town America: Stereoscopic Views from the Robert Dennis Collection, 1850–1920; and Touring Turn-of-the-Century America: Photographs from the Detroit Publishing Company, 1880–1920.

American Museum of Photography

http://www.photography-museum.com/

Galleries of historical interest deal with slavery, spirit photography, and Commodore Matthew Perry's expedition to Japan.

Center for Creative Photography

http://www.library.arizona.edu/branches/ccp/ccphome.html

Offers an index of the center's collection of more than 60,000 photographs as well as selected online images. The center maintains more than one hundred collections of papers, manuscripts, and artifacts pertaining to photographers and photographic organizations.

Center for Documentary Studies

http://cds.aas.duke.edu/index.html

The Center for Documentary Studies promotes documentary work encompassing photography, filmmaking, oral history, folklore, and writing.

Charles Cushman Collection

http://www.dlib.indiana.edu/collections/cushman/

A searchable archive of more than 14,000 Kodachrome slides taken by the amateur photographer Charles Cushman from 1938 to 1969.

Collected Visions

http://cvisions.cat.nyu.edu/mantle/

The Collected Visions project offers a provocative perspective on how photographic images shape personal memory. The site invites visitors to submit photographs and to create photo essays from their own photographs or from other visitors' submissions.

The Daguerreian Society

http://www.daguerre.org

The Daguerreian Society's site features a selection of digitized daguerreotype images and informative explanatory text. The site's resource page offers a history of the daguerreotype, nineteenth- and twentieth-century published sources, a bibliography, and information on the daguerreotype process.

Denver Public Library Photography Collection

http://photoswest.org/

This site features exhibits based on the photography collection in the Denver Public Library's Western History/Genealogy Department.

Digital Media Lab, University of Virginia

http://www.lib.virginia.edu/clemons/RMC/DML/index.html

Offers thousands of digitized images. Recent projects include The Atlantic Slave Trade, Viewing Pompeii, and the Tibet and Himalayan Digital Library.

Frank Lloyd Wright: Designs for an American Landscape, 1922–1932

http://www.loc.gov/exhibits/flw/flw.html

The online version of an exhibit at the Library of Congress, this site integrates many of Wright's drawings into an essay on his work. The project includes images of hypothetical study models based on Wright's drawings.

George Eastman House International Museum of Photography and Film

http://www.eastmanhouse.org/

The George Eastman House, an important resource for research in the history of photography, offers many digitized photographs, stereo views, and lantern slides.

Images From the History of Medicine

http://wwwihm.nlm.nih.gov/

Provides online access to almost 60,000 images in the prints and photographs collection of the U.S. National Library of Medicine's History of Medicine Division. Includes portraits, caricatures, and graphic art.

Images of African Americans From the 19th Century

http://digital.nypl.org/schomburg/images_aa19/

A selection of images from the New York Public Library's Schomburg Center for Research in Black Culture. The archive can be searched by keyword or subject area.

Japanese Old Photographs in Bakumatsu-Meiji Period

http://oldphoto.lb.nagasaki-u.ac.jp/unive/

More than 5,000 digitized photographs of Japan from 1860 to 1899, made available by Nagasaki University Library.

LIFE

http://www.life.com/Life/lifeclassic.html

Front covers from 1936 to 1972, the period when *LIFE* was published weekly, can be searched by keyword or date. The site also offers a selection of photographs.

Motion Picture & Television Reading Room

http://lcweb.loc.gov/rr/mopic/

The Library of Congress offers many early motion pictures online in QuickTime, MPG, and Real Media formats. Subject areas and periods range from popular entertainment in the 1870s to the consumer economy of the 1920s.

Museum of the City of New York

http://www.mcny.org

Many of the museum's online exhibitions on New York history make use of images. Among the site's photographic projects is New York During the War: Photographs from the Office of War Information. Other exhibitions of historical interest are Looking North: Upper Manhattan in Photographs, 1896–1939; Gotham Comes of Age: New York Through the Lens of the Byron Company, 1892–1942; and Berenice Abbott: Changing New York.

National Aeronautics and Space Administration

http://www.nasa.gov/multimedia/highlights/index.html

NASA's multimedia gallery features a searchable archive of hundreds of thousands of still images. The gallery also provides access to NASA-related audio, video, and works of art.

National Archives and Records Administration: Exhibit Hall

http://www.archives.gov/exhibit_hall/index.html

Features numerous exhibitions of historical images including Picturing the Century, a photographic retrospective of the twentieth century; Powers of Persuasion, a collection of World War II propaganda posters; Panoramic Photography, a sampling of panoramic images; and Portrait of Black Chicago, an exhibition of photographs of 1970s Chicago.

National Museum of Photography, Film & Television

http://www.nmpft.org.uk/home.asp

Provides an introduction to the museum's collections and online images.

New York Public Library

http://www.nypl.org/research/chss/spe/art/photo/photo.html#online

Provides online access to the exhibition Berenice Abbott: Changing New York, 1935–1938 and to two projects on Lewis Hine: Work Portraits, 1920–1939 and Construction of the Empire State Building, 1930–1931.

Online Archive of California

http://www.oac.cdlib.org/

Provides image searching in many collections throughout California.

Photographs From the *Chicago Daily News:* 1902–1933

http://memory.loc.gov/ammem/ndlpcoop/ichihtml/

A major collection of more than 55,000 images by *Chicago Daily News* photographers. The photographs are from the Chicago Historical Society and have been made available through the American Memory site at the Library of Congress.

Princeton University: Seeley G. Mudd Manuscript Library

http://www.princeton.edu/~mudd/

Features recent exhibits from the library including photographs and audiovisual items. Among recent exhibits is Testing Boundaries: Cartoon Visions of Roosevelt's Third Term.

Royal Photographic Society

http://www.rps.org/

Offers an archive of recent exhibitions held at the society's Octagon Galleries in Bath.

The Siege and Commune of Paris, 1870–1871

http://www.library.northwestern.edu/spec/siege/

Provides more than 1,200 digitized, searchable photographs and images from the Siege and Commune of Paris.

Small Towns, Black Lives

http://www.blacktowns.org

Created by Wendel White, professor of art at Richard Stockton State College of New Jersey, this project presents documentary images of historically African-American communities in southern New Jersey. The project includes photographs, documents, video clips, and panoramic images.

Smithsonian Institution

http://photo2.si.edu/

Offers numerous online exhibitions and a searchable database of images. A few of the projects of historical interest are Magic Lanterns, Magic Mirrors: A Centennial Salute to Cinema, Recent Presidential Inaugurals, and Reflections on the Wall: The Vietnam Veterans Memorial.

Temple of Liberty: Building the Capitol for a New Nation

http://www.loc.gov/exhibits/us.capitol/s0.html

A Library of Congress exhibit on the history and meaning of the U.S. Capitol, including many maps, prints, architectural drawings, and photographs from the eighteenth to the twentieth centuries.

They Still Draw Pictures

http://orpheus-1.ucsd.edu/speccoll/tsdp/

A collection of more than 600 drawings made during the Spanish Civil War by schoolchildren in Spain and in French refugee centers. The images are from the Southworth Spanish Civil War Collection at the University of California–San Diego.

UCR/California Museum of Photography

http://www.cmp.ucr.edu/

An outstanding site based on the museum's collection of historical and contemporary images. More than 33,000 stereographic images from the museum's Keystone Mast Collection are available online. Visitors to the site can use 3-D red/blue glasses to simulate the effect of a stereoscopic viewer. The site features numerous exhibits and searchable image collections.

United Nations Photo

http://www.un.org/av/photo/

Provides a selection of images from the United Nations Photo Library. The site's history section includes a time line of images from the League of Nations to the present.

Chapter 35

Resources for Teachers of History
K–12 and College

Stephen Kneeshaw

Metasites

Academic Info

http://www.academicinfo.net/table.html

Academic Info is a subject directory designed for college-level use that provides both annotated listings of Internet sites and gateways to specialized materials. The site offers metaindexes, general directories, and teaching materials to serve needs at many academic levels. Especially useful is the section on U.S. history —Academic Info U.S. History, with a fully annotated directory of Internet resources divided into sections such as period gateways, diversity gateways, and topical resources.

Digital Librarian: A Librarian's Choice of the Best of the Web—History

http://www.digital-librarian.com/history.html

Self-described as "a librarian's choice of the best of the Web" (and run by Margaret Vail Anderson of Cortland, New York), the Digital Librarian covers virtually every academic discipline, many of which are linked to the history page. This site provides an entry point for such diverse topics as the ancient world, genealogy, Judaica, Latin America, the Middle East, and women's resources. For elementary teachers, there are useful connections to children's literature and resources. Lists are alphabetized and annotated briefly, but there is no internal search mechanism.

Index of Resources for Historians

http://vlib.iue.it/history/index.html

http://rmweb.indiana.edu/History/VL/index.html

The oversight of this valuable Web site has switched from the University of Kansas to the European University Institute in Florence, Italy, but this remains an exceptional metasite with more than 3,000 connections arranged alphabetically by subject and name. There are no annotations, but subject breakdowns make this an easily usable Web site. The list emphasizes college and university-level history, but some sites are geared specifically to K–12 audiences. Some sections are foreign-language–based rather than English (e.g., Brazil in Portuguese and Holocaust in German), making them difficult for many American users to access. Users also can access the full index via a mirror site at Indiana University (the second URL above).

Internet Public Library

http://www.ipl.org

The Internet Public Library is an easy-to-use metasite organized by "subject collections" and "ready references." History Web sites (available through arts and humanities or social sciences) have been organized by documents and sources, eras, regions, and topics, with subheadings in each area allowing users to break down their searches in close detail. Short but descriptive annotations for each Web site make the IPL easy to manage for students as well as teachers.

Lesson Plans and Resources for Social Studies Teachers

http://www.csun.edu/~hcedu013/index.html

This site, maintained by Marty Levine at California State University, Northridge, should be the first gateway accessed by elementary and secondary history teachers who want to sample the wealth of the World Wide Web. A clickable table of contents on the opening page leads to nine areas such as Lesson Plans and Teaching Strategies, Other Social Studies Resources (including government and museum sites), Teaching Current Events, and Newsgroups and Mailing Lists. The lengthy lists of links are alphabetized and annotated for a quick reading of contents.

The Ten Best Sites

AMDOCS: Documents for the Study of American History

http://www.vlib.us/amdocs/

This Web site, managed at the University of Kansas, provides users with one of the broadest Web-based lists of documents for American history available on the WWW. Documents range from the fifteenth century into the twenty-first century, from Columbus's letter to Ferdinand and Isabella in 1494 to the presidential debates of 2004. The list is set to both chronological eras (e.g., Age of Exploration, the Civil War) and presidential administrations, making it easy to locate documents for any given time in American history.

American Memory

http://rs6.loc.gov

The rich collections of the Library of Congress come to life in words and pictures in American Memory. This rapidly growing site, now with more than 125 collections online (up from forty-two three years ago), includes documents, maps, photographs and prints, motion pictures, and sound recordings. An easy-to-use search engine and a list of entries alphabetized by subjects and titles provides entry to topics ranging from baseball cards, Civil War images, and the conservation movement (one of my favorites) to Ansel Adams (photographs from the internment camp at Manzanar), posters from the WPA, and the dust bowl.

The Avalon Project: Documents in Law, History, and Diplomacy

http://www.yale.edu/lawweb/avalon/avalon.htm

History teachers frequently use documents to enrich lesson plans and illustrate key ideas. The Avalon Project from the Yale Law School provides connections to a wealth of documents from pre-eighteenth century into the twenty-first century. The one downside is the listing of documents (within a century-based format) in alphabetical rather than chronological order. But a list of major collections and a search engine within the project make this a user-friendly Web site that is accessible for all grade levels.

The Digital Classroom

http://archives.gov/digital_classroom/index.html

The Digital Classroom, from the National Archives and Records Administration (NARA), encourages teachers at all levels to use documents in their classrooms. This is NARA's complement to American Memory from the Library of Congress. The Web site delivers documentary materials from the National Archives, lesson plans, and suggested methods for teaching with primary documents. The topics available online span a wide range—literally A to Z—from the *Amistad* case to the Zimmerman telegram. NARA also provides a reproducible set of document analysis worksheets for written documents, photographs, cartoons, posters, maps, artifacts, sound recordings, and motion pictures that history teachers will find easy to use and attractive for their students.

ERIC—Educational Resources Information Center

http://www.eric.ed.gov/

Reorganized under the auspices of the Department of Education in 2004, ERIC (formerly AskERIC) provides a centralized database to search the ERIC online systems that contain more than 1.1 million entries dating back to 1966. Users also can access more than 100,000 full-text documents. The search engine offers several options: keywords, title, author, or ERIC number. For students and teachers, ERIC will be a valuable source to track down information on every conceivable topic, pointing to resources for teaching, research, and writing.

History Matters

http://historymatters.gmu.edu

Designed for secondary and college teachers in American history, History Matters combines the efforts of the American Social History Project at the City University of New York and the Center for History and New Media at George Mason University. With an express purpose to "focus on the lives of ordinary Americans," History Matters delivers teaching materials, first-person documents, interactive exercises, "syllabus central," and threaded discussions on teaching history. A keyword search option allows users easy access to materials in the site.

Kathy Schrock's Guide for Educators

http://school.discovery.com/schrockguide

Kathy Schrock created and maintains one of the best-known Web sites for educators. This "categorized list of sites" on the Internet, which Schrock updates often "to include the best sites for teaching and learning," covers the whole span of academic subjects. Clicking the link for history and social studies opens connections to American and world history as well as general history and social studies sites. Schrock's annotations give brief but useful signposts to the various links.

SCORE History–Social Science

http://score.rims.k12.ca.us

Schools of California Online Resources for Education (SCORE) designed this Web site primarily for K–12 teachers in California, but the site will be useful to teachers in all states. SCORE links users to resources and lessons by grade level, resources by theme and topic, virtual projects and field trips, and more. All the materials have been evaluated and rated on a 1 to 5 scale by a team of educators, assuring quality control in such areas as accuracy, grade appropriateness, depth, and variety.

Studying and Teaching History

http://www.tntech.edu/history/study.html

This fine Web site from Tennessee Technological University offers a database of valuable materials for history teachers and students on a wide range of topics. Currently available are study guides for history classes from several universities, reference works, guides for research and writing, links for oral history, maps and audio-visual materials, portfolios, living history and reenactments, studying and teaching history at K–12 levels, and graduate schools.

Teaching History: A Journal of Methods

http://www.emporia.edu/socsci/journal/main.htm

Designed and maintained at Emporia State University, Kansas, by the publication team for the journal *Teaching History,* this site reflects the main objective of the journal, to provide teachers at all academic levels "with the best and newest teaching ideas for their classrooms." Besides information on the journal, this site provides links to a rich list of resources in nine history-related categories, from American and world history to genealogy, writing aids, and teaching resources.

WWW Resources for History Teachers

Agents of Social Change

http://www.smith.edu/libraries/ssc/curriculum/index.html

Working with a grant from NEH, Smith College, Massachusetts, processed eight manuscript collections addressing issues centered on the major theme of "agents for social change." Smith took as its mission "to reach beyond the traditional community of archival users—beyond senior scholars, graduate students and undergraduates" and to design lesson plans directed toward middle and high school students. Through this Web site students can get better acquainted with such diverse topics as the fight for civil rights, for urban reform, and for women's rights from the 1930s into the 1980s.

Awesome Library

http://www.awesomelibrary.org/

Awesome Library for teachers, librarians, students, and parents gives users links to all teaching fields and to more than 26,000 reviewed resources. Under the social studies link, users can click into history and lesson plans or make connections to specialized history-related fields such as conservation, current events (including hunger and civil liberties), holidays, multicultural resources, and terrorism.

Biographical Dictionary

http://www.s9.com/biography

Biographical Dictionary offers biographies of more than 28,000 men and women "who have shaped our world from ancient times to the present day." Users can search the list by names, birth or death years, professions, literary and artistic works, and other keywords, making these men and women easily accessible for students and teachers.

Center for Teaching History With Technology

http://thwt.org/

As the name suggests, the Center for Teaching History with Technology provides a variety of materials to aid teachers at K–12 levels (with carryover value for college-level teaching) who wish to incorporate technology into their classrooms. The Web site is easy to navigate, using links brought together under "resources." Teachers will find activities, games, quizzes, and e-texts, as well as lesson plans, PowerPoint tips, and Advanced Placement resources.

Center for the Liberal Arts at the University of Virginia

http://www.virginia.edu/cla/

This Web site is dedicated to "opportunities for continuing content education for K–12 teachers," although many of the materials are appropriate for college and university levels as well. Clicking on "History" takes the user to a wonderful collection of Web sites on American history, geography, government, world history, and Virginia state history, which, of course, is rich in early American and Civil War–related topics.

Core Documents of U.S. Democracy

http://www.gpoaccess.gov/coredocs.html

This Web site from the Government Printing Office delivers more than the title suggests. Beyond such cornerstone documents as the Declaration of Independence, Constitution, and Bill of Rights, and Supreme Court decisions, users get a statistical abstract of the United States, a weekly compilation of presidential documents, and more. This Web site will be useful for history teachers who bring current events into their classrooms.

Ditto.com

http://www.ditto.com

For teachers wanting to liven up PowerPoint and lecture presentations and bring more visuals into their classrooms, Ditto.com provides "visual search of the web using pictures." The search engine is fast and user-friendly, but teachers might feel overwhelmed with the number of choices. For example, searches on topics such as Vietnam, Yellowstone, and Civil War provide thousands of images. For each visual, source information is available to ensure proper citations.

EDSITEment

http://edsitement.neh.gov/

EDSITEment provides subject-based connections to top humanities sites in four fields: art and culture, literature and language arts, foreign languages, and history and social studies. EDSITEment draws from collections "from some of the world's great museums, libraries, cultural institutions, and universities." All the sites have been "reviewed for content, design, and educational impact in the classroom." The materials are set into grade-specific categories from K–2 through 9–12, with many of the 9–12 materials suitable for college and university classrooms.

FREE: Federal Resources for Educational Excellence

http://www.ed.gov/free/index.html

FREE is the result of a "partnership" of teachers and more than fifty federal agencies to develop Internet-based learning modules and learning communities. The agencies include the CIA, FBI, National Park Service, Library of Congress, National Archives and Records Administration and White House. A site map provides connections to various topic areas, including the social studies. Topics are arranged alphabetically with the sponsoring agency identified. Brief annotations give good direction for users.

From Revolution to Reconstruction . . . and What Happened Afterwards

http://odur.let.rug.nl/~usa/

This hypertext Web site comes largely from materials prepared by the United States Information Agency, starting with "an outline of American history." This Netherlands-based site delivers one of the best collections of materials on American presidents, including full texts of inaugural addresses and State of the Union speeches.

Helping Your Child Learn History

http://www.ed.gov/pubs/parents/History/

This Web site, aimed primarily at parents, brings history to life for children, especially ages four through eleven. The suggestions, of course, are equally pertinent for lower-grade teachers. Topics include History Education Begins at Home (e.g., "history is a habit"), History as Story (e.g., "cooking up history"), and History as Time (e.g., "put time in a bottle").

The Heritage Education Network (THEN)

http://histpres.mtsu.edu/then/

Many indifferent students turn on to history when teachers introduce them to family and local history. THEN—The Heritage Education Network—provides a nice mix of resources for teachers who want to make "nearby history" part of their curriculum. As the Web site notes, "Heritage Education is the use of local cultural and historic resources for teaching the required curricula of grades K–12." In fact, it can work at the college level too. Run through Middle Tennessee State University, THEN spotlights such diverse resources as family history, historic buildings and structures, cemeteries, farms, and photographs. THEN also provides a list of contacts in each of the fifty states, including local historical societies and state agencies, who can assist in program development.

The History Channel

http://www.historychannel.com

This Web site provides an easy gateway into video materials from the History Channel. The History Store is the place to order videos, but this is more than just a commercial site. The speeches and video section lets students "watch, listen, [and] explore" such diverse characters as Franklin D. Roosevelt, Neil Armstrong, Martin Luther King Jr., Babe Ruth, and Yasir Arafat. Classroom materials, including vocabulary terms, discussion questions, and extended activities, are available online to accompany videos.

The History Net: Where History Lives on the Web

http://www.thehistorynet.com

The History Net, with its clickable list of historical times and topics along the edge, might seem to be just another history Web site. In fact, its major role is to provide links to published articles on times and topics, using journals such as *Civil War Times, Military History, Vietnam, British Heritage, Wild West,* and *American History*. The Web site also provides discussion forums related to topics addressed by the journals.

History Now: American History On-Line

http://www.historynow.org

This new Web site started in late 2004 is from the Gilder Lehrman Institute of American History (a sure sign of quality) and appears in journal form. History Now will offer four "issues" per year, with each separate issue focusing, through documents, on a topic with significance in American history, such as American elections and slavery. From the Teacher's Desk offers lesson plans for different grade levels, and Interactive History delivers interactive time lines, maps, and more. Topic specialists offer their thoughts in short but pointed essays in The Historian's Perspective. This Web site operates much in the manner of the *Magazine of History* from the OAH, focusing on one topic per "issue," providing teachers with a variety of ideas to bring into their classrooms.

The History Place

http://www.historyplace.com/index.html

The History Place provides a variety of links that will be useful to history teachers, especially at the secondary level. At this point, the site emphasizes American history, but there are strong sections on Hitler and the Holocaust, the Irish potato famine, and genocide in the twentieth century. Other European topics are "in development." Users will find time lines (e.g., the Civil War "with quotes and photos"), photographs, and "points of view," which are reviews and reflections from established writers and historians. The site also offers "movie reviews" for films with historical themes.

History Timelines on the Web

http://history.searchbeat.com/

The title promises time lines, but this Web site delivers much more that will be useful to history teachers and students at all levels. For example, the section on the Depression and New Deal includes a short history of the era, an annotated list of online resources, a section on people, places, and events, and links to collections of photographs, as well as time lines.

H-Net Teaching

http://www.h-net.msu.edu/teaching

H-Net Teaching provides a gateway to several Web sites on teaching maintained by H-Net (Humanities and Social Science Online) at Michigan State University. Each of these Web sites includes edited, threaded discussions on topics of interest to list subscribers and archives, complete with search mechanisms, on previous discussions. H-Net Teaching includes the following:

> EDTECH—on educational technology
> H-AfrTeach—teaching African history and studies
> H-High-School—teaching high school history and social studies (an indispensable site for secondary history teachers)
> H-Mmedia—high-tech teaching, multimedia, CD-ROM
> H-Survey—teaching United States history survey courses (a must-see site for college American survey teachers)
> H-Teach—teaching history at all levels (my personal favorite of the H-Net sites with enlightening discussions on a wide range of important topics for history teachers)
> H-W-Civ—teaching Western Civilization courses (a companion to H-Survey).

Internet History Sourcebook Project

http://www.fordham.edu/halsall/

This Web site provides a gateway to a collection of public-domain and copy-permitted historical texts developed and maintained by Paul Halsall of Fordham University. The three key "sourcebooks" cover ancient history, medieval history, and modern history. In addition, Halsall has developed several subsidiary sourcebooks that draw from the three key sourcebooks. The subsection on multimedia and history in the modern history sourcebook is rich in audio and visual materials that will enliven teaching and learning.

Learning Space—Social Studies for Washington Students and Teachers

http://www.wscss.org/

The Learning Space provides many links specific to a single state, here Washington State, but the site has great value for all history teachers. Using general indicators such as social studies subjects, frameworks, and teacher resources, the Learning Space links users to broad topics (American and world history) as well as specialized topics such as flags, Lewis and Clark, and Native Americans.

The Library in the Sky

http://www.nwrel.org/sky/index.asp

Run by the Northwest Regional Educational Laboratory in Portland, Oregon, the Library in the Sky offers more than 1,200 links to educational resources for teachers, librarians, students, and parents, in every field of study. History and the social studies get enough attention to make this a useful site for the K–12 community.

Marco Polo: Internet Content for the Classroom

http://www.marcopolo-education.org/index.aspx

Started in 1997 as a nonprofit consortium of educational organizations, Marco Polo provides K–12 teachers access to seven content-based Web sites tied to national standards plus professional development resources. Teachers will find lesson plans keyed to specific grade levels, downloadable worksheets, links to other Web sites, and more. Content partners include EDSITEment (for the humanities—from NEH) and Xpedition (for geography—from *National Geographic*).

National Center for History in the Schools

http://www.sscnet.ucla.edu/nchs

The National Center for History in the Schools, located at the University of California, Los Angeles, publishes online the National Standards for United States History, K–4 and 5–12, the National Standards for World History, and the Revised Standards for History. In addition, Bring History Alive introduces sourcebooks for U.S. and world history, grades 5–12, with more than 1,200 activities arranged by grade level and keyed to the revised standards (available for purchase rather than free use by teachers).

National Portrait Gallery

http://www.npg.si.edu

The National Portrait Gallery, a branch of the Smithsonian Institution, provides online access to many of its collections that teachers and students can tap for PowerPoint and lecture presentations. The Web site includes several virtual past exhibitions and the permanent collection of the NPG, including the Hall of Presidents. For some of the special exhibitions, teacher resources packets are available.

Our Documents—100 Milestone Documents

http://www.ourdocuments.gov

Promising "to help us think, talk, and teach about the rights and responsibilities of citizens in our democracy," this Web site introduces "100 milestone documents" that shaped the American experience. A teacher sourcebook delivers an annotated time line, key themes, and lesson plans. The Web site also provides quick links to curriculum standards and ideas for librarians, making this useful across many grade levels.

ParkNet—National Park Service

http://www.nps.gov

The National Park Service, through ParkNet, delivers one of the best Web sites run and maintained by a U.S. government agency. "History and Culture" and "Interpretation and Education" (link to "Learn NPS") provide entry points to a variety of teaching resources, including lesson plans, Parks in Your Curriculum, and Teaching with Historic Places (which gets a full description below). The Parks and Recreation heading opens links for all NPS properties. Some of these—Olympic National Park in Washington State, for example—have expanded Web sites that provide attractive resources for teachers such as lesson plans that they can pick up and use with ease.

Popular Songs in American History

http://www.contemplator.com/america/index.html

This innovative Web site provides "tunes, lyrics, information, historical background and tune related links" for a wide range of songs from the seventeenth century into the early twentieth century. The songs are arranged by time frame and topic (e.g., gold rush, Civil War, and cowboys). For each song, users get a brief introduction, lyrics, and music. One notable section, developed "in response to requests," spotlights sea shanties and songs of the sea.

Project Gutenberg

http://www.promo.net/pg

One of the best-known early WWW sites, Project Gutenberg, started in 1971, provides digital versions of classic works in world history and literature for the classroom. The collection now numbers more than 13,000 electronic books (e-Books) in more than thirty languages. An in-site search engine—called an online book catalog—allows users to find e-texts by checking alphabetical lists of authors and titles, which can be downloaded via FTP or the Web. Two lists—on the top hundred books and authors of the week—make interesting browsing.

Smithsonian Institution Social Studies Lesson Plans

http://smithsonianeducation.org/educators/index.html

Under the heading Field Trips, the Smithsonian Center for Education and Museum Studies provides detailed information that will aid teachers preparing students for visits to the Smithsonian Institution or to other museums (see Teaching Strategies and Preparation Materials). Teachers can jump quickly to lesson plans and easily identify useful resources with a search engine keyed to subject, grade level, and keyword. The section on Heritage Teaching Resources will prove useful to teachers looking for materials to celebrate "heritage months" in their classrooms.

Teachers Helping Teachers

http://www.pacificnet.net/~mandel/

Teachers Helping Teachers opened in 1995 under the direction of Scott Mandel, a classroom teacher in California, who updates the site each week during the school year. Now with more than 4 million hits—testimony to its value for teachers—the site provides lesson plans (all submitted by teachers) for K–12 grade levels. Many of these plans are easily adaptable to a variety of teaching situations. Another useful section is links to educational resources on the Web that have been alphabetized by subject.

Teaching With Historic Places

http://www.cr.nps.gov/nr/twhp/index.htm

This site, run through the National Park Service, focuses on the teaching opportunities presented by properties on the National Register of Historic Places.

The purpose is to "turn students into historians as they study primary sources, historical and contemporary photographs and maps, and other documents, and then search for the history around them in their own communities." The NPS provides lesson plans (categorized according to the National Standards for United States History for Grades 5–12), education kits, and workshops to facilitate the integration of historic places into the curriculum. In a nice invitation to get teachers to add new materials, the NPS also provides an online author's packet to "help [teachers] create materials to convey the meaning and importance of these places to students from upper elementary to high school."

THOMAS: Legislative Information on the Internet

http://thomas.loc.gov/#thomas

THOMAS bills itself as "legislative information on the Internet." It is certainly that and much more. Run through the Library of Congress, THOMAS follows the work of the U.S. Senate and House of Representatives, providing summaries, status reports, and full texts of legislation in Congress. The site also provides directories for members of Congress, making it a critical tool for teachers who use current events in their classrooms.

Timelines of History

http://timelines.ws

Timelines of History operates with a simple format: Click on dates (centuries, decades, years, even months for the most recent dates) and follow time. The time lines include American and world history. Other sections allow users to search time by countries, American states, cities (notably New York City and San Francisco plus others off site), and subjects of various sorts, such as disasters, environment, pop and rock music, technology, women, and writers. Regular updates keep this Web site current (literally up to date), making it a useful resource for teachers and students.

United States Department of Education

http://www.ed.gov

The official home page of the U.S. Department of Education is a good place to learn about federal educational initiatives. The "teachers" link opens some useful sites such as FREE (described above) and GEM (Gateway to Educational Materials). Those who are interested also can find a variety of policy documents online at this site.

Virtual Field Trips Site

http://www.field-guides.com/

This Web site provides a way for teachers to take their students around the world without leaving their classrooms. They can "travel" to Antarctica; visit deserts, oceans, salt marshes, and volcanoes; encounter dinosaurs, fierce creatures, and insects ("a creepy crawly experience"); and then live through hurricanes and tornadoes. At the individual field trip sites, users will find terms to learn, concepts, and teachers' resources.

Words and Deeds in American History

http://lcweb2.loc.gov/ammem/mcchtml/corhome.html

Here is one more site from the Library of Congress (LOC). Actually an offshoot of American Memory (described above), Words and Deeds gives a condensed collection of manuscript materials (with some ninety "representative documents") that can enrich the teaching and study of history. The LOC has provided a detailed description to accompany each document and links to other resources in the library's collection that connect to the documents.

Chapter 36

Libraries

Jessie Bishop Powell, Merriman

Library of Congress

Library of Congress

Library of Congress http://www.loc.gov

Library of Congress catalog http://catalog.loc.gov/

Library of Congress authorities http://authorities.loc.gov/

The Library of Congress's Web page provides a digital gateway to a variety of online collections and government sites, including the U.S. Copyright Office. The Library of Congress collects in all areas *except* medicine and technical agriculture. Most items are available through interlibrary loan.

On the Web site, researchers can search the library's holdings, including some links to digitized materials. Basic searching allows standard library searches, including title, author, and International Standard Book Numbering (ISBN). A more specific guided search allows for Boolean and index limits. Searchers, particularly historians, should be aware that many materials cataloged before 1980, while available to the public, are not represented in the digital catalog. Some collections are represented with collection level catalog records only, meaning that individual items within the collections are not shown in the online catalog.

Metasites (American and Worldwide)

East Asian Libraries Cooperative

http://pears.lib.ohio-state.edu/

A project of Ohio State University, this catalog aims to support researchers interested in East Asia.

ETANA: Electronic Tools and Ancient Near Eastern Archives

http://www.etana.org/

ETANA is the project of several American Oriental studies programs, funded by the Andrew W. Mellon Foundation and a National Science Foundation grant. In addition to housing the Abzu database for studies of the Near East, ETANA also contains digitized versions of some of the core texts for ancient Near East studies and a digital library with archaeological data.

National Libraries of the World

http://www.publiclibraries.com/world.htm

Contains links to many nations' public libraries.

Public Libraries.com

http://www.publiclibraries.com/

Lists contact information, including Web sites, for many U.S. public libraries. The section is organized by state and includes links to metasites for state and presidential libraries (below).

Presidential Libraries

http://www.publiclibraries.com/presidential_library.htm

Lists contact information, including Web sites, for all eleven presidential libraries.

RLG

http://www.rlg.org/

Research libraries belonging to RLG (RedLightGreen) offer digital and print access to a variety of collections. The RLIN (Research Libraries Information Network) database has been frozen and replaced by RLIN21, and these catalogs are both accessible only to members. However, the Web site also offers links to a variety of research-oriented articles and the RedLightGreen research database, which is available to the general public.

State Libraries

http://www.publiclibraries.com/state_library.htm

Lists contact information for most official state libraries.

Yale's Other Libraries Page

http://www.library.yale.edu/orbis/othercats.html

Though designed for Yale students, this page represents an excellent collection of library and research links, including information about Yale's Special Catalogs and a link to the Center for Research Libraries (CRL).

American Libraries and Collections

American Memory: Historical Collections of the National Digital Library

http://memory.loc.gov/ammem/index.html

American Memory contains items that the Library of Congress considers important to U.S. cultural history. The most recently cataloged records have the highest-level information, while older collections may have less detailed information online. Most collections are searchable and many have finding aids such as subject and author lists.

The Beinecke Library

Beinecke library home page: http://www.library.yale.edu/beinecke/

ORBIS: http://orbis.library.yale.edu/

Searchable through ORBIS, Yale's online catalog, the Beinecke Library, Yale's rare books and manuscripts library, also offers access to its events and educational programs, as well as searcher tips on its own home page.

CRL: The Center for Research Libraries

http://www.crl.edu/catalog/index.htm

A consortium of college and university libraries from all over the United States, CRL holds materials important to researchers that librarians could no longer keep on their own institutions' shelves. Member libraries and their patrons may access these materials. Currently, 98 percent of the nearly 5 million entries in the CRL's catalog are available online, including books, newspapers, serials, microforms, archival collections, and other research materials.

The Getty Research Institute for the History of Art and the Humanities

http://opac.pub.getty.edu

Collections available in the Getty include Western art, archaeology, and architecture from the Bronze Age to the present. There are also extensive collections on the conservation of cultural heritage and historic preservation and an unparalleled auction catalog collection with more than 110,000 volumes of materials from the late seventeenth century to the present. Included in the Special Collections are artists' journals and sketchbooks, albums, architectural drawings, early guidebooks, emblem books, prints, and drawings. The Getty Collection's strengths are French, German, Russian, Italian, and American avant-garde materials, futurism, Dada, surrealism, the Bauhaus, Russian constructivism, and Fluxus. Many items from the research library are available for interlibrary loan.

The Hagley Library

http://www.hagley.lib.de.us/

Located in Deleware, the Hagley Museum and Library's focus is American business and technological history.

The Kinsey Institute for Research in Sex, Gender and Reproduction

http://www.indiana.edu/~kinsey/

Collections searchable via KICAT at Indiana University catalog (IUCat):
http://www.iucat.iu.edu/

KICAT does not contain records for all items in the Kinsey library, nor does it contain records for the institute's art and archival collections. Records are continually being added to the online catalog as part of the library's retrospective conversion project. For help in using the library's holdings of sex-related magazines, films and videos, newspapers and tabloids, pulp fiction, and books still cataloged according to Dr. Kinsey's system of categories, users must consult with library staff.

Labriola National American Indian Data Center at Arizona State University

Labriola: http://www.asu.edu/lib/archives/labriola.htm

ASU's online catalog: http://catalog.lib.asu.edu/

The Labriola National American Indian Data Center, part of the ASU Libraries, brings together current and historic government, culture, religion and worldview, social life and customs, tribal history, and information on individuals from the United States, Canada, Sonora, and Chihuahua, Mexico. All materials held by the center are searchable via ASU's online catalog.

The Library Company of Philadelphia

http://www.librarycompany.org/

Founded in 1731 by Benjamin Franklin, the Library Company of Philadelphia has over half a million items covering American history and culture from the seventeenth to the nineteenth century. The online catalog, WolfPAC, currently has nearly 100 percent of the library's rare book collection and roughly 10,000 graphic materials. It also includes records from the union catalog of the Philadelphia Area Consortium of Special Collections Libraries (PACSCL): the Academy of Natural Sciences, the Balch Institute for Ethnic Studies, Saint Charles Borromeo Seminary, the Philadelphia Museum of Art, the Rosenbach Museum and Library, the Presbyterian Historical Society, the Athenaeum, and the Historical Society of Pennsylvania. Several other PACSCL member libraries have, or will soon have, catalogs available through the PACSCL Web site or through their individual institution's Web site. These include the American Philosophical Society, the Free Library of Philadelphia, the University of Pennsylvania, Winterthur, the Hagley Museum and Library, Temple University, the College of Physicians of Philadelphia, the Wagner Free Institute of Science, Bryn Mawr, Haverford, and Swarthmore.

The Lilly Library

http://www.indiana.edu/~liblilly/

Searchable at the Indiana University Catalog (IUCat):
http://www.iucat.iu.edu

The Lilly Library's online resources include searchable indexes of the manuscript collections, chapbook collection, and French Revolution documents.

National Center for Education Statistics

http://nces.ed.gov/

The National Center for Education Statistics offers digital access to many of its reports and selected publications at this address.

The Newberry Library

http://www.newberry.org/

Library Catalog: http://i-share.carli.illinois.edu/nby/cgi-bin/Pwebrecon.
cgi?DB=local&PAGE=First

Currently, about 20 percent of the Newberry Library's collection is searchable.
Online records exist for materials cataloged by the library since 1978. (This includes some materials published before 1978, but cataloged later by the library.)
Starting in 2004, the library began a retrospective conversion from catalog cards
to online MARC records for approximately 725,000 items.

The New York Public Library

http://catnyp.nypl.org/

CATNYP is the online catalog of the Research Libraries of The New York Public
Library. This catalog includes nearly 2 million records for materials added to the
collections before 1972 and nearly 2 million records for materials added to the
collection after that time. A very few items are still only to be located in catalog
cards or retrospective collections. Publisher G.K. Hall's 800-volume *Dictionary
Catalog of The Research Libraries* is one such retrospective catalog.

OhioLink

http://www.ohiolink.edu

This is the communal catalog for all libraries (public, private, college, and
university) in Ohio.

Online Archive of California

http://www.oac.cdlib.org/

This site is a compilation of items contributed to the California Archives, including the Bancroft Library, and the California Heritage Digital Image Access
Database.

RedLightGreen

http://www.redlightgreen.com

A project of the RLG corporation, and a massive searchable database, RedLight-
Green is currently available to the general public (unlike RLIN and RLIN21)
and offers a search of over 120 million books, and tells whether they are at
your local library.

The Schlesinger Library, Radcliffe College

http://www.radcliffe.edu/schles/

http://holliscatalog.harvard.edu/

The Schlesinger Library is the foremost library on the history of women in America. Its holdings of audiovisual materials, books, ephemera, manuscripts, oral histories, periodicals, and photographs document the social history of women in the United States, primarily during the nineteenth and twentieth centuries—including the recently acquired papers of the late chef Julia Child. It is searchable via Harvard's online catalog, HOLLIS. To search for manuscript and archival collections, users should choose the Expanded Search option in HOLLIS.

Schomburg Center for Research in Black Culture

http://www.nypl.org/research/sc/sc.html

(Holdings searchable via CATNYP, the New York Public Library catalog, http://catnyp.nypl.org)

The Schomburg Center for Research in Black Culture is a national research library devoted to collecting, preserving, and providing access to resources documenting the experiences of peoples of African descent throughout the world. The center provides access to, and professional reference assistance in, the use of its collections to the scholarly community and the general public through five research divisions. The center's collections include art objects, audio and videotapes, books, manuscripts, motion picture films, newspapers, periodicals, photographs, prints, recorded music discs, and sheet music.

University of Oklahoma Western History Collections

Library catalog: http://libraries.ou.edu/eresources/catalog/

Western History Collection: http://libraries.ou.edu/info/info.asp?id=22

This collection aims to provide research opportunities into the development of the Trans-Mississippi West and Native American cultures. Catalog information for many of the materials within the Western History Collections may be accessed through the University of Oklahoma Libraries online catalog. Inventories of several individual collections can be found at the library's Western History Collections page.

Ten Largest Research Libraries in the United States*

1. Harvard University
http://hollisweb.harvard.edu/

2. Yale University
http://orbis.library.yale.edu/

3. University of Illinois at Urbana-Champaign
http://www.library.uiuc.edu/

4. University of Texas at Austin
http://utdirect.utexas.edu/lib/utnetcat/

5. University of California at Berkeley
Bancroft Library (GLADIS): http://sunsite5.berkeley.edu:8000/

UC Berkeley Library Guide: http://www.lib.berkeley.edu/Catalogs/guide.html

6. University of California at Los Angeles
http://www2.library.ucla.edu/

7. University of Michigan, Ann Arbor
http://www.lib.umich.edu

8. Stanford University
http://jenson.stanford.edu

9. Columbia University
CLIO: http://www.columbia.edu/cu/lweb/

Pegasus: http://pegasus.law.columbia.edu/

EduCat: http://educat.tc.columbia.edu/

Library of the Jewish Theological Seminary: http://alpha3.jtsa.edu:4525/F

---

* *Digest of Education Statistics*, U.S. Department of Education. National Center for Education Statistics, 2002, 492, table 420.

10. The University of Chicago
http://www1.lib.uchicago.edu/e/index.php3

Selected Worldwide Libraries
and Collections

ABZU: Oriental Institute Research Archives

http://www.etana.org/abzu/

Rebuilt in partnership with ETANA (Electronic Tools and Ancient Near Eastern Archives), ABZU is a guide to resources for the study of the ancient Near East. Created, compiled, and updated by Charles E. Jones, research archivist at the Oriental Institute's Research Archives at the University of Chicago, the catalog consists of primary and secondary indexes of information.

Bibliothèque Nationale de France

http://www.bnf.fr/

Home page of the French National Library, in French, with an English gateway under construction. The above link is to the summary page for all four catalogs, including GALLICA—an effort to chronicle nineteenth-century France through digitized images and sound.

British Library Integrated Catalogue

http://catalogue.bl.uk/

Manuscript catalog: http://www.bl.uk/catalogues/manuscripts.html

British Library Integrated Catalogue provides access to the major catalogs of the British Library in London and Boston Spa. The collections include humanities, social science, hard science, and technology. There are also business collections cataloged from 1975 to the present, as well as all music cataloged from 1980 to the present and all humanities reference materials cataloged before 1975 (including the archives and materials of the former India Office and colonial Africa). In the older reference materials, the appearance of "D-" before items means the original was destroyed during World War II and has since been replaced. Finally, all serials from 1700 to the present are included in the catalog.

EuroDocs: Primary Historical Documents From Western Europe

http://eudocs.lib.byu.edu/index.php/Main_Page

Compiled by Richard Hacken, a librarian at Brigham Young University, this list of links connects to Western European (mainly primary) historical documents that are transcribed, reproduced and, in some cases, translated.

Japan's National Diet Library

http://www.ndl.go.jp/en/index.html

This site offers English-language access to Japan's National Diet Library Web page. It contains links to both Japanese-only and English-language searches of its catalog.

The National Archives—UK

http://www.nationalarchives.gov.uk

Britain's national archives Web site is searchable online. Some documents have been scanned into the site and are viewable via the DocumentsOnline link. There is also a catalog of immigration into Britain in the last 200 years at the MovingHere link, as well as access to documents from the Macmillan government of 1957–1963, digital datasets collections, and collections related to medieval and early modern taxation.

The National Library of China

http://www.nlc.gov.cn/old/english.htm

Non–Chinese-speaking visitors to this site submit questions to librarians who then search for the information. The site, which is fully searchable in English, explains the collections of China's National Library. Regrettably, English-speaking visitors cannot search the library's actual collections.

OLIS—Oxford's Bodleian Library

http://www.bodley.ox.ac.uk/

OLIS, Oxford University Library's online catalog:
http://www.lib.ox.ac.uk/olis/

The library is searchable through OLIS, Oxford University Library's online catalog. Most materials found in the Bodleian Library are available for inter-library loan.

Chapter 37

Archives and Manuscript Collections

Donnelly Lancaster

Information for Researchers

Introduction to Archives

http://www.umich.edu/~bhl/bhl/refhome/refintro.htm

This Web page is a brief, general introduction to archives and manuscript materials. It clearly states in the text that it provides helpful, basic information for those researchers unfamiliar with special collections. Hyperlinks provide examples of materials and additional information on researching at the library.

Library Research Using Primary Sources

http://www.lib.berkeley.edu/TeachingLib/Guides/PrimarySources.html

This site is a comprehensive, detailed introduction to archives and manuscript use. Not only does it answer the question "What Are Primary Sources?" but it also provides step-by-step strategies and instructions that patrons can use to find the information they seek.

Primary Sources at Yale

http://www.library.yale.edu/instruction/primsource.html

This site contains a detailed introduction to finding primary sources along with instructions. Tailored to the Yale University library resources, it includes finding aids to collections. It also contains information on how to use bibliographic tools and gives links to comprehensive lists of such tools available at Yale's Sterling Library.

Using Archives: A Practical Guide for Researchers

http://www.collectionscanada.ca/04/0416_e.html

This is found on the National Archives of Canada or Library and Archives Canada Web site. It is listed as an online publication. Unlike some of the other sources listed in this chapter, this resource contains more narrative description and instruction than lists, tables, and bibliographies.

Information for Archivists

Archives of the Archivist Listserv

http://listserv.muohio.edu/archives/archives.html

This site contains the archives of the Archives Listserv, maintained by the Society of American Archivists. The listserv is an open forum for discussion about archival issues. The archives Web site contains postings dating back to 1993. A search option allows users to search by date, subject, or author.

Archives Resource Center

http://www.nlc.gov.cn/old/english.htm

Sponsored by the Council of State Historical Records Coordinators, the Web site contains information and links to educational programs, state archives, and other facilities, training available on the Web, and programs that educate on the use of primary sources. In addition, it contains lists, with Web sites when available, of a variety of information useful to archivists and those interested in the profession, including lists of archival associations, state agencies, forms used by institutions, and fees charged by institutions for services.

CoOL Conservation OnLine

http://palimpsest.stanford.edu/

The result of a project of the Preservation Department of Stanford University Libraries, this Web site contains vast resources on conservation and related issues. Resources may be searched by author name or by subject. Users are invited to submit additional resources.

Introduction to Archival Organization and Description: Access to Cultural Heritage

http://www.getty.edu/research/conducting_research/standards/introarchives/

An excellent resource for students or those new to the archival profession, this site provides a concise, step-by-step introduction to archival theory and work. An excellent section on processing provides the reader with an over-the-shoulder view of this often mentioned and rarely disseminated piece of the archival workflow. Maintained on the Getty Institute Web site and funded by the J. Paul Getty Trust, the Web site was created by prominent members of the American archival community.

Society of American Archivists

http://www.archivists.org/

The Society of American Archivists is the preeminent organization for archivists in the United States. Its Web site contains information about the organization itself and its activities, as well as online resources for education, employment, and publications.

Archives, Manuscripts, and Special Collections

Metasites

ArchiveNet

http://www.archiefnet.nl/index.asp?taal=en

Maintained by the Historical Centre Overijssel, this site focuses on the Netherlands and Flanders, providing links to repositories in provinces and towns there. In addition, the site provides links to repositories around the world. The site is primarily in Dutch with sections in English.

The European Library

http://www.theeuropeanlibrary.org/portal/index.html

Launched as a pilot project in 1995, this metasite for forty-three libraries from forty-one member nations in the Conference of European National Librarians allows users to search the collections of all libraries. There are links to each of the forty-three libraries' Web sites along with the language option for each site. In addition, the site contains additional information about the national libraries of Europe, including online exhibits and a news bulletin board dating to 1995.

Guide to the Archives of Intergovernmental Organizations

http://www.unesco.org/archives/guide/uk/index.html

A joint project of the United Nations Educational, Scientific and Cultural Organization (UNESCO) and the International Council on Archives, Section of Archivists of International Organizations, this Web site contains a list of the archives of about eighty intergovernmental organizations. A history of the organization, description of materials held, and rules and guidelines for archival use and access are among the information provided about each archive.

Ready, 'Net, Go! Archival Internet Resources

http://www.tulane.edu/~lmiller/ArchivesResources.html

Created and maintained by Tulane University's Howard-Tilton Library's Special Collections Division, this metasite is clear, concise, and easy to use. Its introductory language is geared to a general audience, and the site contains links to archival resources on the Net, organized by category.

Repositories of Primary Resources

http://www.uidaho.edu/special-collections/Other.Repositories.html

Maintained by Terry Abraham, head of Special Collections and Archives at the University of Idaho, this site contains lists of links to other repositories around the world. The sites are arranged by geographic region. In addition, there are lists of Web sites for organizations, other metasites, and other useful sites for archivists and researchers. Updated monthly, this is an excellent starting point for any researcher seeking primary sources.

Area Specific Sites

Africa

Africa South of the Sahara: Libraries/Archives

http://www-sul.stanford.edu/depts/ssrg/africa/libs.html

Sponsored by the Stanford University Library, this metasite contains links to Internet resources related to Africa and is organized by both country and topic. Within the topical index, the links are annotated and contain valuable information for researchers. In addition, the site is searchable. Researchers interested in Africa should consult this site before venturing further.

Schomburg Center for Research in Black Culture

http://www.nypl.org/research/sc/sc.html

Located at the New York Public Library, the Schomburg Center contains vast holdings related to African-Americans. Its excellent Web site offers online exhibits, a large number of finding aids to its manuscript collections, searchable access to digital images of its visual holdings, and an online catalog for its books.

Asia and the Pacific

Directory of Archives in Australia

http://www.archivists.org.au/directory/asa_dir.htm

Maintained by the Australian Society of Archivists, this is a directory of archival repositories in Australia.

National Archives of Japan

http://www.archives.go.jp/index_e.html

An excellent Web site for those researching Japanese history and interested in the archives' holdings, this site offers an introduction for first-time users to the site and to archives in general. Finding aids to collections are available and easy to use, as are digital images.

National Archives of Singapore

http://www.museum.org.sg/NAS

This user-friendly Web site should be the first stop for those interested in Singapore's history. The site's features make it easy to search different collections and types of materials, including online exhibits. The site provides easy access to Web sites of the other members of the National Heritage Board, including the Singapore History Museum, Singapore Art Museum, Heritage Conservation Centre, and Asian Civilizations Museum.

Canada

Canada Archival Resources on the Internet

http://www.archivescanada.ca/english/index.html

Developed and maintained by the Canadian Council of Archives, this Web site is geared toward a wide audience, from a school-age child doing a report for class to a scholar doing research. A search engine allows the user to search for material across Canada. Search results include information about collections along with physical location of material and any digital material available. Users may also view online exhibits and search for digitized material. Available in French and English.

Europe—Eastern

PIASA Archival Information Center

http://www.piasa.org/archives.html

This Web site is part of the Polish Institute of Arts and Sciences of America, Inc. (PIASA) Web site. PIASA does not hold archives collections itself, but the Archival Information Center provides links to archival collections around the world relating to Polish history.

Slavic and Eastern European Library, University of Illinois Urbana-Champaign

http://www.library.uiuc.edu/spx/

Although the library holds more than 670,000 volumes related to Slavic and Eastern European countries, the archives and manuscripts held by the library are hard to find on the main library's Web site. A link to the Russian and Eastern

European Library (http://web.library.uiuc.edu/ahx/russia/russia.htm) identifies archives and manuscripts related to Russia and other former Soviet Union countries. Links to Internet resources by country contain links to Web sites administered by repositories and agencies in those countries rather than holdings at the Slavic and Eastern European Library. This is an excellent gateway to Eastern European archives and manuscripts.

Slovene Archives

http://www.pokarh-mb.si/index.php?is=2&L=1&L=2

The introductory page is in English and provides only a small amount of information about the archive and its holdings. The introduction page also links to a database searchable in Slovenian only.

Europe—Western

Archives Hub

http://www.archiveshub.ac.uk/

An excellent source for finding archival materials from colleges and universities throughout the United Kingdom, the Hub provides helpful information about everything from the site itself to a glossary of archival terms. The Hub, developed and maintained by representatives from different archives in the United Kingdom, allows users to search the almost 190,000 descriptions of holdings in ninety colleges and repositories in the United Kingdom.

Archives in Germany

http://home.bawue.de/~hanacek/info/earchive.htm

This helpful site about archival resources in Germany provides users with a glossary of terms they might encounter while doing online research, as well as links to different Web sites for repositories in Germany.

ARCHON Archives Online

http://www.archon.nationalarchives.gov.uk/archon/

This is the Web site of the National Archives of the United Kingdom. The Web site includes numerous search mechanisms that allow the user to search for a variety of records, including census records, wills, tax records, and cabinet records. Searching the records is free, but there is a small fee to see some records.

Bundesarchiv Online

http://www.bundesarchiv.de/

This site is in the German language only; the English version is under construction.

Latin America

Benson Latin American Collection, University of Texas at Austin

http://www.lib.utexas.edu/benson/

The Benson Latin American Collection holds materials about Latin America and Latinos in the United States. The Web site contains online exhibits of digital materials. Users may browse through finding aids for manuscript collections and search the online catalog for other materials in the Benson Collection's holdings.

H-LatAm Archives

http://www.h-net.org/~latam/archives/

Displayed partially in Spanish and English, this site contains information about holdings and access to more than twenty repositories.

Latin American Library Tulane University

http://lal.tulane.edu/

The Web site contains a list of manuscript collections, along with finding aids for a portion of the collections.

Military History and Peace Collections

Hoover Institution on War, Revolution, and Peace Library and Archives

http://www-hoover.stanford.edu/hila/

This Web site provides users with access to complete finding aids to a wide variety of manuscript collections dealing with the military, politics, war, and peace around the world.

National Archives and Records Administration (NARA)

http://www.archives.gov/

The National Archives holds vast resources documenting the activities of all branches of the U.S. armed forces.

Swarthmore College Peace Collection

http://www.swarthmore.edu/Library/peace/

This Web site contains access to lists of manuscript collections, photographic collections, artifacts, and other collections. Some of these lists include links to complete finding aids. In addition, the site includes links to repositories with similar collections.

U.S. Army Military History Institute

http://carlisle-www.army.mil/usamhi/

This institute holds unofficial historical records relating to the U.S. Army. The Web site contains descriptions of its archival holdings. In addition, the site contains links to similar repositories for other branches of the armed forces.

Virginia Military Institute Archives

http://www.vmi.edu/archives/

The VMI Archives Web site provides researchers with access to some of their 450 manuscript collections. These collections include personal papers of military personnel who served in the nineteenth and twentieth centuries. The lists of manuscript collections include descriptions, and many have online finding aids and/or digital images of the collections themselves.

Russia and the Former Soviet Union

Estonian Historical Archives

http://www.eha.ee/

Users may choose to read the English version of the Web site, which provides a catalog and other databases for searching the archives' holdings. Some of the databases, however, are offered only in Estonian.

National Library of Russia

http://www.nlr.ru:8101/eng/

Most of the materials that users may access on this site are current published materials rather than manuscripts and archives. There is a database, however, for eighteenth- and nineteenth-century books. In addition, the site contains a link to the Virtual Reference Library, which has links to repositories in other former Soviet states.

State Archives of Latvia

http://www.arhivi.lv/engl/en-lvas-frame.htm

This Web site is in English with searchable databases of its holdings in a mixture of Latvian and English.

United States

Congressional Collections at Archival Repositories

http://www.archives.gov/records_of_congress/repository_collections/

Provides users with links to archival repositories that hold congressional collections. These links are arranged by repository, state, and congressional member's name.

The Library of Congress

http://www.loc.gov/

The largest library in the world, the Library of Congress holds over 128 million items. Funded by the United States Congress, the library is the oldest federal cultural institution in the country. The American Memory collection, which makes available to users over 5 million items online, is an excellent resource for those interested in research using primary sources.

National Archives and Records Administration

http://www.archives.gov/

The National Archives, which holds the nation's official records and those of its federal officials, has a Web site offering excellent resources for researchers of all ages. In addition, the National Archives directs the presidential library program. Its Web site includes searchable catalogs providing access to vast sources documenting American history.

Presidential Libraries

http://www.archives.gov/presidential_libraries/

Contains information about the presidential libraries and links to the individual libraries' Web sites.

State Archives and Historical Societies

http://www.ohiohistory.org/textonly/links/arch_hs.html

A list of state archives and historical societies' Web pages.

Topic Specific Sites

African-Americans

African American Archives, Manuscripts, and Special Collections

http://www2.lib.udel.edu/subj/blks/internet/afamarc.htm

This University of Delaware Library Web site includes an excellent list of links to repositories holding African-American collections.

Amistad Research Center

http://www.amistadresearchcenter.org/

Located at Tulane University in New Orleans, the Amistad Research Center holds materials related primarily to African-Americans, as well as other minority groups in the United States. Its holdings are significant, but only a few finding aids to these holdings are available on the Web site at present. There is a list of manuscript collections.

Moorland-Spingarn Research Center, Howard University

http://www.founders.howard.edu/moorland-spingarn/

Located at Howard University, Washington, DC, this center's holdings include 175,000 volumes, thousands of journals, 17,000 feet of manuscript and archival materials, and about 100,000 prints, photographs, and maps relating to African-American history. The site, however, does not provide information about any of these holdings.

Sexuality

Human Sexuality Collection, Cornell University

http://rmc.library.cornell.edu/HSC/

The Web site contains descriptions and links to finding aids for numerous manuscript collections. Users may search for published material through the online catalog. In addition, there are lists of available periodicals and helpful annotated bibliographies that describe and highlight some of their books.

Kinsey Institute for Research, Indiana University

http://www.indiana.edu/~kinsey/

The Web site contains information about some of the Kinsey Institute's manuscript, archive, art, photography, film, and video collections. The Web site also has a searchable catalog, but this does not contain records for all of their holdings.

United States Immigration History

California Ethnic and Multicultural Archives (CEMA), University of California Santa Barbara

http://cemaweb.library.ucsb.edu/cema_index.html

This Web site includes information about manuscript collections, arranged by ethnicity, including African-American, Asian/Pacific American, Chicano/Latino, and Native American. Some collections have brief descriptions of a few words, while others contain links to complete finding aids along with digital images. Users can also follow links to the Online Archive of California for additional finding aids. In addition, the Web site includes excellent links to other related collections in the United States.

Chicano Research Collection, Arizona State University

http://www.asu.edu/lib/archives/chicano.htm

The collection focuses on Mexican-Americans in Arizona and the Southwest, and the Web site contains descriptions of some manuscript collections. Online exhibits featuring digital images illuminate the Mexican-American experience. Links to other web resources for Mexican-American history make this Web site a must for users researching Mexican-Americans.

Immigration History Research Center, University of Minnesota

http://www.ihrc.umn.edu/

This Web site features a user-friendly search engine for searching descriptions of the collections, or the user can browse through an alphabetical list of collections. Users may also search a separate database of images. The Web site includes a helpful list of links to other Web sites for similar collections.

Women

Archives for Research on Women and Gender, University of Texas, San Antonio

http://www.lib.utsa.edu/Archives/WomenGender/

The collections housed here focus on women and gender issues in south Texas. An annotated guide to resources around the United States and the world makes this site stand out.

The Arthur and Elizabeth Schlesinger Library on the History of Women in America, Harvard University

http://www.radcliffe.edu/schles/index.php

The library holds over 2,500 manuscript collections in women's history. Although users cannot browse through lists of collections, the online catalog on the Web site provides access to finding aids for some of the collections.

Sallie Bingham Center for Women's History and Culture, Duke University

http://scriptorium.lib.duke.edu/women/

This Web site contains helpful information about the Bingham Center's holdings, including annotated subject guides to resources.

Sophia Smith Collection, Smith College

http://www.smith.edu/libraries/libs/ssc/home.html

The Web site gives access to finding aids not only from the Sophia Smith Collection, but also links to the Five College Finding Aid Database, which holds over 900 finding aids from Smith College, Mt. Holyoke College, Amherst College, Hampshire College, and the University of Massachusetts Amherst. The Smith Collection Web site also provides subject lists of manuscript collections in its holdings. Links to other women's history resources on the Web make this a valuable site for researchers.

Chapter 38

Special Collections

Anne Rothfeld

Metasites

ARCHON: Archives On-Line

http://www.archon.nationalarchives.gov.uk/archon/

The main gateway to repositories with manuscript material for British history, ARCHON is a key British resource for both archivists and researchers. The Royal Commission on Historical Manuscripts maintains the site. Researchers will be most interested in the British National Register of Archives (NRA). The NRA leads researchers to a wide variety of manuscript collections, including papers of individuals of note, estates, local authorities, and societies, located both inside and outside the United Kingdom. Users may search the indexes by name of individual or corporate body, type of corporate body, and place name.

Gateway to Library Catalogs

http://lcweb.loc.gov/z3950/

This important search gateway will lead the researcher to descriptions of holdings for a large number of manuscript and archival repositories, predominantly, but not exclusively, in the United States. Select from one of three straightforward, fill-in-the-blank search forms. This electronic catalog derives from the print source, the *National Union Catalog of Manuscript Collections*, a project of the Library of Congress. Check the List of RLIN Library Identifiers on the search forms to see a list of the participating institutions.

Repositories of Primary Sources

http://www.uidaho.edu/special-collections/Other.Repositories.html

With over 5,000 links, this Web site is by far the most complete listing of Web sites for actual (not virtual) archives and special collections departments. Updated frequently by Terry Abraham of the University of Idaho, the site arranges its links by geographical region (continent, country, state, and province). Additional Lists is a good jumping-off point for other archive and special collections metasites.

UNESCO Archives Portal

http://www.unesco.org/cgi-bin/webworld/portal_archives/cgi/page.cgi?d=1

Not nearly as complete as Terry Abraham's Repositories of Primary Sources, this UNESCO site is worth knowing about for the important role UNESCO plays in helping archives around the world. This listing of over 4,000 links covers archives in Europe, North America, Latin America, Asia, and the Pacific as well as international archival organizations, professional associations, archival training, international cooperation, and Internet resources.

General Sites

American Memory: Historical Collections for the National Digital Library

http://lcweb2.loc.gov/ammem/

Over one hundred multimedia collections containing over 9 million digitized documents, photographs, recorded sound, moving pictures, and text selected from the Library of Congress's vast Americana holdings cover topics as diverse as twentieth-century architectural design and ballroom dancing. The collections may be searched by keyword or browsed by titles, topics, or collection type. A fun spin-off is Today in History, which presents people, facts, and events associated with the current day's date. Finally, educators are particularly targeted in the Learning Page with activities, lesson ideas, and other information to help teachers use the primary source material at American Memory in their classrooms.

Annuaire des archives et des bibliothèque nationales, des bibliothèque parlementaires et des centres nationaux d'information scientifique et technique de la Francophonie

http://www.bief.org

This directory, originally published in print form in 1996, has been converted into a searchable Web database by the publishers, Canadian-based BIEF (Banque internationale d'information sur les États francophones). The directory includes basic contact information for the national archives and libraries of forty-seven francophone countries. Further descriptive information about many of the listed institutions can be found in a BIEF companion Web site, titled Profis géo-documentaires des états et gouvernements membres des sommets francophones. Together, these databases are an important source of scarce information about archives for many small, non-Western countries. The Web site is available in French and English.

Archives and Knowledge Management: Scholarly Online Resource Evidence and Records

http://www.academic-genealogy.com/archives.htm

Created and maintained by V. Chris and Thomas M. Tinney Sr., retired genealogical specialists, this Web site includes links to resources of particular interest to genealogists, such as Genealogy on the Web and the Salt Lake City LDS Family History Center. The Tinney Family organizes links to archives, libraries, and many other types of resources in a variety of categories, from Business and Community and Geography to Religion and Surnames.

Archives of American Art

http://americanart.si.edu/museum_info/index.cfm

The Smithsonian maintains the Archives of American Art (AAA) and its Web site to provide researchers with access to "the largest collection of documents on the history of the visual arts in the United States." With 13 million items, including the papers of artists, dealers, critics, art historians, museums, and art-related organizations of all kinds, the Smithsonian's claim can easily be believed. The letters, sketchbooks, diaries, and other paper archives are supplemented with a large oral history interview collection and a sizable photograph collection. General collection descriptions of AAA treasures can be found in the Smithsonian online catalog (SIRIS) as well as RLIN, and the Smithsonian is beginning to make more detailed finding aids available as well.

Archives of Traditional Music at Indiana University

http://www.indiana.edu/~libarchm/

A Web site that provides information about an important and unusual archive of ethnographic sound materials housed at Indiana University. The largest such university-based archive in the United States, the Archives of Traditional Music preserves commercial and field recordings of vocal and instrumental music, folktales, interviews, and oral history from the state of Indiana, the United States, and the diverse cultures of the world. Holdings can be searched using Indiana University's online catalog, IUCAT.

ArchivesUSA

http://archives.chadwyck.com/

Chadwyck-Healey Inc. has developed a product that is an important tool for researchers interested in locating archival material in the United States. Although ArchivesUSA is a subscription service and therefore not available for free over the Web, it is an important resource that some libraries and archives make available to the public. ArchivesUSA integrates the entire print edition of the National Union Catalog of Manuscript Collections with other sources of information to create a more complete record for a greater number of repositories than is available through RLIN AMC.

The Avalon Project at Yale Law School: Documents in Law, History and Diplomacy

http://www.yale.edu/lawweb/avalon/avalon.htm

Directed by William C. Fray and Lisa A. Spar, the Avalon Project is a major source of digital primary source documents in the fields of law, history, economics, politics, diplomacy, and government. Access to the documents is by time period (mainly century), author/title, and subject. Major collections include the Nuremberg Trials Collection and the Native American Treaty Collection. A recent addition to the digital repository is the Cuban Missile Crisis and Aftermath section, with over 250 documents (including editorial notes), prefatory essay, and lists of persons and abbreviations—a good example of the Avalon Project's aim to not simply mount static text, but to add value.

Black Film Center/Archive

http://www.indiana.edu/~bfca/

By and about African-Americans, the historic 700 films housed at the Black Film Center/Archive at Indiana University consist of both Hollywood and independent efforts. Supplementing the films and videotapes are interviews, photographs, and other archival material. The Web site gives access to descriptions of the repository's holdings, the Frame by Frame database, and related Internet sites.

Canadian Archival Resources on the Internet

http://www.archivescanada.ca/car/menu.html

A comprehensive list of links to Canadian archives and associated resources on the Internet, this guide is the work of two Canadian archivists: Cheryl Avery of the University of Saskatchewan Archives and Steve Billinton of the Archives of Ontario. Researchers can locate archives by name, type (provincial, university, municipal, religious, and medical), and Canadian region or find links to archival educational resources, associations, listservs, and multirepository databases.

Directory of Archives in Australia

http://www.asap.unimelb.edu.au/asa/directory/asa_dir.htm

The updated Web version of a directory originally printed in 1992, this directory of Australian archives allows researchers to browse archives alphabetically and by Australian states and to search them by keyword. There are also handy lists of links to Australian archives and finding aids on the Web.

Directory of Corporate Archives in the United States and Canada

http://www.hunterinformation.com/corporat.htm

The fifth edition of this important print directory, put out by the Society of American Archivists, Business Archives Section, has recently moved to the Web. From Amgen to Walt Disney Corporation, each corporate archive entry supplies contact information, type of business, hours of service, conditions of access, and holding information. "Corporate" is interpreted broadly and includes "professional associations" ranging from the American Psychiatric Association to the International Longshoreman's Union. The directory may be searched by name of corporation, name of archivist, or geographical location.

DPLS Online Data Archive

http://dpls.dacc.wisc.edu/archive.html

The Data and Program Library Service at the University of Wisconsin is creating access to a large selection of archival machine-readable datasets (raw data and documentation files) that can be downloaded for use by social science researchers. The datasets, listed in reverse chronological order or alphabetically by title, cover raw data from an extremely diverse range of historical and current topics, such as French Old Regime bureaucrats (1661–1790), vegetation change in the Bahamas (1972), and the effects of the Learnfare Program (1993–1996).

EuroDocs: Primary Historical Documents From Western Europe: Selected Transcriptions, Facsimiles and Translations

http://eudocs.lib.byu.edu/index.php/Main_Page

Aiming to provide digitized documents that shed light on "key historical happenings" in political, economic, social, and cultural history, EuroDocs links to a wealth of digitized resources organized under twenty-three Western European countries from Andorra to Vatican City. Documents are also accessible from pages devoted to medieval and Renaissance Europe and to Europe as a supernational region. EuroDocs is a project of Richard Hacken, European studies bibliographer, at the Harold B. Lee Library, Brigham Young University in Provo, Utah.

Guía preliminar de fuentes documentales etnográficas para el estudio de los pueblos indígenas de Iberoamérica

http://www.lanic.utexas.edu/project/tavera/

An important guide in the Spanish language, made available on the Web, the Guía describes the holdings related to indigenous peoples at hundreds of libraries and archives throughout Latin America, the United States, and Europe. A project of La Fundacién Histérica Tavera in Spain, the Guía is organized by country and type of archive (civil or ecclesiastical) and provides contact information and holdings descriptions for all of the institutions listed.

Historical Maps: The Perry-Castañeda Library Map Collection

http://www.lib.utexas.edu/maps

A wonderful collection of digitized historical maps from all regions of the world offered by the Libraries at the University of Texas at Austin. Maps are organized by continent (including the polar regions and oceans) and each map listing gives both publication information and file size. Although most maps are in JPEG format in the 200 to 300K range, some map files are much larger, so users should expect some slow load times. The site also includes Historical Maps at Other Web Sites with links to other historical map collections.

History of Medicine—National Library of Medicine

http://www.nlm.nih.gov/hmd/

The History of Medicine Division at the National Library of Medicine houses one of the world's largest history of medicine collections. The collection consists of print and nonprint materials including archival resources, photographs, and historical audiovisuals that document the history of medicine, health, and disease in all time periods and cultures. Arabic and Persian manuscripts dating back to the eleventh century are available.

International Institute of Social History

http://www.iisg.nl

Founded in 1935 in the Netherlands, IISH is one of the world's largest archival and research institutions in the field of social history, particularly labor history. Its 2,700 archival collections cover a range of topics not always well represented in traditional archives, like anarchism, revolutionary populism in nineteenth-century Eastern Europe, the French Revolution and Utopian socialism, and World War II resistance movements. Collections may be identified using an online catalog, a list of archival collections, or other finding aids. Other IISH resources include the William Morris Archive on the Web, Occasio (a collection of digital social history documents), and numerous electronic publications. The institute's image collections are highlighted by a number of virtual exhibitions with titles like The Chairman Smiles and Art to the People.

National Archives and Records Administration

http://www.archives.gov

NARA's Web site is a rich source of information for historians, genealogists, teachers, and students. For historians, the Research Room organizes information about historical archival records by branch of government and type of material. For genealogists, the Genealogy Page publishes not only practical information about using NARA's facilities nationwide, but also a growing list of "quick guides" on census, military, immigration, and other types of records. Teachers and students will appreciate the Digital Classroom: Primary Sources, Activities, and Training for Educators and Students, with reproducible documents and teaching activities. The Online Exhibit Hall is a showcase for NARA treasures. Finally, NARA's Archival Research Catalog (ARC) is a searchable database that contains and describes more than 1,235,359 cubic feet of selected NARA holdings in Washington, DC, and Maryland (Archives II), the regional archives, and presidential libraries, including 106,215 digital copies of selected textual documents, photographs, maps, and sound recordings.

New York Public Library for the Performing Arts

http://www.nypl.org/research/lpa/lpa.html

"The world's most extensive combination of circulating, reference and rare archival collections" in the performing arts, this Web site describes the library's important collections of recordings, videotapes, autograph manuscripts, correspondence, sheet music, stage designs, press clippings, programs, posters, and photographs in the areas of dance, music, and theater.

Online Archive of California

http://www.oac.cdlib.org/

The Online Archive of California is an umbrella site bringing together information on a steadily increasing number of archival institutions in California. Its most important resource is a centralized database of over 8,000 searchable electronic finding aids, which allows a level of precision searching for archival materials not available in more traditional online library catalogs, like RLIN AMC. Digital images of photographs and correspondence are also available.

Social Science Data Archives–Europe

http://www.nsd.uib.no/cessda/europe.html

A map of Europe organizes links to fourteen important European social science data archives, with separate links to similar non-European institutions. Maintained by the Council of European Social Science Data Archives (CESSDA), this Web site also allows researchers to search the holdings of eleven electronic data repositories through its Integrated Data Catalogue.

Television News Archive

http://tvnews.vanderbilt.edu/

Vanderbilt University holds "the world's most extensive and complete archive of television news," including 30,000 evening news broadcasts and 9,000 hours of special news-related programming. These news broadcasts have been consistently recorded and preserved by the archive since 1968. The Web site makes several searchable indexes available, including Network Television Evening News Abstracts, Special Reports and Periodic News Broadcasts, and Specialized News Collections (containing descriptive summaries of news material for major events like the Persian Gulf War of 1991). The archive is willing to loan videotapes to researchers worldwide.

United States Holocaust Memorial Museum

http://www.ushmm.org/research/collections

The Archive of the Holocaust Memorial Museum in Washington, DC, has gathered together 13 million pages of microfilmed documents, 50,000 photo images, 200 hours of historical motion picture footage, 250 documentary or feature films, and 2,900 oral interviews—all related to the Holocaust, its origins, and aftermath. The document and photographic archives may be searched individually or together using the USHMM Information Access query form available at the Web site.

USIA Declassified Historical Information

http://dosfan.lib.uic.edu/usia/

Pursuant to Executive Order 12958, the United States Information Agency Declassification Unit prepares a listing of declassified documents in order to alert the general public, especially academic researchers, to information no longer classified. Researchers may do keyword searching of this listing or browse by broad topic, from Africa to Youth, to find the titles of more than 5,300 classified and unclassified one-cubic-foot boxes of records coming from the National Archives and many other document-holding federal agencies.

Women and Gender Project, UTSA Archives

http://www.lib.utsa.edu/Archives/WomenGender/

This guide to the archives, libraries, and other repositories on the Web with archival materials by or about women is maintained by the Archives for Research on Women and Gender Project at the University of Texas at San Antonio. Arranged by states in the United States (plus a link devoted to institutions outside of the United States), each listing includes annotations indicating which materials in a given collection may be of interest to researchers in the field of women's history.

Chapter 39

Online Reference Desk

Anne Rothfeld

Metasites

Avalon Project at Yale Law School

http://www.yale.edu/lawweb/avalon/avalon.htm

Documents in law, history, and diplomacy from the pre-eighteenth, eighteenth, nineteenth, and twentieth centuries. "The Avalon Project will mount digital documents relevant to the fields of Law, History, Economics, Politics, Diplomacy and Government. We do not intend to mount only static text but rather to add value to the text by linking to supporting documents expressly referred to in the body of the text."

Center for History and New Media

http://chnm.gmu.edu

The center shows historical works in new media and offers a forum to discuss the usage of archival sources in historical research and presentation. In addition, the center's Web pages provide electronic access to extensive directories, journals, sources, and professional discussions related to historical issues. The center's resources are designed to benefit professional historians, high school teachers, and students of history.

Google

http://www.google.com

The world's largest search engine—for free!

History Cooperative

http://www.historycooperative.org

A collaboration between the American Historical Association, the Organization of American Historians (OAH), the University of Illinois Press, and the National Academy Press, this Web site is a gateway to full-text articles in recent journals including *American Historical Review* and *Journal of American History*. Access to some portions of the Web site is restricted.

History Departments Around the World

http://chnm.gmu.edu/resources/departments/

Sponsored by the Center for History and New Media at George Mason University, a search engine of university history departments.

H-Net Humanities and Social Sciences Online

http://www.h-net.org/

H-Net is an international organization of historians, teachers, and students of history contributing to discussion of numerous historical subjects thematically, geographically, and chronologically. H-Net offers discussion listservs, job announcements, book reviews, and calls for papers. Each list is monitored by a committee of scholars.

InfoMine

http://infomine.ucr.edu/

Created by librarians, InfoMine is a gateway of resources for faculty, students, and research staff at the university level. Organized by topics and material medium, this reference tool contains databases, electronic journals, electronic books, bulletin boards, listservs, online library card catalogs, articles, and directories of researchers.

Internet Public Library (IPL), Reference Center

http://www.ipl.org/ref

Provides all the basic reference information and specific subject areas of a regular brick-and-mortar library. When users click on a topic, IPL takes them to additional subject-related sites. Links are subdivided and annotated.

Research-It! Your One-stop Reference Desk

http://www.iTools.com

A metasearch site for information. Each area has its own search screen. Hosted by iTools!, the site is broken into sections or "tools" including language, research, financial, maps, people search, and a link to other links.

Scout Report for Social Sciences and Humanities

http://scout.wisc.edu/

Since 1994, the Internet Scout Project of the Computer Sciences Department at the University of Wisconsin-Madison has been offering a selective collection of Internet resources, covering a myriad of topics. The Scout Report staff consists of content specialists aiming at an audience of faculty, students, staff, and librarians in the social sciences and humanities. Subscription is free with no solicitations and pop-up ads, and the report conveniently arrives in your e-mail inbox.

Archives

ArchivesUSA: Integrated Collection and Repository Information

http://archives.chadwyck.com

Fee-based service providing information and access to primary source holdings of over 5,500 repositories, indexes to over 149,000 special collections, and links to over 5,000 online finding aids. ArchivesUSA includes three major references: Directory of Archives and Manuscript Repositories in the United States (DAMRUS); National Union Catalogue of Manuscript Collections (NUCMC); and National Inventory of Documentary Sources in the United States (NIDS). ArchivesUSA is updated quarterly.

Historical Text Archive

http://www.historicaltextarchive.com

Now with its own domain name, the site is divided into three sections: articles, e-books, and Web links. Organized by geographical and topical subject headings, this site provides links to other sites. Sites focus on the studying and teaching of history.

Manuscripts Catalogue

http://molcat.bl.uk/

The British Library's Department of Manuscripts catalog covers accessions from 1753 to the present day in all types of handwritten materials, with the focus on Western languages. Users can search the multiple catalogs by name, language, year, and other modifiers.

Repositories of Primary Sources

http://www.uidaho.edu/special-collections/Other.Repositories.html

With over 5,000 links, this Web site is by far the most complete listing of Web sites for actual (not virtual) archives and special collections departments. Updated frequently by Terry Abraham of the University of Idaho, the site arranges its links by geographical region (continent, country, state, and province). Additional Lists is a good jumping-off point for other archive and special collections metasites.

Acronyms

Acronym Finder

http://www.acronymfinder.com

Searches over 398,000 common acronyms with definitions, including technology, telecommunications, computer science, and military acronyms. Contains search hints and links to other acronym sites.

Almanacs

CIA World Factbook 2000

http://www.cia.gov/cia/publications/factbook

Complete resource of statistics, maps, and facts for over 250 countries and other entities. The *Factbook* is in the public domain. The site has links to other excellent resources, including Chiefs of State and Cabinet Members of Foreign Governments and selected task force reports. Prepared by the CIA with information provided by numerous federal agencies, including Bureau of the Census, Bureau of Labor Statistics, Department of State, Defense Intelligence Agency, and U.S. Board on Geographic Names.

Biographies

Biographical Dictionary

http://www.s9.com/biography

Includes over 28,000 notable men and women from ancient times to the present day. Users can search the database by name, birth year, death year, and other keywords. Links to biography-related sites, arranged by subject, and has tips for students and teachers on how to use this resource in the classroom.

Biography.com

http://www.biography.com

Searchable database with over 25,000 biographical entries and over 2,500 video clips. Features discussions and materials for the classroom.

Copyright

Intellectual Property Law

http://www.cs.utexas.edu/users/ethics/prop_rights/IP.html

Connects visitors to Web site links including patents, trademarks, intellectual property law, and copyright.

U.S. Copyright Office

http://www.loc.gov/copyright

Housed in the Library of Congress in Washington, DC, this is the main office for copyright information on usage and copyright registration. The site describes how to file for a copyright, what can be copyrighted, and the terms of a copyright. Includes copyright information regarding digitization, the Digital Millennium Copyright Act, legislation, and publications.

Corporations

Directory of Corporate Archives in the United States and Canada

http://www.hunterinformation.com/corporat.htm

The fifth edition of this important print directory, put out by the Society of American Archivists, Business Archives Section, has recently moved to the

Web. From Amgen to Walt Disney Corporation, each corporate archive entry supplies contact information, type of business, hours of service, conditions of access, and holding information. "Corporate" is interpreted broadly and includes professional associations ranging from the American Psychiatric Association to the International Longshoreman's Union. The directory may be searched by name of corporation, name of archivist, or geographical location.

Dictionaries and Thesauri

The Alternative Dictionaries

http://www.notam.uio.no/~hcholm/altlang

Contains foreign words and expressions that would not be found in a standard dictionary. Over 3,100 words and phrases in 120 different languages. Readers and users can add words to the site.

Merriam-Webster Dictionary

http://www.m-w.com/dictionary.htm

Sponsored by Merriam-Webster Inc. Full definitions with an online thesaurus available. Features words recently added, word of the day, and word games.

Oxford English Dictionary On-line

http://www.oed.com/

Fee-based service. Second edition is now available.

Roget's Thesaurus

http://www.thesaurus.com

Like Merriam-Webster, this is the print version now searchable with links to other words and phrases, word of the day, and word games.

Wordsmyth English Dictionary-Thesaurus

http://www.wordsmyth.net

Through this Web site, researchers can search words exactly or as a phrase, find definition and pronunciation guides, and access additional dictionaries with words of the week.

YourDictionary.com

http://www.yourdictionary.com

A portal linking over 2,500 multilingual dictionaries, thesauri, and other sites relating to words and phrases in over 300 languages. Grammar guides in selected languages are also available.

Dissertations and Theses

UMI's On-Line Dissertation Services

http://www.umi.com/umi/dissertations/

This site links to published and archived dissertations and theses, including those available for purchase. Maintains a comprehensive bibliography of over 2 million doctoral dissertations and master's theses. A listing of best-selling dissertations is also available.

Encyclopedias

Encyclopedia Britannica Online

http://www.eb.com

This is a fee-based resource. Content is taken from the print edition and also includes information from *Britannica Books of the Year, Nations of the World, Merriam-Webster's Collegiate Dictionary,* 13,000 graphics and illustrations, and links to related Web sites.

Encyclopedia.com

http://www.encyclopedia.com

Because knowledge is cool, this user-friendly Web site offers a free encyclopedia featuring more than 57,000 articles from the *Columbia Electronic Encyclopedia,* sixth edition. Users can search over 32 million full-text documents, photographs, and maps provided by HighBeam Research.

Symbols.com—Encyclopedia of Western Signs and Ideograms

http://www.symbols.com

Site contains over 2,500 Western signs with discussions of histories, uses, and meanings. Search using the graphic index or the word index.

FAQs (Frequently Asked Questions)

Encyclopedia Smithsonian

http://www.si.edu/resource/faq

Encyclopedia Smithsonian features answers to Smithsonian's frequently asked questions with links to available Smithsonian resources. Topics are filed alphabetically.

Flags

Flags of the World (FOTW)

http://www.fotw.ca/flags

Users can view more than 9,800 pages about flags and over 18,000 images. Site contains news and reports posted to the site's mailing list, and flags can be searched by country, title, maps, and keywords. There is also a glossary and bibliography.

General

Find-A-Grave

http://www.findagrave.com/index.html

This site locates the graves of famous people. Database is organized by last name and geographic location and some photos of graves are included. Users can search by name, location, claim to fame, and date. Database currently contains over 7.2 million names.

The HistoryNet: Where History Lives on the Web

http://www.thehistorynet.com

Contains an archive of different topical areas including eyewitness accounts, historic travel, and people profiles. The site has links to history magazines and newspaper articles and sponsors daily quizzes and factoids.

HyperHistory Online

http://www.hyperhistory.com/online_n2/History_n2/a.html

A 3,000-year time line is available to access over 2,000 files with relevant maps, biographies, and brief histories of people, places, and events. The People section reaches from 1000 BCE to the present for over 800 individuals in science, culture, religion, and politics. The History section displays time lines for major civilizations. The Events section continually grows on the site, ranging from 1790 to the present.

Internet Scout Project

http://scout.wisc.edu/

Published every Friday on the Web and by e-mail, this site provides valuable information about new electronic and online resources, free of charge. Subject report areas include social sciences, science and engineering, business and economics, and the site's general weekly report. Librarians and educators contribute to the site offering reviews of useful and not so useful pages. Searchable archives.

Geographic Names and Maps

Getty Vocabulary Names

http://www.getty.edu/research/conducting_research/vocabularies/

Sponsored by the Getty Research Institute, this site currently has information for the Art and Architecture Thesaurus (AAT), the Union List of Artist Names (ULAN), and the Getty Thesaurus of Geographic Names (TGN). AAT contains over 133,000 terms and notes for describing fine art, archival materials, and material culture. ULAN contains over 225,000 names and biographical information about artist and architects. The TGN currently has over a million geographic names and places. Users can search displays by using geographic hierarchy displays, definition or description of term, other known names, and sources.

Perry-Castañeda Library Map Collection

http://www.lib.utexas.edu/maps/

Links to historical maps at other Web sites. Scope of site includes historical maps from Africa, Asia, the Pacific, North America, South America, Europe, and the Middle East. Also includes astronomical maps.

USGS Mapping Information—Geographic Names Information System (GNIS)

http://geonames.usgs.gov/

This Web site contains over 2 million physical and cultural geographic features in the United States supplied by the Geographic Names Information System and U.S. Board on Geographic Names (BGN). Includes a search engine and links to online geographic resources.

Government and State Resources

FedStats

http://www.fedstats.gov

Statistical information gateway for over a hundred federal government agencies and departments. Users can search FedStats by topic for information on demographics, education, and labor. Each site provides annotated links. Includes the Statistical Abstract of the United States.

Social Statistics Briefing Room

http://www.whitehouse.gov/fsbr/ssbr.html

Access to current federal social statistics on crime, demographics, education, and health. Links are produced and provided by numerous federal agencies.

THOMAS: U.S. Congress on the Internet

http://thomas.loc.gov/

Users can search for congressional bills, the *Congressional Record,* committee bills, and historical documents. FAQs regarding THOMAS Are available.

Grants

FinAid! The Smart Student Guide to Financial Aid

http://www.finaid.org/

"One of the most comprehensive annotated collections of information about student financial aid on the web." Includes links to loans, scholarships, and military aid; information on other types of aid; and tips for applying for aid.

The Foundation Center: Your Gateway to Philanthropy on the World Wide Web

http://fdncenter.org

A subscription-based Web site, the Foundation Center provides grant information, funding trends and analysis, libraries and locations, and Foundation Center publications. Searchable links to over 80,000 private, commercial, and corporate funding sources.

Indices

Librarians' Index to the Internet

http://lii.org

Annotated subject-directory to over 7,900 Web resources arranged by subject. The index is linked to over 200 history-related sites. Using the available search engine can focus a search.

Internet Tutorials

Evaluating Internet Resources

http://library.albany.edu/internet/evaluate.html

Discusses what elements should be included in a reliable Web site and why, including the intended audience, the source of the content, the accuracy and comprehensiveness of the content, and the style and functionality of the page.

Searching the Internet: Recommended Sites and Search Techniques

http://www.internettutorials.net/search.html

Discusses and describes searching tips for successful usage of subject directories and search engines within Web pages.

Libraries

The Library of Congress

http://www.loc.gov/

America's oldest federal cultural institution and the world's largest library. The library's collection contains over 128 million items and includes the largest map, film, and television collections in the world. Its primary mission is to serve the research needs of the U.S. Congress, but the Library assists all Americans through its popular Web site American Memory, which currently contains over 5 million images.

The National Agricultural Library

http://www.nal.usda.gov/

NAL is the primary source of agricultural information for researchers, educators, policy makers, consumers of agricultural products, and the public. The library is one of the world's largest and most accessible agricultural research libraries. Users can search for books and journal articles in NAL's online catalog, AGRICOLA.

National Library of Education

http://ies.ed.gov/ncee/projects/nat_ed_library.asp

NLE is the federal government's main resource for education information.

National Library of Medicine

http://www.nlm.nih.gov/

The National Library of Medicine is the world's largest biomedical library. Users can search for books and journal articles on NLM's online catalog, LocatorPlus.

Listservs

H-Net

http://www.h-net.org

For historians, librarians, and archivists, H-Net hosts over a hundred different topical listservs and includes a call for papers page, conference announcements, and employment.

Tile.Net: The Comprehensive Internet Reference

http://tile.net

Users can search for discussion lists, newsgroups (usenet), and FTP sites by entering a subject search. All the results are linked to a page describing the listing and how to subscribe.

Quotations

John Barlett's Familiar Quotations (1901)

http://www.bartleby.com/100/

Sponsored by Columbia University's Bartleby Library Archive. Includes English and French writers and wisdom from the ancients. Users can browse by author or search by keyword. Indices are available to browse by author, both alphabetically and chronologically.

The Quotations Page

http://www.quotationpage.com

Read motivational quotes of the day on numerous topics including successes, families, authors, and sports.

Statistics

Historical U.S. Census Data Browser

http://fisher.lib.virginia.edu/collections/stats/histcensus/

Descriptions of people and economy of the United States for each state and county from 1790 to 1960. Information on individuals is not available.

Statistical Abstract of the United States

http://www.census.gov/compendia/statab/

Excellent resource for statistical information: demographics, employment, industrial production, and government financial information. Online information covers data from 1995 to 2005.

U.S. Census Bureau: U.S. Gazetteer

http://tiger.census.gov/cgi-bin/gazetteer

Census data from 1990 on all incorporated municipalities in the United States. Maps provided.

Student and School Information

American Universities

http://www.clas.ufl.edu/CLAS/american-universities.html

An alphabetical listing of universities and colleges in the United States offering undergraduate and advanced degrees.

CollegeNet

http://www.collegenet.com

Search engine helps students find the ideal college by using such categories as region, sports, major, and tuition. Users can also find scholarships and financial aid, college Web applications, and information on college recruiting. Virtual tours allow users to see campuses from the desktop with links to the schools' Web sites.

Peterson's College Search and Guide: Colleges, Career Information, Test Prep, and More

http://www.petersons.com

Prospective students can find their ideal college by major, region, and size of student population. This education resource has links to colleges and universities, graduate programs, and international programs. Users can search the database by keywords and subject specialty.

U.S. News and World Report Online: Graduate School Rankings

http://www.usnews.com/usnews/edu/grad/rankings/rankindex_brief.php

This site helps prospective students find graduate programs meeting their requirements. Includes methodology of rankings.

U.S. News and World Report Online: Undergraduate School Rankings

http://www.usnews.com/usnews/edu/college/rankings/rankindex_brief.php

Users can locate a school by using categories from the most expensive school to one with the best marching band! Includes an explanation of the magazine's methodology of rankings.

Style Manuals and Usage

MLA Online

http://www.mla.org/style

This official site for the Modern Language Association (MLA) provides explanations of the *MLA Handbook for Writers of Research Papers* and *MLA Style Manual and Guide to Scholarly Publications,* especially on citing electronic resources. Official site for Modern Languages Association (MLA).

Strunk's Elements of Style

http://www.bartleby.com/141/

The print edition online.

Glossary

ActiveX: Downloadable Microsoft technology used on the Internet. These controls are activated by the Web browser and perform a variety of different functions, such as allowing users to view Microsoft Word documents via the Web browser, play animated graphical effects, and display interactive maps. As the name suggests, they make the Web page active, and they provide the same functions as Java Applets.

animated GIF File: A special type of GIF file. A collection of GIFs, presented one after the other with each picture slightly different from the previous one, gives the impression of a video.

applet: A brief program written in the Java programming language that can only be used as part of a Web page.

ASCII (American Standard Code for Information Interchange): A way of formatting data so that it can be read by any program, whether DOS, Windows, or Mac.

av (audiovisual): The file extension assigned to the final draft of an AV document.

BBS (bulletin board system): This term usually refers to small, dial-up systems, which local users can call directly. BBS users generally work asynchronously, meaning that they do not have to be connected to the Web the entire time they are uploading, downloading, and posting messages.

bit: The smallest unit of information understood by a computer. A bit can take a value of 0 or 1. A byte is made up of eight bits, which is large enough to contain a single character. A kilobyte is equivalent to 1024 bytes. A megabyte is equivalent to 1024 kilobytes. A gigabyte is equivalent to 1024 megabytes. A terabyte is equivalent to 1024 gigabytes. A petabyte is equivalent to 1024 terabytes and 9,007,199,254,740,992 bits.

blog: A Web log, which is a log on the Web of a person's (or group's) ideas normally on a certain subject, such as American history or current events, and contain the log and posts about the ideas.

broadband: This refers to a variety of ways to access the Internet, all of them faster than dial-up. Included in this category are cable modems, wireless connections, and DSL lines. Availability greatly varies, and people in urban areas generally have more access than those in rural areas.

browser: A program used to access the World Wide Web. The most popular browsers —Netscape, Linux, AOL, and Internet Explorer—allow users to interact audio-visually with the World Wide Web. AOL provides its own browser solely for its subscribers to use.

burn: To record music or data from a computer onto a storage device (usually a CD or DVD).

cable modem: A modem that works through a cable TV network to send and receive information.

client: A synonym for Web browser or browser.

desktop: The screen that appears once a computer has started up and launched its operating system, but before any programs are launched. This is the background that appears on the base screen of the computer.

dial-up: A type of modem that works through telephone lines to send and receive information. Also, the act of using such a modem.

discussion list: A program that allows an asynchronous discussion between various members of the list by sending a message from one member to all the rest and then allowing the rest to respond. Most discussion lists also have archives of past messages.

DNS (domain name system): DNS is the system that locates addresses on the World Wide Web. When a DNS error message is given by a browser, it means the address it is looking for cannot be found.

document: On the World Wide Web, documents are files or a set of files that can be accessed with a Web browser. Also, most people use the term to refer to any word-processing file.

download: The process of getting a file or files from a remote computer, which is a computer other than the one on a user's desk or local area network.

DSL (digital subscriber line): A faster way to access the Internet than the standard dial-up process, often available through the phone company but generally more expensive.

e-mail: Sending typed messages and attachments through an electronic mail network.

encryption: A method of converting data into unreadable code so that prying eyes cannot understand the content.

FAQ (frequently asked questions): A document that contains answers to the most frequently asked questions about a given topic.

file: A collection of data stored on a disk or other storage device under a certain name.

flame: The practice of sending extremely negative or insulting e-mail.

Flash: A program developed by Macromedia Corporation used by many Web sites to present graphics quickly on Web pages.

FTP (file transfer protocol): A tool for moving files from a computer site to a user's local service provider's computer, from which they can be downloaded.

GIF (graphic interchange format): A set of standards for compressing graphic files so that they occupy less space in a computer's memory or on a storage device. CompuServe and Unisys developed GIF.

hits: Internet slang for both the number of times a site is accessed and for the number of sites found when using any Web search engine.

H-Net (Humanities and Social Studies Online): An organization dedicated to exploiting the potential of electronic media for history. H-Net was originally supported by the National Endowment for the Humanities, the University of Illinois–Chicago, and Michigan State University. Now, H-Net is supported by grants, donations, and job ads paid for by the universities advertising. H-Net sponsors discussion lists, Web sites, book reviews, conferences, and other activities.

home page: The designated beginning point for accessing a World Wide Web site.

HTML (Hypertext Markup Language): One computer language used to construct documents on the World Wide Web. Most home pages are written in HTML.

HTTP (Hypertext Transfer Protocol): A method of coding information that enables different computers running different software to communicate information. It permits the transfer of text, sounds, images, and other data.

hypertext: Data that provides links to other data, allowing users to move from one resource to another.

icon: A graphic image that is used to represent (and usually activate) a file or program.

Internet: The worldwide network of computers that are linked together using the Internet protocol TCP/IP.

ISP (Internet service provider): Any organization that provides connections to the Internet.

Java: A programming language developed by Sun Microsystems that allows programmers to create interactive applications that can be run within Web browsers on any type of computer. Java programs are referred to as applets.

JavaScript: A programming language for developing Internet applications. A Web browser interprets JavaScript statements embedded in an HTML page to create interactivity.

JPEG (Joint Photographic Experts Group): This is now the standard format for compressing graphic files so they occupy less space in a computer's memory or on a storage device.

kbps (kilobits per second): A unit frequently used to measure how fast data is transferred between devices on a network. One KBPS is 1,000 bits per second.

LAN (local area network): A group of computers connected together by cable or some other means so they can share common resources.

link: A connection point that takes the user from one document to another or from one information provider to another.

Listserv: A computer that serves a discussion group by processing, distributing, and storing messages and files for all members of the list.

log in: To gain access to a remote computer system or network by typing a login name and password.

login name (user-ID): The name used for security purposes to gain access to and identify oneself on a network or computer system.

modem: A way to connect to the Internet. A modem can operate through a phone line (dial-up or DSL) or through a TV (cable modem). Generally a user must both buy a modem (although a modem may come with the computer) and pay for service from an Internet service provider (ISP) in order to gain access to the Web.

MPEG (Moving Pictures Expert Group): This is the standard for compressing video images so they occupy less space in a computer's memory or on a storage device.

netiquette: Etiquette for the Internet.

network: A group of interconnected computers.

nickname: A name used in place of a real name. Aliases are often shorter or cleverer than a person's real name, and they offer a measure of privacy in the online community.

page: Either a single screen of information on a Web site or all of the information on a particular site.

PDF (portable document format): A file type developed by Adobe Systems to allow the preservation of complex formatting and symbols.

POP (post office protocol): A standard for exchanging e-mail between a user's computer and an Internet service provider.

RAM (random access memory): The memory that a computer uses to temporarily store and manipulate information. RAM does not hold information after a computer is turned off.

RealAudio: Software that allows sound files to be transmitted from the Internet back to the user's computer in streams, allowing the experience of immediate and simultaneous playing.

rip: To copy music or data from a CD or DVD onto a computer. The first user burns the information from a computer onto a CD or DVD and then a second user rips the information from the storage device onto another computer.

SMTP (simple mail transfer protocol): An accepted standard used extensively on the Internet to allow the transfer of e-mail messages between computers.

snail mail: A term that e-mail users employ to describe the traditional mail or post office service.

spam: To send e-mails to people who in no way asked for that information. Spamming is usually done as bulk e-mailing in order to hassle people, to promote a product, or to send a virus. Named for the Monty Python sketch in which a restaurant served almost nothing but Spam.

TCP/IP (transfer control protocol/Internet protocol): Essentially this is the most basic language on the Internet. The rules of TCP/IP govern the sending of packets of data between computers on the Internet, and they allow for the transmission of other protocols on the Internet, such as HTTP and FTP.

telnet: An Internet protocol enabling users to log on to a remote computer.

T-1 line: A leased Internet line connection. The maximum speed at which data can be transmitted is 1.45 megabits per second on a T-1 line.

UNIX: Like DOS or Windows, UNIX is an operating system run by most of the computers that provide access to the Internet.

URL (Uniform Resource Locator): The address for an Internet site.

USENET: A network of newsgroups dedicated to thousands of different topics.

User-ID (Login name): The name used for security purposes to gain access to and identify oneself on a network or computer system.

Web browser: A program used to access the World Wide Web. The most popular browsers—Netscape and Internet Explorer—allow users to interact audiovisually with the World Wide Web.

Webmail: An e-mail program, based at a Web site, that allows users to pick up their e-mail wherever they are in the world, as long as they have access to the Web. Users log onto a Web site to pick up their e-mail rather than having to access the server at their own institution. Useful and becoming a more universal way to administer and access e-mail.

WiFi (wireless access): A pun on "HiFi"(high fidelity), WiFi is the term used to describe any computer or location capable of making a wireless Internet connection.

Windows Media Player: A program, available for computers using Windows, that allows users to play audio and video files.

.wma: Windows Media Audio. This extension refers to an audio file that is playable by the Windows Media Player on a Windows-based machine.

.wmv: Windows Media Video. This extension refers to a video file that is playable by the Windows Media Player on a Windows-based machine.

WWW (World Wide Web): An Internet service that enables users to connect to all the hypermedia documents on the Internet. The Web is like a network within the Internet.

Zip: Zip files (or Zipped files) are files that have been compressed by a software package to reduce the amount of space that the data take up. The file type is popular on the Internet because smaller files can be sent faster. To create or open a Zip file, a user needs a special software package such as WinZip or PKUNZIP. The .zip extension indicates a Zip file.

About the Editors
and Contributors

John Barnhill is an independent scholar in Oklahoma (PhD, Oklahoma State University) whose publications deal with immigration, civil rights, energy, and other aspects of the twentieth-century United States. He is author of *From Surplus to Substitution: Energy in Texas* and numerous articles and reviews.

Jeremy Boggs is a PhD student in the Department of History and Art History, George Mason University, and a graduate assistant at the Center for History and New Media. His research interests include nineteenth-century U.S. cultural history, race and racism in U.S. history, and history and new media. Jeremy is currently working on a project that assesses the current state of historical scholarship on the Web and an annotated index of online history journals. Jeremy maintains a blog, ClioWeb, at http://www.clioweb.org.

David Calverley has a PhD in history from the University of Ottawa (1999). His particular specialty is Canadian history (with a focus on First Nations history). He has taught postsecondary students and currently is teaching secondary-level history at the Crescent School in Toronto. His book, *Who Controls the Hunt? Ontario's Game Act, the Canadian Government and the Ojibwa, 1800–1940,* is under consideration for publication by McGill-Queen's University Press.

Mary E. Chalmers teaches European history at Butler University, Indianapolis, Indiana, and is currently president of the American Association for History and Computing. She has taught European and world history for almost a decade at a variety of institutions.

Samuel Dicks holds a doctorate from the University of Oklahoma and has been a member of the history faculty at Emporia State University since 1965. He is the publication director of *Teaching History: A Journal of Methods* and edits its Internet Web site. In addition to courses in ancient and medieval history, he also teaches historiography and an introductory class in genealogy.

Bambi L. Dingman is a freelance writer from New Jersey. She has been the French and Indian War editor for *Smoke and Fire News,* an internationally recognized living history newspaper, and has also written for *Recreating History Magazine.* She currently serves as the regimental adjutant for the Seventh Vermont Infantry Regiment as part of the Web-based project Vermont in the Civil War.

Benjamin Frederick is a research consultant for ChaCha Search. He received his BA from DePauw University, where he was a member of the Information Technology Fellows Program. Prior to joining ChaCha, Frederick held various consulting and technology positions in both major corporations and non-profit organizations.

Mary Anne Hansen is an assistant professor at Montana State University Libraries. She has authored numerous articles and presented papers at several scholarly conferences, including the Association of College and Research Libraries Biennial Conference.

Mariah Hudson is a PhD student in early American history at The Ohio State University in Columbus, Ohio, where she teaches early American history. Her research interests are in urban development and gender, ethnicity, and race in the nineteenth century trans-Mississippi West. For her dissertation, she is writing a comparative study of public health systems and their relationship to mortality in Cleveland, Savannah, Denver, and Atlanta. Mariah holds an MA in American studies from the University of Dallas (2001), where she studied American economic history, and a BA in English from the University of Oregon (1999).

Ranin Kazemi is a second-year MA student in the Department of History at The Ohio State University. Islamic history is his primary academic focus. He acquired his BA degree in English and history from Middle Tennessee State University in May 2002. His interests within his primary field include Iranian history, cultural and intellectual exchange between Iran and its neighbors, and social and intellectual movements on the greater Iranian plateau.

John A. King holds degrees in history and political science from Emory University, Atlanta, Georgia, and Vanderbilt University in Nashville, Tennessee, including a PhD in history, with an emphasis on Chilean history and U.S.-Latin American relations. He taught at Vanderbilt University as a teaching fellow and instructor and served as a history professor at Belmont University in Nashville, Tennessee, before coming to Ransom Everglades Schools in Florida in 1999. He is currently also a member of the adjunct faculty at Barry University, Florida, teaching courses on modern America, the history of Florida, and the contemporary world.

Stephen Kneeshaw is professor of history at College of the Ozarks in southwest Missouri. He is also involved with the teacher education program, specifically history and social studies education. He completed his BA in history and English at the University of Puget Sound and his MA and PhD in American history at the University of Colorado, Boulder. Since 1972 he has been on the history faculty at College of the Ozarks, where he was named the first recipient of the college's Distinguished Faculty Award for excellence in teaching, scholarship, and service. He has held fellowships for study and research at the Newberry Library, Chicago, Illionois, Harvard, MIT, and the U.S. Military Academy at West Point. Steve is the founder and editor of *Teaching History: A Journal of Methods* and for several years has presented workshops on "Active Teaching and Learning" at high schools and colleges. His publications cover a wide range of topics from diplomatic history-to-history education, active learning, and writing to learn.

Jessica Lacher-Feldman serves as the public and outreach services coordinator at the W.S. Hoole Special Collections Library at the University of Alabama. As part of the libraries faculty, she coordinates reference services and instruction, curates archival exhibitions, arranges public events, and manages the Hoole Web site. A native of New York state, Jessica holds a BA in French studies and master's degrees in history and library science (archives concentration) from the State University of New York at Albany. She is active in the American Association for History and Computing, the Society of American Archivists, and the Society of Alabama Archivists.

Donnelly Lancaster is a faculty member of the University of Alabama Libraries, where she is archival access coordinator for the W.S. Hoole Special Collections Library and manages the manuscript department. She holds a master's degree in history with an emphasis in archival studies from Auburn University. A former junior fellow of the Library of Congress Manuscript Division, she is an active member of the Society of American Archivists and the Society of Alabama Archivists and serves on the editorial board of *Provenance,* the journal of the Society of Georgia Archivists.

Robert Lee is a manuscript cataloger for the Gilder Lehrman Collection, on deposit at the New York Historical Society. He works with archival holdings concerning the political and social history of the United States, focusing on the periods of the American Revolution and the early republic.

Jeffrey W. McClurken worked on the *Valley of the Shadow* online project at the University of Virginia for fifteen months. He graduated from Johns Hopkins University, Baltimore, Maryland, in 2002 with a PhD in American history. He is currently completing a manuscript titled, "After the Battle: Reconstructing the Confederate Veteran Family in Pittsylvania County and Danville, Virginia, 1860–1900." He is an assistant professor of history at the University of Mary Washington, in Fredericksburg, Virginia.

Scott A. Merriman teaches at the University of Kentucky and the University of Maryland University College. He received his PhD in modern American history from the University of Kentucky in 2003. He has previously taught history at the University of Cincinnati, Northern Kentucky University, Midway College in Kentucky, and Thomas More College in Kentucky. His books include *The History Highway: A Guide to Internet Resources, The History Highway 2000: A Guide to Internet Resources, The History Highway 3.0: A Guide to Internet Resources,* and *History.edu: Essays on Teaching with Technology.* He currently is an associate editor for *Journal of the Association for History and Computing.* He has contributed to the *Register of the Kentucky Historical Society, Historical Encyclopedia of World Slavery, American National Biography, American Decades Primary Sources,* and *Buckeye Hill Country,* among other publications.

Martin V. Minner is a PhD candidate at Indiana University who specializes in urban history and photographic history. His current research is on civic politics and cultural memory in Newark, New Jersey. He is also a technical communication consultant and has worked in software development and computer publishing.

Melissa Ooten received her MA in history from the College of William and Mary, Virginia, in 2001. She currently teaches history and women's studies there, and she defended her dissertation, "Screen Strife: Movie Censorship in Virginia, 1922–1965," in the fall of 2005.

S. Mike Pavelec received his PhD in history from The Ohio State University in 2004. He is an assistant professor of history at Hawaii Pacific University and teaches classes within the Master's in Diplomacy and Military Studies program. He is an active contributor to the historical field with recent book reviews, presentations, and upcoming publications. His first book, *The Development of Turbojet Aircraft in Germany, Britain, and the United States: A Multi-national*

Comparison of Aeronautical Engineering 1935–1946, is undergoing revisions for publication with Texas A&M University Press. He focuses on military history, aviation history, science and technology studies, and the interaction between technology and society.

Jessie Bishop Powell, Merriman received a master's degree in English from the University of Kentucky in 2000 and a master's degree in library and information science from the same institution in 2001.

Edward Ragan received his PhD in early American and Native American history from Syracuse University. Currently, he is a visiting assistant professor at the State University of New York, College of Environmental Science and Forestry. His dissertation explores seventeenth-century Anglo-Indian relations in Virginia. Through his research, he has become involved with Virginia Indians in their efforts to gain federal acknowledgment. He has worked most closely with the Rappahannock Tribe. In 2002, he drafted the recognition petition that the Rappahannocks submitted to the United States Congress and the Bureau of Indian Affairs. In addition, he works with the Rappahannock's community education and cultural recovery programs.

J. Kelly Robison teaches at San Juan College in New Mexico. He holds a PhD in American history from Oklahoma State University and an MA in American history from the University of Montana. His research and teaching focus is the history of the American West and Native America, with a special emphasis on the Spanish borderlands and cross-cultural acculturation. He is also interested in the use of computer technology in teaching and researching history. He is a consulting editor for the *Journal of the Association for History and Computing.*

Anne Rothfeld is an information specialist at the University of Maryland, Baltimore. She earned her MA in library science from the Catholic University of America, Washington, DC, concentrating in special collections and archives. Previously she was the archivist technician at the U.S. Holocaust Memorial Museum in Washington, DC.

Thomas Saylor is associate professor of history and director of the Faculty Scholarship Center at Concordia University, St. Paul, Minnesota. He studied at the University of Akron, Ohio, and the University of Rochester, New York, where he received his doctorate in 1993. Professionally active in the field of oral history, since 2001 he has founded and directed two oral history projects dealing with World War II. He is the author of *Remembering the Good War* (2005), on the varied experiences of women and men in the Upper Midwest between 1941 and 1945. He is currently working on a book on Minnesotans held as POWs during World War II, having completed more than seventy-five interviews across the nation.

David J. Staley is director of the Harvey Goldberg Program for Excellence in Teaching at The Ohio State University. He is executive director of the American Association for History and Computing. His areas of interest include visual thinking, historical methodology, the history of science and technology, and the philosophy of history. His publications include *Computers, Visualization and History: How New Technology Will Transform Our Understanding of the Past* (M.E. Sharpe, 2003).

Kathleen A. Tobin received her PhD in history from the University of Chicago. She currently works as assistant professor of Latin American studies at Purdue University Calumet in Hammond, Indiana. Her interests are U.S.-Latin American relations and population policy.

Dennis A. Trinkle Dr. Dennis A. Trinkle is the inaugural Chief Information Officer for Valparaiso University. Formerly the Chief Information Officer and Tenzer University Professor in Instructional Technology at DePauw University, Trinkle has more than twenty years experience in information technology and higher education leadership. He received his B.A. from DePauw University; his M.A. and Ph.D. from the University of Cincinnati; and his M.B.A. from the University of Phoenix. The founding President of the American Association for History and Computing (AAHC), Trinkle served two terms as Executive Director of the AAHC from 1998-2004. He currently serves on the organization's Board of Directors. He has been a Fellow of the Frye Leadership Institute and the International Center for Computer-Enhanced Learning at Wake Forest University.

Trinkle serves on the Board of Trustees of Tri-State University and on the Board of Directors for Opelin Corporation and College Mentors for Kids and on Advisory Boards for Askahistorian.com., Student Advantage, Localités/Localities, and the Gale Group. He co-chairs the Educause Constituent Group on Change Leadership and is a member of the Educause Advisory Committee on Teaching and Learning and the Educause Fellowship Advisory Board.

Trinkle publishes and speaks widely on technology, teaching and learning, and IT planning and management. The author or editor of more than a dozen books, his recent works include: *The History Highway: A Twenty-first Century Guide to Internet Resources; Writing, Teaching, and Researching History in the Electronic Age*; and *History.edu: Essays on Teaching with Technology*.

Alexander Zukas is an associate professor of history at National University in San Diego. He received his PhD in history from the University of California, Irvine, in 1991. He has written on the European working class and gender history, innovative approaches to the teaching of world history, and using music and theater to teach historical subject matter. His publications include the articles "Lazy, Apathetic, and Dangerous: The Social Construction of Unemployed Workers in the Late Weimar Republic," *Contemporary European History* (forthcoming); "Cyberworld: Teaching World History on the World Wide Web," *The History Teacher* (August 1999); "Age of Empire," *Radical History Review* (Winter 1997); and "Different Drummers: Using Music to Teach History," *Perspectives* (October 1996). He is currently working on articles about teaching world history courses on the Internet, the phenomenology of teaching online, Karl Korsch's Marxism, unemployed workers in the Ruhr region of Germany during the Weimar Republic, and the ecology of the Ruhr from 1850 to 1930. He serves as director of the Institute for Community and Oral History of the Center for Cultural and Ethnic Studies at National University.

Index